BEYOND THE RHETORIC

The Economics of India's Look East Policy

Centre de Sciences Humaines (Centre for Social Sciences and Humanities): Created in New Delhi in 1989 the CSH, is part of network of research centres of the French Ministry of Foreign Affairs. The Centre's research work is primarily oriented towards the study of issues concerning the contemporary dynamics of development in India and South Asia. The activities of the Centre are focused on four main themes, namely: Economic growth and sustainable development, International and regional relations, Institutional structures and political constructions of identity and Urban dynamics.

(Centre de Sciences Humaines, 2, Aurangzeb Road, New Delhi 110 011, Tel: (91 11) 23 01 62 59/23 01 41 73, Fax: (91 11) 23 01 84 80, E-mail: public@csh-delhi.com, Website: http://www.csh-delhi.com)

The Core Group for the Study of National Security (CSNS) is a research of programme of Jawaharlal Nehru University set up in collaboration with the Indian Council for Social Science Research. It is the nodal point for the research, study, analysis and discussion of the strategic implications of major international issues, events and trends as they affect India. By providing long-range, anticipatory, and integrated thinking on a wide range of policy issues, CSNS seeks to fill an intellectual vacuum in the study of India's security,

(Core Group for the Study of National Security, School of International Studies, Jawaharlal Nehru University, New Mehrauli Road, New Delhi 110 067, India - Tel : (91 11) 26 10 76 76 - Fax: (91 11) 26 16 58 86 - Website: http://www.jnu.ac.in)

BEYOND THE RHETORIC

The Economics of India's Look East Policy

VOLUME II

Edited by

FRÉDÉRIC GRARE
AMITABH MATTOO

MANOHAR

CENTRE DE SCIENCES HUMAINES

CORE GROUP FOR THE STUDY OF NATIONAL SECURITY

2003

First published 2003

ISBN 81-7304-490-2

Published by
Ajay Kumar Jain for
Manohar Publishers & Distributors
4753/23 Ansari Road, Daryaganj
New Delhi 110 002

in association with

Centre de Sciences Humaines
2 Aurangzeb Road
New Delhi 110 001

Core Group for the Study of National Security
Jawaharlal Nehru University
New Mehrauli Road
New Delhi 110 067

Printed at
Lordson Publishers Pvt Ltd
Delhi 110 007

Contents

Contributors

MANMOHAN LAL AGARWAL is Professor at the Centre for Studies in Diplomacy, School of International Studies, Jawaharlal Nehru University. Professor Agarwal has taught at the Catholic University in Belgium and the University of Western Ontario in London, Canada, and worked at the World Bank and the International Monetary Fund. His research interests are in the areas of international economics and environmental economics.

MUKUL G. ASHER is Professor in the Public Policy Programme at the National University of Singapore. Earlier, he was a Visiting Professor at the Fiscal Affairs Department of the International Monetary Fund and a Visiting Scholar at the Asian Development Bank in Tokyo. He has authored or edited several books, and has published numerous articles in national and international journals. His most recent book is *Public Policy in Asia: Implications for Government and Business.*

BALADAS GHOSHAL, is a Professor of South-East Asian and South-West Pacific Studies and a former Chairman, Centre for South and South-East Asian Studies, Jawaharlal Nehru University. He had been Visiting Professor of Strategic and International Studies at the National University of Malaysia and University of Malaya, Visiting Ford Professor at the University of Illinois, Urbana Champaign, Senior Fulbright Fellow at Rutgers and Cornell Universities and Fellow in Regional Strategic Studies Programme at the Institute of Southeast Asian Studies in Singapore.

FRÉDÉRIC GRARE is presently Cultural Counsellor, Embassy of France in Pakistan. Earlier he was Director of the Centre de Sciences Humaines, New Delhi, and worked for the Programme for Strategic and International Security Studies in Geneva. Dr Grare's recent publications include: *Political Islam in the Indian Subcontinent: The Jamaat-i-Islami*; *India and ASEAN: The Politics of India's Look-East Policy* (co-edited with A. Mattoo); *India's*

Energy: Essays on Sustainable Development (co-edited with P.R. Shukla and Pierre Audinet); *Islamism and Security: Political Islam and the Western World*; *Tajikistan: The Trials of Independence* (co-authored with Shirin Akiner and Mohammed-Reza Djalili).

AMITABH MATTOO is the Vice-Chancellor of the University of Jammu. He was Professor of International Relations at Jawaharlal Nehru University, and Director of the Core Group for the Study of National Security at JNU. Dr Mattoo is also a member of the National Security Advisory Board appointed by the Prime Minister of India. He has been a visiting Professor at Stanford University and the University of Notre Dame. Dr Mattoo has published extensively, including seven books and more than forty articles in leading international journals.

PRADEEP KUMAR MEHTA is Reader in Economics at the SGTB Khalsa College, University of Delhi. He has served as Honorary Associate Director in the projects entitled India's Export to EC and Promoting Economic Cooperation with ASEAN states at the Indian Statistical Institute, New Delhi. In addition, he has been a Visiting Fellow at the Institute of Asian Studies, Chulalongkorn University (Bangkok) and has served as a consultant to the National Commission on Urbanization, Ministry of Urban Development, Government of India, New Delhi. He has been involved in various research programmes of Indian Council of Social Science Research, New Delhi.

R.K. MISHRA is currently Professor and Dean, Institute of Public Enterprise, Hyderabad. He has had research stints at London Business School and Maison Des Sciences De L'Homme, Paris. He has also been a researcher for the Planning Commission, Finance Commission, Prime Minister's Economic Advisory Council, Indian Council of Social Science Research, Commonwealth Secretariat, International Civil Service Consortium, State Bureaus of Public Enterprises, Financial Institutions and Banks.

SAKULRAT MONTREEVAT is a Fellow at the Institute of Southeast Asian Studies (ISEAS) in Singapore. She was formerly Chief of Macroeconomics at Siam Commercial Bank Research Institute (SCBRI) in Bangkok and Vice-President of SCBRI. Dr Montreevat also acted as Managing Editor of SCBRI's economic journals over the same period and Co-editor of *ASEAN Economic Bulletin* during 2000-1. Her recent research reports/articles have been published in *Thammasat Economic Journal* and various ISEAS's publications.

MAHESH C. PUROHIT is a Professor at the National Institute of Public Finance and Policy, New Delhi. He has also worked as the Member-Secretary of the Empowered Committee of State Finance Ministers to Monitor Sales Tax Reforms, Government of France. In addition, he has been a Visiting Professor at the Maison Des Sciences De L'Homme, Paris; Institute of Fiscal and Monetary Policy, Tokyo; and International Tax Programme, Harvard Law School. He has worked for the UNDP as an advisor in Tax Policy and Chief Technical Advisor and for the IMF as a member of a Fiscal Mission.

ISABELLE SAINT-MEZARD is at present working as a post-doctoral fellow at CERI, Paris. She is also a former Fellow at Hong Kong Baptist University on the evolution of India's external relations at the turn of the century and its putative rise to great power status in the new millennium.

ATUL SARMA is Professor of Economics and previously Head, Indian Statistical Institute, Delhi Centre. He is also noon-executive Director of Steel Authority of India Limited. He has previously been on the faculty of Economic and Social Science Research, Ahmedabad, a post-doctoral fellow at MIT, Cambridge and Visiting Professor at a number of universities in India and abroad. Professor Sarma has been a consultant to international agencies such as ADB, FAO, ESCAP and UNIDO and has served as Economic Adviser to the Eighth and Tenth Finance Commission.

RAHUL SEN is a research scholar at the Department of Economics, National University of Singapore.

DIPANKAR SENGUPTA, is a research associate at the CSH. He is on leave from the International Trade and Development Division, at the School of International Studies, JNU, where he is a Ford Foundation Fellow. He has also been a guest lecturer at the National Institute of Financial Management (Faridabad).

SADHANA SRIVASTAVA is a research scholar at the South Asian Studies Programme, Faculty of Arts and Social Sciences, National University of Singapore.

Introduction

Frédéric Grare and Amitabh Mattoo

India's engagement with South-East Asia is not new. Historically, India's political and cultural influence extended to the Indonesian archipelago. In its current incarnation, however, India's 'Look East Policy' was officially launched in 1991 during the tenure of Prime Minister Narasimha Rao. It is a part of the new *realpolitik* in evidence in India's foreign policy, and the engagement with ASEAN is a part of the recognition on the part of India's elite of the strategic and economic importance of the region to the country's national interests.

This new realism is based, at least in part, on a new consciousness in New Delhi of the political and economic dynamics within India's extended neighbourhood and the international system. Four factors in particular have changed India's policy towards the region. First, India's economic reforms, coupled with the integrative forces of globalization, made it essential for the country to extend its economic vision beyond the confines of its traditional policy. Second, frustration with the process of integration within South Asia, and the manner in which Pakistan was seen to be subverting the efforts at energizing the South Asian Association of Regional Cooperation (SAARC), convinced India's policy-making community that it was necesarry to look beyond the region. Third, there was renewed concern about the consequences of an ascendant and powerful China and its impact on India's security, as well as India's unease at Beijing's growing assertiveness in the Asia-Pacific region. While a Sino-Indian rapprochement had been in evidence since the late 1980s, China still is identified, directly or indirectly, by a significant section of the Indian elite as the principal source of insecurity and the greatest potential threat to India's long-term interests. A closer relationship with South-East Asia was, therefore, vital if India was to seek to set limits on China's influence in the region and, even more ambitiously, to balance its expanding economic and political power. Finally, India's engagement with the ASEAN countries is also rooted in the recognition that if India wants to be taken seriously as a power of consequence it must widen the ambit of its foreign policy. In other words, the willingness of the United States and other powers to allow India to take greater responsibility for the management of the international system would be dependent, to a large extent, on the manner in which India itself assumes greater responsibility in strategically important regions, and South-East Asia is undeniably one such region.

Understandably, therefore, ASEAN gradually has assumed a central place in India's perception of Asia and its future and has slowly emerged as a potential pivot in the construction of a security order that would benefit New Delhi. 'Deeply concerned about the uncertainties of the future, including China's role, India's elite [wanted] to fashion a multilateral security in the Asia-Pacific in partnership with ASEAN', thus demonstrating a willingness to assume a more assertive role in the future.[1] There is, however, still a disjunction between thought and practice, and New Delhi's engagement has still not acquired the thrust, or indeed the institutional requirements, to be able to pursue its interests in the region in a systematic and purposeful manner. Be that as it may, India's efforts to engage ASEAN will, in all likelihood, become more determined in the years to come.

With a market of around 500 million people and a combined gross domestic product of US $800 billion, ASEAN, one of the most dynamic groups of nations in the world economy, was also perceived as a zone of economic opportunity for India. Economic considerations were part of the 'new realism': the conviction that neither a significant influence in world affairs nor a strong military might could be obtained without a strong economic base. Recognition of the need to reform the country's economy had been present since the 1980s. In 1985, Prime Minister Rajiv Gandhi had already made an effort towards initiating reforms. But the attempt resulted in very modest changes. Imports expanded without any improvement in the international competitiveness of state-run enterprises. This led to a deficit in both the government budget and the international balance of payments. The Gulf War aggravated the situation even further. At the beginning of the 1990s, India was confronted with a severe balance of payment crisis. Under IMF pressure it had to undertake far-reaching economic stabilization measures. What followed was a privatization programme and additional incentives to look for new markets. India, however, was not interested only in South-East Asian markets but also in attracting foreign capital. The then quick generating capital-surplus economies of ASEAN appeared as an obvious target for the Indian decision makers. Starting from a very low level, trade and investments between the two partners developed rapidly. However, they remain even today far below their full potential. The Asian financial crisis of 1997-8 is only a partial explanation for this unrealized and untapped potential. Although improving at a remarkable pace, India's attractiveness remains limited while its economy is still not export driven.

This volume examines the potential for increased economic relations between India and ASEAN, as well as the manner in which the structural problems of the Indian economy could undermine these relations. The various essays also seek to draw some lessons for India from the Asian financial crisis.

The volume is part of a research programme on 'India's Foreign Policy at the Turn of the Millennium: Forging New Partnerships in South-East Asia', initiated by the Core Group for the Study of National Security (CSNS), Jawaharlal Nehru University, New Delhi, the Institute of South-East Asian Studies (ISEAS), Singapore, and the French Centre de Sciences Humaines (CSH), New Delhi. A previous volume, *India and ASEAN: The Politics of India's Look East Policy* (2001), dealt with the strategic and security issues between the two regions. The project had initially four major objectives:

(1) To identify India's economic and security strategies in the conduct of its policy vis-à-vis the ASEAN states, to evaluate national versus local strategies, and to examine the complementarity or contradictory aspects of various strategies;
(2) To identify the specific goals determining the substance and forms of India's policy vis-à-vis ASEAN and the South-East Asian states. Particular attention was to be paid to the objectives actually pursued by India in seeking closer relationships with the ASEAN states in order to determine whether the rhetoric matched the actual practice;
(3) To examine the various perceptions and policies of the ASEAN states towards India in the economic and security spheres. Was there, or is there, an overlap in their economic and security objectives?
(4) To determine the domestic, economic, and political impediments to India's increased interaction with ASEAN.

As the strategic and security issues have been addressed in the earlier volume, the present volume deals exclusively with economic issues. It comprises eight contributions, and is the result of a second workshop organized in Delhi in April 2001.

The book is divided into two parts, each addressing two different sets of issues. The first four chapters explain the rationale behind the 'Look East Policy' as well as the opportunities offered by the emerging relationship between India and ASEAN, both in terms of trade opportunities as well as the potential offered by the presence of a significant Indian diaspora in South-East Asia.

In the first chapter, Isabelle Saint-Mézard explains how the 'Look East Policy' was the outcome of the economic liberalization initiated in 1991. Following the balance-of-payment crisis of June 1991, the government of Narasimha Rao had to embark on a programme of structural adjustment under IMF pressure. Another important dimension of the reform process was the opening up of the Indian economy. Indian diplomacy began to promote India's economic potential abroad, in particular in capital-surplus economies. Indian diplomats now had to project the image of the country as an emerging new economic giant. Moreover, they had to convince the investors that the liberalization process would be irreversible despite political instability. South-East Asia was targeted as one of the fastest growing areas in the world and, consequently, as a source of foreign direct investments. It soon became a model of growth for the Indian reform process. The 'Look East Policy' was implemented through a number of high-profile delegations which visited the countries of South-East Asia. Political leaders highlighted the opportunities of co-operation in the priority sectors of development such as the infrastructure of communications (ports, railways, roads), telecommunications, power, etc. Prime Minister Rao personally visited most South-East Asian countries between 1993 and 1995. As they could not not be interested by India's large population and growing middle class, the South-East Asian countries responded in kind, the most proactive state being Singapore. This rapprochement, initiated by the governments, was also the result of a perceived exclusion from the major regional trade groups. As it was opening to the world market, India became aware of the growing trend towards regionalism and feared that it might be marginalized. Western Europe had embarked on a process of deepening and enlarging its integration, while the United States was sponsoring the creation of the Asia-Pacific Economic Cooperation group (APEC). Although New Delhi had sought an entry into APEC ever since it came into existence, it was rejected and has still not become a member of this group. At the same time other fora such as the Group of 77, UNCTAD, and the Non-Aligned Movement were quickly losing their influence. The 'Look East Policy' became one of the springboards of India's integration into the world economy.

Mukul Asher, Rahul Sen, and Sadhana Srivastava discuss the factors contributing to the deepening and expanding economic relations between India and ASEAN. Taking note of the absence of major political or security issues between India and ASEAN, they argue that a broader and deeper engagement between the two is an essential component of Asia's attempt to enhance its role in the world. Moreover, according to the authors, India's GDP increase at a rate of 6.4 per cent between 1992-3 and 2000-1 provided real economic opportunities for its ASEAN partners. This perception materialized during the 1990s in the strengthening of the institutional foundations of the relationship. India became a sectoral dialogue partner of ASEAN in 1992 and a full dialogue partner in 1995, which allowed it to become a member of the ASEAN Regional Forum (ARF) a year later. In the economic field relations have also considerably evolved. Merchandise trade has more than tripled. Investment in ASEAN by Indian companies remains low but it is likely to grow as their financial capacity increases and the regulations become more liberal. Similarly, tremendous potentialities exist in the fields of infrastructure, energy, food security, human resource development, etc. However, this potential will not be realized unless high-level political commitment is made to pursue this goal. India suffers in particular from an 'image deficit' which slowed down and sometimes impeded foreign direct investment. ASEAN is systematically and strongly urged to facilitate an improvement and enhancement of India's image in all regional fora but India itself needs to vigorously pursue its efforts to engage each member of ASEAN in a mutually beneficial manner.

Atul Sharma and Pradeep Kumar Mehta take a closer look at trade possibilities as reflected in trade complementarity between India and the five ASEAN states: Indonesia, Malaysia, Philippines, Singapore, and Thailand. Like the authors of the preceding essay they also observe that India's reforms to achieve a market-driven system and globalization will facilitate trade on the basis of resource endowment and competitive strength. Although India was integrated to a far less degree within the global economy than its ASEAN counterparts, it did manage to expand trade at a rapid pace in the 1990s with the five above-mentioned states. However, the presence of India and ASEAN remains limited in each other's markets. Several complementary products are not traded at all, and where they are traded they have an almost insignificant market presence. The problem is structural. India's exports do not enjoy complementarity with the imports of the ASEAN states to any significant degree, although ASEAN exports show a far higher degree of correspondence with Indian imports. The complementarity of several product groups has declined. Hence there is a need for restructuring trade in alignment with the changing demand and supply conditions between India and the ASEAN trade partners.

Finally, Baladas Ghoshal examines the role of the Indian diaspora in the emerging economic relations between India and the ASEAN. Analysing the specificities of the Indian diaspora as compared to the Jewish and Chinese diasporas, he notes that although prosperous and confident in their identities, 'non-resident Indians' do face the hostility of the lesser developed minority communities and they are further handicapped by the weakened position of India in the global political and economic stage. According to Ghoshal, there is an increasing recognition that the further success of the Indian diaspora, both in the countries of settlement and in the context of their possible contribution to India's economic development 'requires [an] economically rising, strong and resilient India'.

At the same time, the economic structure presents to a large extent the same characteristics as the Indian economy, and as such it is not always prepared to face the demands of globalization. Firms are mostly family owned and need to be transformed into competitive business ventures. Hence there is a need for the introduction of professional management practices, the strengthening and expansion of existing community-based trade networks, and the need to diversify economic activities. The Indian diaspora in South-East Asia inevitably suffers from the comparison with its Chinese counterpart. It is estimated that the Indian community controls one to two per cent of the economy as opposed to three-fifths of the regional economy controlled by the Chinese community. Not only is the Indian community small in size but it has also suffered from decades of neglect by the Indian government and, more importantly, from the years during which the Indian economy was closed to the outside world. The Indian government is only now starting to woo NRI capital, gradually overcoming their initial resistance. The effort sometimes has come from abroad. In 1996 Singapore launched the first initiative to organize the 'Global Indian Entrepreneurs Conference' in a bid to network with the Indian diaspora. The powerful FICCI (Federation of Indian Chambers of Commerce and Industry) has also launched a huge network of business people and is constantly generating attention focused on India, its investment climate, and economic reforms. Other initiatives have followed. Since the launch of economic reforms in India, 20 per cent of the Foreign Direct Investment has come from NRIs. Still, the Indians in South-East Asia are not strong economic players. But the potentialities exist as a new breed of expatriate Indians (software engineers, chartered accountants, financial analysts, and management consultants) are slowly emerging on the scene. It is hoped that their linkages with India will lead them to develop a stake not only in the welfare of India but also to cultivate closer interactions with their adopted countries. Providing the right efforts are made by the Government of India, the expatriate Indians should be a driving force in improving the still uncertain relationship between their motherland and South-East Asia.

The second part of the book addresses the structural problems of the Indian economy. Although these problems are not necessarily specific to the relationship between India and ASEAN, they do impede the broader and deeper development of this relationship. Moreover, the four chapters also seek to identify some lessons which India can draw from the ASEAN experience.

Manmohan Agarwal and Dipankar Sengupta examine the factors which led to the balance of payment crisis at the beginning of the 1990s and look at the early impact of the reforms as well as their stagnation in the mid-1990s. They underline the improvement of the Indian economy in the aftermath of the stabilization programme (exports and GDP grew while the fiscal deficit was reduced). They also note that it has stagnated during the last five years. Hence, the need for further reforms still exists although there is no consensus in India on the nature of these reforms. The authors argue that the lessons which India should draw from ASEAN are both positive and negative. On the negative side, the financial crisis has shown how otherwise fundamentally sound economies can be driven into recession because of panic. As a result, the authors oppose capital account convertibility which they hold responsible for engendering such a situation. Nevertheless, they argue in favour of removing barriers on production and investment. Similarly, they argue that India should emulate ASEAN in the way it attracts foreign direct investments, although they call the attention of policy makers to the need to introduce the reforms in order to ensure that they do not further aggravate social inequities in the country.

Sakulrat Montreevat seeks to draw some lessons for India from the Asian financial crisis which affected India's economy in various ways. In 1997-8, funds were withdrawn from Indian markets. Indian companies lost access to various financial markets. Exports to South-East Asia fell. As a result, industrial and service activities slowed down, putting additional pressures on the currency. Surprisingly, the Indian economy recovered quickly, and did not suffer as much as the more open economies of the region. Montreevat underlines, however, a contradictory trend. If India has been relatively protected because of this lower degree of openness, it is nevertheless now increasingly integrated into the world economy. Deregulation has been an important factor and trade barriers have declined significantly while exports and imports assume a larger share of the GDP. Hence it is important to take appropriate measures to reduce India's vulnerability to external shocks. Public deficits, which undermine foreign investor confidence, and fiscal imbalances have to be addressed. A serious effort has to be made to reform the banking system. The financial sector, still largely dominated by state-owned banks, needs to be strengthened and a second generation of reforms should be put in place in order to limit crisis risk. This will require new strategies of privatization as well as prudent regulations and effective systems of supervision.

The need to reform the Indian fiscal system is the focus of Mahesh Purohit's essay. In this area, too, lessons can be drawn from the ASEAN experience. The fiscal policy was originally intended to raise large amounts of resources from the wealthier sections of society to direct massive investments in the public sector, in particular 'in infrastructure development and the areas having large externalities'. However, if notable results were achieved in some fields, such as agriculture, they remained below target in many others. The lack of growth of the Indian economy soon created problems in the balance of payment situation and, at the end of the 1980s, threatened the monetary stability of the country. Hence the coupling, in 1991, of fiscal reforms with the structural adjustment programme. The reforms aim at reducing the combined centre-state high fiscal deficit by controlling expenditures, reducing interest payments, increasing the number of taxes, simplifying procedures, rationalizing subsidies, etc. But other measures also have to be taken following the ASEAN example. Fiscal consolidation needs to be carried out in such a way that it reduces the size of the public sector and curtails the current account deficit to reduce external vulnerability. Quantitative controls of capital inflow will also have to be eliminated. Overall, the challenge for India will be to adapt the tax system to meet the requirements of globalization, as the ASEAN countries have already done, and to make sure that its fiscal system protects the poor from the effects of globalization.

Finally, R.K. Mishra critically analyses some of the structural problems impeding the development of economic relations between India and ASEAN and looks in particular at the privatization trends in the country. He observes that economic trends converge the world over, in both the developed and the developing countries, about the need to privatize and reduce government control. However, despite the reform of the public sector enterprises initiated as early as 1992, India has not been able so far to register a significant breakthrough in its privatization/disinvestment programme. Several reasons explain the lack of progress in this area. The objectives were never really clearly formulated and enunciated, and in addition the absence of transparency has deprived the programme of public support. Moreover, the administration remained largely in control of the privatization mechanism which itself has not been adequately defined. While the institutional set-up, the selection of techniques, and the implementation strategy have all played important roles in the success of privatization elsewhere in the world, and in particular in the ASEAN countries, these elements have been insufficiently considered in the case of India.

Overall, the book underlines the uncertainty of the emerging economic relationship between India and ASEAN. Although it has significantly improved over the last ten years, this relationship remains largely virtual and is still in the gestational stage. Many hurdles will have to be overcome before this relationship can develop to its full potential. What is at stake here is not only a trade increase between these two particular entities, but also the very capacity of India to integrate into the world economy.

NOTE

1. Amitabh Mattoo, 'ASEAN in India's Foreign Policy', in Frédéric Grare and Amitabh Mattoo (eds.), *India and ASEAN: The Politics of India's Look East Policy*, New Delhi: Manohar, 2001, pp. 91-118, especially pp. 104-5.

The Look East Policy: An Economic Perspective

Isabelle Saint-Mézard

The transition from the 1980s to the 1990s was challenging for many countries in the world. India was no exception. Internally, the country was unsettled by social unrest, serious political instability and poor economic performance. India's situation was as uncomfortable on the international scene. First, the collapse of the Soviet Union came as a shock; New Delhi had lost a major economic partner and its closest strategic ally. The intimate Moscow-New Delhi relationship that had developed over more than three decades, starting with the successful bilateral visits by Nikita Khrushchev and Jawaharlal Nehru in 1955, was coming to an end. The Yeltsin administration was not particularly interested in maintaining a privileged relationship with India, all the more so as Indian diplomacy failed to support the reformers during the attempted coup of August 1991 in Moscow. This Indian misperception was revealing of the country's bewilderment regarding the historic transformations that were affecting the Eastern bloc. One of the major concerns for New Delhi was that it could not any longer rely on Soviet diplomatic support at the Security Council of the United Nations. Thus, India was more exposed to international pressures on vital interests like disarmament, non-proliferation, and the Kashmir issue.

Second and related to this first development, one of the main tenets of Indian foreign policy, non-alignment, seemed to have become obsolete. Because it was a co-founder of NAM and one of its most influential members, India could assume the status of a leading Third World country and enjoy some sort of international aura. But with the end of the Cold War and only one effective superpower left, the very concept of non-alignment was undermined. The triumph of the United States, its political world view and its free-market economic system also posed a new challenge to India's foreign policy.

The Indian predicament in post-bipolar international politics was further accentuated by the worldwide trend towards regionalism. The ASEAN success story (at least until the economic crisis of 1997), the resumption of the integration process of the European Union and the negotiations for NAFTA and APEC gave India the impression that it was in danger of isolation from the dynamics pushing the global economy. This was a major cause of concern as New Delhi was engaged in the process of economic liberalization. Indeed, following the balance of payments crisis of June 1991, the new Congress government of Narasimha Rao had to embark on a programme of structural adjustment. If this financial crisis was triggered off by the Gulf War of 1990 and the subsequent rise in international oil prices, it was also the result of the macro-economic choices made during the 1980s. The option to boost growth through external borrowing and a programme of public expenditure closed. At the beginning of the 1990s, the time had come to launch the most sweeping programme of economic liberalization.

India had therefore to rethink the basic parameters of its foreign policy. As a result of these new compulsions, a Look East Policy was officially launched in 1991 by the Prime Minister, with the aim of developing multi-faceted relations with countries of North-East and South-East Asia. This policy appeared as a new trend in Indian foreign policy. Until then, New Delhi had made little effort to develop relationships with this region. But India had realized the rapid economic growth achieved by its South-East Asian neighbours and also that it was lagging behind. Notwithstanding its inferiority complex, the Indian elite came to the conclusion that the so-called East Asian economic miracle could be a model for its own development policies. New Delhi also sought to enlarge ties with these high performing economies, in the hope of getting integrated into the process of economic regionalization in East Asia. India was indeed eager to associate itself with what was, by then, the most dynamic region of the world. Thus it appears that economic considerations were the prime incentive in the Look East Policy.

This paper concentrates on the launching of the Look East Policy, that is the first years of the 1990s, when India was under the coalition government of Prime Minister P.V. Narasimha Rao. The point of view is mainly Indian. The major questions to answer are as follows. What caused the Rao government to launch the look east policy? What did India expect from it? How did it implement this policy thrust towards East Asia? In other words, this paper tries to identify the major actors and to understand their motivations and expectations. It also focuses on the institutional implementation of the policy and on the role of the governments concerned. Last, it should be underlined that the Look East Policy is not about ASEAN alone, since it is meant to cover the whole East Asian region, if not the

Asia-Pacific.[1] Thus while the focus of this paper is on ASEAN, Japan and South Korea are also taken into account.

This paper first shows that the Look East Policy has been an outcome of the economic liberalization initiated in 1991. In the second part, it observes the way the Look East Policy has been implemented. Finally, this paper argues that the policy has to be understood in the wider context of the world trend towards regionalism.

THE LOOK EAST POLICY AS AN OUTCOME OF THE ECONOMIC LIBERALIZATION INITIATED IN 1991

The liberalization process and the opening up to the world economy have led to a reshaping of the role of the Indian state, not only in economic management but also in foreign policy. Indeed, in the context of India's globalization drive, the primary task of the diplomacy has been to contribute directly to economic development. For that matter, New Delhi has sought to improve the functioning and the efficiency of its economic diplomacy.

ECONOMIC DIPLOMACY AND NEW ORIENTATIONS IN INDIAN FOREIGN POLICY

Economic diplomacy can be broadly defined as the conduct of foreign policy in the economic field. There are two aspects related to such a policy. On the multilateral level, economic diplomacy consists in improving the international economic environment for the benefit of India's own development policies. In other words, India has to make sure that the negotiations for the multilateral trading system at the WTO will be favourable to its economic interests. The Union Ministries of Commerce and Finance are the most involved in this process.

Another important dimension of economic diplomacy is to promote India's economic potential abroad, especially in capital-surplus economies. This has now become one of the primary tasks of the Ministry of External Affairs. Indeed, with its external oriented strategy for development, India has to expand its foreign trade and to bring in more finances so as to maintain a high growth path. But efforts to integrate into the world economy have been hampered by a past image of a centrally planned economy. Because of the inward-looking policies in place until the 1980s, India was not regarded as an economy open to foreign investment and international trade. Therefore, the task of economic diplomacy is to create an international awareness about the reform process and to present India as an attractive destination for business. In other words, Indian diplomacy has to project an image of a country emerging as a new economic giant, with stable institutions, a transparent legal system and a vibrant private sector. In this regard, one of the most important aspects of this international public relations operation is to convince investors that the liberalization process will be irreversible, in spite of the political instability.

This new emphasis on economic diplomacy has induced some re-orientations in the role and functioning of the Ministry of External Affairs. By the end of the year 1991, Prime Minister Narasimha Rao issued a note asking the Foreign Office and its diplomatic posts abroad to focus more on the economic aspects of India's external relations.[2] Since then, the heads of the diplomatic posts abroad have been made directly responsible for the conduct of trade relations with the countries of their accreditation. Indian embassies and High Commissions have been encouraged to work as information agencies on the evolution of the economic reforms and to play a more active role in the promotion of India's exports.

The Ministry of External Affairs has been invited to integrate itself more intensively into the economic work of the government. For instance, under the Rao government, the Foreign Secretary was allowed to participate as a regular member in high-ranking bodies dealing with economic issues, such as the Foreign Investment Promotion Board and the Apex Committee of Secretaries on economic policy. Within the Ministry of External Affairs, the Economic Division has been revamped and strengthened. In addition, an Investment Promotion Unit was created in 1993 to take charge of investment promotion activities. The Economic Division has been directed to coordinate action with other ministries dealing with economic matters such as the ministries of finance and commerce. The implementation of an efficient economic diplomacy has also required better collaboration between the government departments and the representative organizations of the private sector, in terms of exchange of commercial information as well as co-sponsoring seminars, exhibitions and delegations abroad. In this regard, the Ministry of External Affairs has sought to forge a new partnership with apex chambers like FICCI, CII and ASSOCHAM. The CII, in particular, has turned out to be a dynamic partner, dedicated to the promotion of India's economic reforms abroad.

Economic diplomacy was a new trend in the Indian foreign policy of the 1990s. Until the end of the 1980s, the economic dimensions of foreign relations were not given so much importance in the Ministry of External Affairs.[3] Indian foreign policy was more driven by ideological or political factors than economic factors. But with the end of the Cold War and the worldwide trend towards free-market reforms, economics became a major structuring factor in international relations. The Indian leadership has had to acknowledge that the international status of the country would depend a lot on its wealth. In this regard, the East Asian example is telling: the region has emerged as a major pole on the international scene because of its economic dynamism.

The Look East Policy: Catching up with the Fastest Growing Region in the World

Under the framework of economic diplomacy, the East Asian region has been seen as a priority area of cooperation. Indeed, India realized that its economic ties with this region were underdeveloped whereas it was one of the fastest growing areas in the world. Until then, India had adopted a primarily politico-strategic approach to the region and had considered it of secondary interest.[4] Because of its friendship with the Soviet Union, India used to regard ASEAN as a 'Trojan Horse' of the United States and cultivated closer ties with socialist Vietnam. On the whole, from the 1960s to the 1980s, India's traditional attitude towards most of the East Asian countries was one of contempt and negligence. But in the early 1990s, the Indian leadership in its admiration for their economic achievements, became eager to cooperate with the East Asian countries.

As a matter of fact, East Asia became a model for the Indian reform process. In this regard, it should be underlined that some members of the governmental team coming into power in 1991 used to work in international institutions. For that reason, they were well aware of the growing development gap between India and its eastern neighbours. For instance, before he became Finance Minister in the Rao government, Dr Manmohan Singh was General Secretary of the South-South Commission in Geneva. This position enabled him to study the development process of the East Asian economies and to compare it with India's options. As Finance Minister and as one of the 'fathers' of the reform process, Dr Singh often drew a parallel between India's poor performance and South Korea's high growth path.

The comparison between India and this small country is striking indeed. Both of them became independent in 1947, and all along the 1950s, India was industrially more developed than South Korea and most other East Asian countries. However, during the 1960s and the 1970s, South Korea's annual growth rate was well over 10 per cent, whereas India's 'Hindu' rate of growth was stuck at 3 per cent a year only. As a result, in the 1990s, around 90 per cent of the South Korean population belonged to the middle class. In India, the percentage of the population living under the poverty line was at least 40 per cent. India was thus very impressed to learn that South Korea was about to be admitted among the OECD countries.[5] India has also been an admirer of the city-state of Singapore, the first state to boast of a development level superior to that of its erstwhile colonial power, Great Britain. But the most significant influence of all has probably been China's recent economic take-off. China is the country most comparable in size and complexity to India. Both started off in the 1950s with centrally-planned economies, but China began to liberalize in 1979, with Deng Xiaoping's 'Four Modernizations'. As a result, China emerged as the first destination for foreign investment and it has been pronounced as one of the three major economic powers of the twenty-first century.

The Rao government was thus prompted by a desire to emulate the East Asian miracle through the reform process. Prime Minister Narasimha Rao confirmed this when he stated to a Japanese audience: 'Indeed, it is the success of Japan, the Asian NIEs and ASEAN that have in a way contributed to the dynamic revision in plans and policies for foreign investments in India, and the rest of the South Asian region in recent years.'[6] Furthermore, the Indian leadership couldn't remain indifferent to the prophecy of the 'Asian century' that was then much talked about. In fact, it has been anxious to be a part of it since the initiation of the liberalization process. But, to catch up with the fast developing countries of East Asia, India has had to increase its economic interdependence with the region as a whole. In other words, the Indian economy has had to integrate with the process of economic regionalization in East Asia.

Economic integration in East Asia has been driven by shifts in the pattern of comparative advantages. This process has originally been epitomized in the model of the 'flying geese', theorized by Japanese economists. This model highlights the investment strategies of North-East Asian firms that relocate activities from countries that no longer have a comparative advantage in the production of certain goods to other countries that do. The model also shows the intra-regional links between the trade exchanges in goods and services and the flows of investments. Japan has been the leading goose in the Asian formation and the foreign investment strategies of Japanese companies have been at the source of the functional interdependence between East Asian economies. As Japanese manufacturing industries have been climbing up the technological ladder, rising domestic production costs in labour-intensive industries have caused Japanese companies to relocate their production bases initially in the Newly Industrialized Countries

(Singapore, Hong Kong, Korea and Taiwan). But when the Asian NIEs began to lose their comparative advantage in the production of certain goods, Japanese investments gradually shifted to ASEAN countries (Thailand, Malaysia, Indonesia) and more recently to China. At the same time, the Asian NIEs started to transfer some of their labour-intensive manufacturing activities to the ASEAN countries and China. Even some ASEAN countries like Malaysia or Thailand have initiated a reorientation of their non-competitive activities to new locations, in China, Vietnam or Myanmar.

After China, therefore, India expects to be the next economy to benefit from the relocating of the manufacturing activities of Japan, the NIEs and the economies of ASEAN. In other words, India hopes to develop in the pattern of intra-regional complementarities as defined by the 'flying geese paradigm'. These expectations were clearly expressed by the then External Minister, I.K. Gujral, at the Post Ministerial Conference of ASEAN, in 1996: 'In terms of intra-industry collaboration and production mobility, we look forward to becoming part of the East and South-East Asian Flying Geese formation.'[7] With its availability of low wage labour, India could indeed emerge as an attractive FDI location and develop as a low cost manufacturing base. More generally speaking, a successful integration into the Asian regionalization process would imply a strengthening of trade, investment and technology flows between India and East Asia. In the end, the cooperation with East Asia is expected to be the engine of growth of the Indian economy. This is precisely the reason why New Delhi has been so keen on 'Looking East'.

THE IMPLEMENTATION OF THE LOOK EAST POLICY AT THE BEGINNING OF THE 1990s

It appears that the Look East Policy was first and foremost a product of the liberalization process. Consequently, the implementation of this policy thrust towards East Asia comes as a good example of the new tenets of Indian economic diplomacy.

How to Woo East Asia?

In East Asia, the industrially advanced economies of Japan and South Korea have been identified as major sources of investment and technology transfer. As regards Japan, the second economic power in the world, Finance Minister Manmohan Singh sought to enhance channels of communication with the Japanese leadership, right from the beginning of the reform process, in mid-1991. The Indian embassy in Tokyo was asked to establish direct links not only with their official counterparts but also with the Japanese business communities.

South-East Asia has been at the core of the Indian Look East Policy because of its potential as a major trading partner and as a source of FDI flows. By 1991-2, Prime Minister Narasimha Rao suggested a streamlining of the institutional mechanisms in the Ministry of External Affairs so as to ensure that a new policy thrust would be given to the relations with the countries of ASEAN. He instructed the Foreign Secretary to take direct charge of the territorial division dealing with South-East Asian countries. Before this institutional restructuring, this region used to be under the jurisdiction of an official of a lower rank. While assuming control of this division, the Foreign Secretary was also dealing directly with the Economic Division.[8] Therefore, this organizational rearrangement reveals that the opening of India to South-East Asia was first and foremost driven by economic considerations.

The Look East Policy has been implemented through a great number of high-profile Indian delegations visiting the countries of East Asia. The most important of them have been usually led either by the Prime Minister himself, or by the Ministers of External Affairs, Finance or Commerce. The primary emphasis of these trips to East Asia has been on economic cooperation. More precisely, one of the prime objectives of the Indian political leaders abroad has been to highlight the opportunities of cooperation in the priority sectors of development such as infrastructures of telecommunication, power, and transport communications (ports, railways, roads), where India needs massive resources. In keeping with the new tenets of economic diplomacy, these diplomatic missions have taken along high-powered business delegations. Furthermore, during trips abroad, Indian political leaders have been eager to meet not only their political counterparts, but also to establish direct contacts with the captains of industries in the countries of their visit. For instance, when he went to Japan, Prime Minister Rao spent two days meeting the leaders of the five major economic organizations of Japan as well as the chairmen of Japanese multinational corporations interested in India.

In order to emphasize the economic aspects of its relations with East Asia, Indian diplomacy has become more flexible and pragmatic on certain political or strategic issues. This is striking in the case of Korea and Japan. Prime Minister Rao went to Japan on an invitation from Prime Minister Miyazawa in June 1992. Although Rao's agenda was mainly economic in content, it could not avoid dealing with the Japanese concerns about nuclear non-proliferation. All the more so as Tokyo was, by then, in search of an international diplomatic role through its world campaign against the atom bomb. In order to avoid tensions, Narasimha Rao accepted a Japanese proposal for the setting up of working level consultations on disarmament and nuclear issues. Japan was too important an economic partner for India to decline to engage bilateral consultations on that vexed question. Narasimha Rao also went on an official visit to the Republic of Korea in September 1993. This was the first visit ever paid by an Indian Prime Minister to this country. Until then, New Delhi had been following a policy of equidistance between North and South Korea. But during his trip to Seoul, Narasimha Rao clearly stated that India's policy towards the two Koreas would be driven by its economic interests first. In other words, South Korea was given precedence because of its importance as a potential economic partner of India.

As for the countries of ASEAN, New Delhi sent a great number of high-level delegations in the post-1991 period, in order to foster closer economic ties. Soon after he was assigned Finance Minister, in April 1991, Manmohan Singh visited Singapore and Malaysia. The fact that he chose these two South-East Asian countries for his first trip abroad gave an added symbolic importance to the visit. Besides, it seems that the Indian diplomacy selected Singapore as a regional centre to disseminate information about its economic reforms in the whole East Asian region. Thus, Prime Minister Goh Chok Tong was one of the first Heads of State to be personally informed about India's liberalization process by the then External Minister, M. Solanki. A conference on India's reforms was jointly organized by the government of India and the Economic Development Board of Singapore as early as October 1991.

Rao went personally to most South-East Asian countries between 1993 and 1995. On the occasion of his visit to Thailand, in April 1993, he agreed with the Thai Prime Minister to give a political impetus to upgrade bilateral trade by at least 20 per cent per year. P.V. Narasimha Rao also made highly publicized trips to Vietnam and Singapore in 1994. No Indian Prime Minister had been to the city-state for about 26 years. On this occasion, Narasimha Rao had the privilege to be invited to give a lecture at the Institute of South-East Asian Studies (ISEAS). This was a unique opportunity to put forward his vision on the Indian Look East Policy to a high-level South-East Asian audience. In August 1995, P.V. Narasimha Rao paid an official visit to Malaysia and was accompanied by a large business team. On this occasion, he signed no fewer than five agreements to promote bilateral trade. It has to be underlined that despite a new Union government coming into power in mid-1996, the Look East Policy kept momentum. For instance, External Minister of the United Front government, I.K. Gujral, went to Jakarta as early as July 1996, for one of his first trips outside the country.

With India's huge population of 950 million and a growing middle class, East Asian economies could not but show an interest in its opening. In fact, from the point of view of many East Asian countries, the Look East Policy came at the right time, when they were in search of new, emerging markets in South Asia and Africa. Thailand for instance launched a 'Look West' Policy to reorient its relations towards India and Africa. In addition, many East Asian countries were eager to balance their investments in China with India. Since the beginning of the 1990s, China has been the largest recipient of FDI in Asia or in the developing countries. The capital-surplus economies of East Asia which have invested a lot in the Chinese market have thus tended to regard India's opening as a good opportunity to diversify their investments and spread risks, all the more so as India's geopolitical evolution seems more predictable than that of China.

For these different reasons, most East Asian countries evinced a keen interest in India's overtures and they sent several delegations to visit the country. But the most proactive state has been Singapore. In his National Day speech for 1993, Prime Minister Goh Chok Tong even talked about sparking off a 'mild Indian fever'. Singapore's interest in India has to be linked to the regionalization programme that the authorities launched that same year, in order to build a more external oriented economy. This regionalization drive consists in investing Singapore's expertise and capabilities in other growth areas in the region and interlocking them with the domestic economy. In this programme, the countries of Indochina, Myanmar, China and India have been promoted as new frontiers of growth.

Thus, between 1991 and 1996, the interactions between Indian and Singapore officials were close and frequent. A brief survey of Singapore's major delegations to India is given here. In December 1991, Foreign Affairs Minister, Wong Kan Seng, was in India. In March 1992, Deputy Prime Minister and Minister of Trade and Industry, Brig Gen Lee Hsien Loong paid a five-day long official visit to India. Later on, B.G. Georges Yeo, Minister for Information and the Arts and Second Minister for Foreign Affairs, came to India, in early February 1993. Then, Prime Minister Goh Chok Tong was invited in January 1994 to participate as Chief Guest in the Republic Day celebrations in New Delhi. He led a delegation comprising Foreign Minister, Minister of Trade and Industry, and CEOs of 36 major business houses. One of the major outcomes of these close interactions has been the launching of the Information Technology (IT)Park near Bangalore. The project was conceived with the involvement of the Karnataka government, the Tata group of India and a consortium of Singapore investors. The IT Park was well-publicized as the Singapore's flagship project in India, and it was meant to boost the private sector relations between the two economies.

Last but not least, the partnership between the Indian government and the representative organizations of the Indian private sector has proved quite successful. CII has turned out to be a major partner, especially in the case of Singapore-India relations. For instance, when Prime Minister Goh Chok Tong visited India in January 1994, he also addressed a gathering of over one hundred captains of Indian industry at a round table conference organized by CII. The Confederation has also established a representative office in Osaka and in Singapore, so as to cover respectively North-East Asia and South-East Asia. Thanks to its overseas office in the city-state, CII has succeeded in networking with important economic institutions such as the Trade Development Board, Economic Development Board and the Singapore Manufacturers' Association.

The CII has also succeeded in forging a network of relations with several East Asian political leaders, such as Prime Minister of Malaysia Mahathir Bin Mohamad, General Secretary of ASEAN Dato Ajit Singh, and Singapore Prime Minister Goh Chok Tong. For instance, the CII Singapore core group meets the Prime Minister of Singapore at least once a year to keep him abreast of progress on the economic and political front from a business point of view. Further, Prime Minister Goh Chok Tong was the Chief Guest for the celebrations of CII Centenary, in Calcutta, in January 1995. He brought with him a 60-member business delegation. To commemorate Goh Chok Tong's visit, CII even decided to observe 6 January as Singapore Day!

Governments as Spearheads of Economic *Rapprochement*

The above analysis shows that government policies play a major role in boosting economic relations between India and the East Asian region. The policy-makers set the framework for the business communities to interact and try to give a kick-start to private sector cooperation. Two examples confirm that the approach adopted by the governments is primarily voluntarist. The first is related to the Indian diaspora, the second to the Indo-ASEAN institutional dialogue. In both cases, the governments of India and South-East Asian countries try to involve the private sectors in their projects. Indeed, the governments may initiate regional integration, but it is the private sector that has ultimately the critical role to play in fulfilling the process.

India expects that its diaspora in South-East Asia will help to further the Look East Policy. The Indian government has thus started to woo the NRIs, mostly in Singapore, Malaysia and Hong Kong. The NRIs in these countries are expected to integrate the Indian economy into East Asian trading networks, to facilitate the creation of joint ventures, and to bring foreign capital investment and high technology to their motherland. In his *Singapore Lecture*, Prime Minister Rao insisted on the specific role that the NRIs could play in the context of the Look East Policy: 'the overseas Indian community which retains strong links with its homeland, but prefers to live and work abroad constitutes a vital link between India and the countries of the Asia-Pacific. We have a stake in their prosperity, as they have a stake in our future.'[9] In fact, India hopes that the Indian diaspora will support its economic take-off in the same way as the overseas Chinese community did in relation to China's open door policy. But the Indian diaspora differs from the overseas Chinese community in many ways, especially in its relation to the motherland. Moreover, the Indian diaspora comprises people with varying skills and resources and is not as much into business as is the Chinese diaspora. In South-East Asia, the majority of the NRIs do not have a high socio-economic status. There are a few tycoons however.

As for the Singapore government, it does not rely only on the NRIs in South-East Asia. Rather, it expects that the *global* Indian diaspora will help to bring about synergies with India. As a matter of fact, it would like to be a 'partnership centre' bringing together in strategic alliances Indian companies, NRI investors and regional companies to invest in India or in third countries in the region. This is in keeping with its desire to play a catalystic role in the development of business linkages between East Asia and India. Singapore even took the initiative to launch a cycle of conferences in order to promote closer links among Indian entrepreneurs, both in India and overseas. The first Global Indian Entrepreneurs Conference was organized by the Singapore Chamber of Commerce and Industry in June 1996. But the acknowledged driving force behind this event was the Prime Minister of Singapore, Goh Chok Tong. The event was supported by Singapore government agencies, such as the Economic Development Board and the Trade Development Board. The government of India also took strong interest in the event. Finance Minister Chidambaram attended the conference as the special representative of Prime Minister Deve Gowda. The second edition of the GIEC took place in November 1997, in New

Delhi. It was arranged by FICCI and the Indian Investment Centre, with active support from the Indian government. The event was inaugurated by the Indian Prime Minister, Atal Behari Vajpayee.[10]

The governments of India and South-East Asian countries have also tried to enhance private sector cooperation under the institutional framework of the Indo-ASEAN dialogue. New Delhi acquired the status of Sectoral Dialogue Partner of ASEAN in January 1992. The fact that the Economic Ministers of the Association supported India whereas the Foreign Ministers were more cautious indicates that ASEAN has had primarily an economic interest in India. Besides, this institutional dialogue has been mainly focused on the boosting of business linkages since the areas mutually identified for cooperation have been the sectors of trade, investment and tourism. A fourth sector of cooperation in Science and Technology was added later. The first official dialogue between India and ASEAN was held in Bali, in January 1994. Both sides agreed on the fact that the enhancement of economic cooperation required the support and involvement of the private sector. In this regard, an expert group was established and asked to propose recommendations on the means to promote trade and investments within the next six months. The officials from India and ASEAN even took the initiative to set up an ASEAN-India Business Council (AIBC) as a representative body for the private sector. The AIBC is meant to help the business communities of India and ASEAN to interact. The council is thus an organization for the private sector but it is born out of an inter-governmental initiative. This is testimony of the voluntarist approach of the governments of India and ASEAN in expanding their economic ties. With India being elevated to the status of full dialogue partner of ASEAN in 1996, the mechanisms of cooperation have been further strengthened.[11]

WORLDWIDE TRENDS TOWARDS REGIONALISM

The launching of the Look East Policy has to be analysed in the light of the evolution of the world trading system at the beginning of the 1990s. Then, this policy appears as a strategy to cope with the challenge arising from the consolidation of major regional groups the world over.

A SENSE OF EXCLUSION FROM THE MAJOR REGIONAL TRADE GROUPS

As it was opening its economy to the world market, India became aware of the growing trend towards regionalism and feared that it might be marginalized from the dynamics pushing the global economy. Being an outsider to the most important regional arrangements, India was increasingly concerned about the adverse impact of the growth of regionalism. Since the 1980s indeed, the number of regional trade agreements effected had increased dramatically. No fewer than thirty-four regional agreements were notified to GATT (General Agreement on Tariffs and Trade) under Article XXIV, between 1990 and 1994. India was then afraid that this proliferation of regional trading arrangements would lead to protectionism and inward looking trade blocs. In the beginning of the 1990s, the world trading system seemed to be on the way to getting fragmented into three major regional blocs, with the North American Free Trade Agreement (NAFTA), the European Union and, possibly, Japan with East Asia.[12]

Western Europe embarked on a deepening and an enlarging of its integration process. The 'Common Market' came into force in 1993 and the ex-socialist economies of Eastern Europe seemed likely to join the European Union in the middle term. The United States also found a renewed interest in transcontinental regional arrangements. The North American Free Trade Agreement took shape in 1993, among the United States, Canada and Mexico. The long-term ambition of the United States through NAFTA was to create a Pan-American free trade area. In other words, all of South America was potentially involved in this project. From New Delhi's point of view, the EC and NAFTA are not in keeping with the non-discriminatory multilateral trading regime advocated by the World Trade Organization. India has been all the more worried about this trends towards regionalism in the West, as the European countries and the United States have been its most important economic partners. The European Union accounts for 26 per cent of India's imports and 28 per cent of its exports. The United States is India's largest trade partner, as it absorbs 18 per cent of its exports and provide 14 per cent of its imports.[13] Therefore, India has been afraid to face a problem of market access in these regions of export interest. It has also worried that these regional groups might affect the prospects of attracting investment flows.

In keeping with its new enthusiasm for transcontinental regionalism, the United States also sponsored the creation of an Asia-Pacific Economic Cooperation group (APEC). The forum was established in 1989 at a ministerial summit in Canberra, but gained momentum with the Seattle Summit of 1993, when the leaders of the member countries put forward a vision of a 'community of Asia-Pacific economies'. At the summit in Bogor, Indonesia, in November 1994, the member countries adopted the goal to set a free trade area in the Asia-Pacific by 2020. The unique feature of APEC lies in its principle of 'concerted unilateral liberalization', which differs from the preferential trade liberalization practised by the UE and NAFTA. By the mid-1990s, APEC appeared as the most rapidly expanding economic region of the world. With its eighteen members,[14] it was the largest market in the world, accounting for nearly half of the world GDP. It was the epitome of Asia-Pacific prosperity and of the incoming Asian century.

New Delhi has sought an entry into APEC since its inception. But it has so far not been accepted as a member. India believes that membership of APEC is likely to boost economic ties with this region. However, exclusion from APEC should not—in theory—alter India's links with Asia-Pacific economies. Indeed, APEC is meant to uphold the principle of open regionalism, that is to say it is not discriminatory towards the non-members and it conforms with WTO provisions. Exclusion from APEC is a handicap inasmuch as it is an important forum for coordinating economic policies and for facilitating business and technical cooperation among member countries. Thus, India is being kept out of the flow of information, the networks of expertise and the databases concerning technology, trade and investment regimes among APEC members.

During the 1990s, India continued to find itself isolated from the mega-groups structuring the global economy while in its own region, the South Asian Association for Regional Cooperation (SAARC) could not succeed in creating major trade relations. SAARC was formally launched in 1985 with the aim of promoting economic cooperation between its seven members, namely Bangladesh, Bhutan, India, the Republic of Maldives, Nepal, Pakistan and Sri Lanka. But this regional organization did not make any significant progress due mainly to the Indo-Pak dispute and to domestic political turmoil throughout the region. In 1992, intra-regional trade only accounted for 3 per cent of the global trade of SAARC members. A South Asian Preferential Trading Agreement (SAPTA) was proposed in 1993 to free trade in the region, through the grant of tariff concessions for products of export interest to the seven member countries of SAARC. In 1995, SAARC members decided to work collectively towards the establishment of a South Asian Free Trade Area (SAFTA). Thus, in October 1995, SAFTA countries agreed to introduce preferential tariffs on 224 items of common trade. However, India cannot expect that SAARC will be a major influential pole in the global economy, in the near future.[15]

In addition, trans-regional multilateral fora such as the Group of 77 (G-77), UNCTAD and the Non-aligned Movement seem to have lost their influence. The regionalist trend of the 1990s brings together developed countries as well as developing countries in the same regional group so that the bargaining power of the Third World as a collective entity has been undermined. For India which used to be very involved in South-South cooperation, this development means that it is likely to be more and more isolated in international trade negotiations for the protection of developing countries' interests. The fact is that regional groups have more leverage in the negotiating process than individual countries. In this regard, India has understood that if it is not part of any major regional group, it will be deprived of a strong bargaining capacity in negotiations on trade issues. India's ability to bargain efficiently in the WTO was especially important during the 1990s as the organization was mandated to start negotiations on contentious issues such as the social clause, labour standards and trade related environment measures. These issues have been of primary interest to India.

Ramesh Behl and L.D. Mago, two researchers from the Indian Institute of Foreign Trade, sum up India's situation in relation to the evolution of the world trade system in the mid-1990s and they draw the general conclusion: 'the world trading system is in the process of splintering into trade blocs in spite of the successful conclusion of the Uruguay Round of Multilateral Trade Negotiations. No trading bloc in South Asia is likely to have enough economic clout to counteract this phenomenon of trading blocs causing a market entry problem to a country like India. This calls for a closer relationship with regional trading blocs on a bilateral basis. Thus a closer relationship with ASEAN is a pre-requisite for India.'[16] In sum, owing to this situation of exclusion from major trade groups, India has been anxious not only to be a partner of ASEAN but also to associate itself more closely to the East Asian region.

The Look East Policy in India's Globalisation Drive

Because of its globalization drive, India is fully committed to economic multilateralism, that is to say to a non-discriminatory multilateral trading system. New Delhi participated in the Uruguay Round of Multilateral Trade Negotiations actively and became part of the final agreements signed at Marrakesh in April 1994. India is thus a founder member of WTO. This international organization aims at reducing tariff and non-tariff barriers and, more generally speaking, it is entrusted with the task of maintaining an open and non-discriminatory global trading system. In this regard, the Look East Policy partakes of New Delhi's globalization drive. This new thrust towards East Asia does not mean that India ignores its other traditional partners, since the aim is rather to establish economic links with as many countries as possible. But with the growing trends towards protectionism in North America and Western Europe at the beginning of the 1990s, India started to regard East Asia as the best option to expand foreign trade relations. As well as its dynamism, East Asia has turned out to be one of the most open areas in the world. Besides, like India, East Asian countries are fully committed to global free trade. During the 1980s, they enforced unilateral liberalization of their trade and exchange payments while developed countries were resorting to protectionist measures. As most of the East Asian economies have adopted export-led growth strategy, they need access to the markets of the developed countries. In the 1990s, the growth of the tiger and dragon economies were still heavily dependent on the openness of the global trade system. East Asian countries also think that preferential trade agreements in Europe and North America affect non-members and they may severely hurt their export growth.

With regard to regionalism, the approach of the East Asian countries has been primarily outward-looking.[17] In fact, the growing economic integration in East Asia is a result of the free play of market forces and not of the adoption of preferential trade agreements. The increase in the share of intra-Asian trade in global Asian trade is mostly the effect of the higher growth among the trading countries themselves and of their unilateral liberalization. For instance, in spite of the launch of the ASEAN Free Trade Area (AFTA), Indonesia, Malaysia, Philippines, Thailand and Singapore have continued to carry out unilateral trade liberalization. From the East Asian point of view, regional cooperation is meant to increase multilateral trade and economic liberalization. Within APEC, the Asian member countries have been anxious to ensure that this regional forum would be a building bloc of economic multilateralism. They opposed the initiatives of the United States to institutionalize the forum and to implement discriminating measures against non-members such as the reciprocal application of APEC liberalization.

The Look East Policy is one of the most important aspects of India's integration in the world economy. The integration into the East Asian region is regarded as the best springboard into the global economy as it is one of the most globalized and open areas in the world. This perspective is in keeping with Singapore which has proposed India to be its gateway to the Asia-Pacific and the world economy. It should also be underlined that India's strategy to integrate into the East Asian region is based on its unilateral economic liberalization and its economic diplomacy and not on any preferential trade agreement. This is consonant with the East Asian approach to regionalism.

INDIA'S 'REGIONAL POLYGAMY'[18]

Since it has not been granted membership in any major trade group, New Delhi has embarked on various regional and sub-regional arrangements which supplement its Look East Policy. The Indian Ocean Rim Association for Regional Cooperation (IOR-ARC) initiative can be regarded as a response to other mega trade blocs, such as NAFTA and APEC. The idea of a region formed around the Indian Ocean was mooted in November 1993 by the then South African Foreign Minister, Mr Pik Botha, during a visit to New Delhi. In 1994, Australia started to get interested in the project. Then, Mauritius took the lead of the campaign for IOR, and Singapore, Oman and Kenya joined the process. From 29 to 31 March 1995, these seven countries of the Indian Ocean rim gathered to launch the IOR-ARC. The next meeting was held five months later, from 15 to 17 August 1995 and welcomed seven other members, namely Indonesia, Madagascar, Malaysia, Mozambique, Sri Lanka, Tanzania and Yemen. IOR-ARC was formally set up in March 1997, with 14 member countries. The IOR-ARC charter states that the objective of the forum is to 'build and expand understanding and mutually beneficial co-operation through a consensus-based, evolutionary and non-intrusive approach'.[19] The association is meant to encourage trade liberalization and facilitate and promote cooperation in trade and investment, science and technology.

For India as well as for South Africa and Australia, the IOR-ARC marks the desire to assert a region in response to the consolidation of other regional mega groups. It is also intended to combat a sense of exclusion. As already shown, India has not been admitted in APEC. If Australia is an APEC member, it is not very comfortable in its own Asian region. Some South-East Asian leaders refuse to consider Australia an Asian country and have consequently opposed its entry in important fora like EAEC and ASEM.[20] As regards South Africa, it has been economically and politically marginalized because of its long held apartheid regime. In India's viewpoint, IOR-ARC could also help to gain some bargaining power in multilateral trade negotiations, through collective action. IOR-ARC should also provide market access to India's exports. Indian Ocean countries account for about 10 per cent of India's global trade. According to the member countries, there is a huge potential of growth in trade cooperation. IOR-ARC appears thus as one more platform from which India can launch its globalization and regionalization drive.

IOR-ARC has been formed on the basis of the APEC model. It is an ocean-based regional cooperation project, advocating the concept of open regionalism. As in APEC, the process is tripartite and involves governments as well as the business communities and academic circles. A major difference between the two mega-groups is that IOR-ARC results from governmental initiatives whereas in APEC, economic cooperation has been primarily market driven. Furthermore, the concept of India Ocean Rim is fraught with fuzziness and, this large heterogeneous region is far from being as developed as APEC. Conflicting interests among member countries may alter IOR-ARC's functioning as well as the lack of political will from most of them. In the end, it seems that IOR-ARC will not deliver great economic benefit to India in the near future.

Aside from large-scale regional arrangement such as IOR-ARC, India is also involved in a sub-regional cooperative scheme, the Bangladesh, India, Myanmar, Sri Lanka, Thailand-Economic Cooperation (BIMST-EC). This regional group results first and foremost from Bangkok's initiatives. In keeping with its Look West Policy, Thailand has been advocating the concept of a Bay of Bengal community since at least 1994. In October 1994, Mr Surin Pitsuwan, Thai Deputy Foreign Minister, proposed the creation of a 'growth triangle' between India, Sri Lanka and Thailand in the Andamans. This proposal was once again formulated by Mr. Supachai Panitchpakdi, in January 1995, who explained that 'Thailand wished to build a four-lane highway between the Andaman Sea and the Gulf of Thailand and envisioned construction of deep-sea port, refineries and industrial ventures alongside the highway'.[21] Thailand may have been keen on developing BIMST-EC to compensate for its exclusion from IOR-ARC. Indeed, while IOR was taking shape between 1995 and 1997, Bangkok sought membership in the forum.[22]

BIMST-EC was eventually launched in June 1997. The unique feature of this cooperation project is that it establishes a link between ASEAN and SAARC. The official declaration states that cooperation within BIMT-EC will constitute an addition to and not be a substitute for bilateral, regional or multilateral cooperation involving member-states.[22] The member-states have also confirmed that the group would be committed to the principle of open regionalism. BIMST-EC is thus consistent with India's other regional projects. Moreover, it supplements its partnership with ASEAN since it aims at intensifying interactions with two ASEAN members, Thailand and Myanmar. In this regard, BIMST-EC is a stepping stone to the Indian Look East Policy.

BIMST-EC aims at creating a sub-regional pole of growth between South and South-East Asia. In fact, it is inspired by the innovative model of the growth triangles that has emerged in South-East Asia. Indeed, the BIMST-EC Concept Paper starts with the following observation: 'successful economic co-operation at the sub-regional level has been a new and encouraging feature of the dynamic growth of the Asia-Pacific region'.[24] Well-known examples of such sub-regional economic zones are the Singapore-Johor-Riau triangle (SIJORI) between Singapore, the southern part of the Malaysian state of Johor and the islands of Riau in Indonesia or the Indonesia-Malaysia-Thailand Growth Triangle (IMT-GT). Most of the time, these sub-regional economic zones involve only some provinces or states of the member countries. As regard BIMST-EC, it could turn out to be a means of integrating some South Asian countries or, at least some South Asian areas, in the process of economic regionalization in East Asia. India's eastern coastal states should be the most involved in the cooperation process. Calcutta, Madras and Visakhapatnam have already been among the sites identified for feasibility studies under the framework of BIMST-EC.

BIMST-EC adopts many characteristics of the East Asian sub-regional cooperative schemes. First, sub-regional Asian cooperative arrangements often try to enhance cooperation among countries at varying stages of economic development. In BIMST-EC's case, as of 1996, the GDP per capita for Thailand was \$2810 compared to \$720 for Sri Lanka, \$370 for India, \$240 for Bangladesh and \$235 for Myanmar.[25] But the fact is that sub-regional cooperation emphasizes the complementarities of the resource bases of the different partners. It helps to increase economies of scale in the production bases and facilitates the spillover of growth across national borders. Moreover, in sub-regional economic zones, the focus is not only on trade, but also on the promotion of tourism, natural and human resource development and infrastructure. This is the case with BIMST-EC, as one of its priority goals is to build infrastructure linkages among member countries, especially transportation linkages. At the inaugural ministerial meeting, on 6 June 1997, the representatives of the member-states decided to consider the feasibility of setting up a regional airline to provide the required network for enhancing business and tourist links between the member countries. The objectives of BIMST-EC are also to enhance intra-regional energy cooperation through an action plan for the development and utilization of natural gas, wind, solar and water/ tidal wave energy sources. Thus, BIMST-EC is a dynamic process of cooperation that tries to expand the resources of the Bay of Bengal sub-region as well as the growth of its future output. This project has benefited from the support of international institutions such as the Asian Development Bank and ESCAP, which have conducted preliminary studies.

IOR-ARC and BIMST-EC help India to strengthen its economic cooperation with South-East Asian countries. As a matter of fact, these two regional arrangements take part in the Look East Policy. Therefore, it turns out that the policy of 'Looking East' is made up of different scales of regional cooperation: sub-regional (BIMST-EC), regional (dialogue partnership with ASEAN), mega-regional (IOR-ARC).[26] These arrangements overlap and complement one another, with the ultimate goal of providing access to the globalization process. The best metaphor to describe the different dimensions of this policy would be that of Russian dolls. To sum up, the Look East Policy can be regarded as a strategy to deal with both regionalism and globalization. This is confirmed by the view of A.N. Ram, former Secretary, Ministry of External Affairs, Government of India: 'the challenge for our diplomacy will be to reconcile both the trends towards inevitable long-term globalisation and the consolidation of regionalism and sub-regionalism co-operation in such a manner that we are able to take advantage of both at the same time, even as we strengthen SAARC and our ongoing and expanding links with South-East Asia, the Pacific Rim and the Indian Ocean'.[27]

CONCLUSION

The focus of this paper has been more Indian *intentions* than the *facts* of the economic exchanges between India and East Asia. As a conclusion, it would be interesting to mention some of the actual results in terms of trade and investment flows between India and the countries of East Asia. On the whole, India has strengthened its economic ties with the East Asian region, even if the full scope of cooperation has not been reached as yet. Between January 1991 and August 1997 (when the financial crisis started to hit the East Asian economies), the total amount of FDI from South Korea and Japan was respectively Rs. 55,684.11 million and Rs. 50,568.28 million.[28] South Korea was the fourth investor in India, just before Japan, which was in the fifth position. South Korea has started to fulfil India's expectations with regard to the 'flying geese paradigm', in the sense that major *chaebols* like Hyundai, Daewoo, Samsung or L.G. have begun to relocate some of their manufacturing activities in India. As regards the level of Japanese investment flows, it is a little disappointing in relation to India's initial expectations.

As for the South-East Asian countries, they also proved to be important investors during that same period of time. As of August 1997, Malaysia was in the ninth rank, with a total amount of FDI flows of Rs. 33,411.36 million. Thailand was the thirtieth, with Rs. 24,491.02 million and Singapore was seventieth, with Rs. 20,113.24 million. Between 1991 and

1996, the total amount of approved FDI from ASEAN was around Rs. 66.2 billion, that is to say 7.2 per cent of the total amount of FDI approved by the Government of India. Total trade between India and ASEAN has also increased fairly substantially since 1991. From Rs. 71,524 million in 1992-3, it rose to Rs. 204,975 million in 1996-7, which is nearly a threefold increase (+ 2.8). Trade between India and ASEAN represented 6 per cent of India's global trade in 1992-3, and 8 per cent in 1996-7. Unfortunately, these upward trends have been affected by the Asian crisis. India's overall trade with ASEAN registered a marginal decline of about 0.2 per cent during the year 1997-8 because of the depression in the ASEAN markets in those two years. But it would seem that the worst of the Asian crisis is already over and, with signs of growth in the ASEAN economies, India hopes to increase trade both in terms of quantity and value with ASEAN countries. However, it should be underlined that India's potential integration into the East Asian economic regionalization will be a long-term process.

NOTES

1. In this paper, East Asia is defined as South-East plus North-East Asia. South-East Asia is more or less embodied in ASEAN, as of in 2000 (Brunei, Cambodia, Indonesia, Laos, Malaysia, Myanmar, Philippines, Singapore, Thailand, Vietnam). North-East Asia comprises Japan, the two Koreas, China (+ Hong Kong) and Taiwan.
2. J.N. Dixit, *My South Block Years: Memoirs of a Foreign Secretary*, New Delhi, UBSPD, 1996, p. 58.
3. P.M.S. Malik, *The Changing Face of India's Economic Diplomacy: The Role of Ministry of External Affairs*, Foreign Service Institute, *Indian Foreign Policy: Agenda for the 21st Century*, vol. 1, New Delhi, FSI & Konark Publishers, 1997, p. 234.
4. Kripa Sridharan, *The ASEAN Region in India's Foreign Policy*, Singapore, ISEAS, 1996.
5. P.V. Narasimha Rao, 'Indo-Korea Economic Interaction', Speech at the luncheon hosted by presidents of Apex Economic Organisations of Republic of Korea, Seoul, 10 September 1993.
6. P.V.N. Rao, 'India and Japan', Speech at the banquet hosted by the Prime Minister of Japan, Mr. Miyazawa, Tokyo, 23 June 1992.
7. Statement by External Affairs Minister of India, I.K. Gujral, on the occasion of the Post Ministerial Conferences of ASEAN (PMC-7+10), 24 July 1996, Jakarta, § 14.
8. J.N. Dixit, *My South Block Years*, op. cit., p. 266.
9. P.V. Narasimha Rao, 'India and the Asia-Pacific: Forging a New Relationship', *The Singapore Lecture Series*, Institute of Southeast Asian Studies, Singapore, 1994.
10. On this occasion, the Indian government confirmed the launching of the People of Indian Origin (PIO) card. He also announced the setting up of a study committee on dual citizenship.
11. An ASEAN-India Working Group on Trade and Investment has been established. An ASEAN-India Working Group Meeting has also been set up in order to streamline the procedural mechanism for expediting approvals and implementation of the mutually agreed ASEAN-India projects.

12. Satinder Palaha and H.L. Sharma, 'Towards Economic Integration through Regional Trade Blocs', *Occasional Paper 4*, Indian Institute of Foreign Trade, New Delhi, 1994.
13. These figures are taken from T.P. Bath, 'Trade Blocs and Global Trade Prospects', *Foreign Trade Review*, vol. XXXI, no. 4, January-March 1997, p. 72.
14. Australia, Brunei Darussalam, Canada, Chile, the People's Republic of China (PRC), Hong-Kong, Indonesia, Japan, the Republic of Korea, Malaysia, Mexico, New Zealand, Papua New Guinea, the Republic of the Philippines, Singapore, Chinese Taipei, Thailand and the United States.
15. The SAPTA scheme would at best augment 0.3 per cent of member countries' global trade in the span of 2-3 years. Taranath P. Bhat, 'Trade Blocs and Global Trade Prospects', *Foreign Trade Review*, vol. XXXI, p. 73.
16. Ramesh Behl and L.D. Mago, *India-ASEAN Trade Cooperation and Investment Opportunities*, New Delhi, Indian Institute of Foreign Trade, 1996, p. 35.
17. Asian Development Bank, *Asian Development Outlook*, Hong Kong, ADB & Oxford University Press, 1995, p. 183. However in 1992, ASEAN decided to launch an ASEAN Free Trade Area (AFTA) to be achieved by the end of year 2003. But, as the ADB explains, 'despite their membership in ASEAN since its formation in 1967 and the establishment of the much more comprehensive ASEAN Free Trade Area (AFTA) in 1992 and their participation in the Uruguay Round, all of the ASEAN countries continued to reduce their barriers to imports unilaterally during the period from the beginning of the Uruguay Round of negotiations in 1986 and since its conclusion in December 1993', ADB, p. 193.
18. J. Coussy, 'L'Inde Face a la Régionalisation de l'Economic Mondiale', les Edudes du CERI, no. 23, 1997, p. 45.
19. Ministry of External Affairs, Government of India, *India in IOR-ARC: Towards a new partnership in the Indian Ocean Rim*, XP Division, 1997.
20. East Asia Economic Caucus (EAEC) is mostly a Malaysian initiative and is limited to ASEAN, Japan, South Korea and China. The Asia Europe Meeting (ASEM) is a forum between the European Union and Asia as defined by the EAEC.
21. *Times of India*, 6 January 1995, quoted in Ganganath Jha, 'ASEAN and India: Dawning of New Partnership', *The Indonesian Quarterly*, vol. XXV, no. 2, 1997, p. 162.
22. Thailand was eventually admitted in IOR-ARC in April 1999.
23. Declaration on the Establishment of the Bangladesh-India-Sri Lanka-Thailand Economic Cooperation (BIST-EC), Bangkok, 6 June 1997, § 3.b.
24. Concept Paper, Bangladesh-India-Sri Lanka-Thailand Economic Cooperation (BIST-EC), Introduction, § 1.1.
25. *Times of India*, 27 November 1997.
26. Micro-regionalism could be added as another level of regional cooperation under the framework of the Look East Policy. Micro-regionalism refers to the regionalist activities of the Indian states. Indeed, some South Indian states like Andhra Pradesh, Karnataka and Tamil Nadu have been especially keen on strengthening their economic ties with South-East Asia. For more details on these different levels of regionalism, see J.H. Mittelman, 'Rethinking the New Regionalism in the Context of Globalisation', *Global Governance*, no. 2, 1996, pp. 189-213.
27. A.N. Ram, 'Challenges to India's Economic Diplomacy', Nancy Jetley, *India's Foreign Policy: Challenges and Prospects*, New Delhi, Vikas Publishing House, 1999, p. 117.
28. Ministry of Industry, Government of India, *SIA Newsletter*, September 1997.

ASEAN-India: Emerging Economic Opportunities

Mukul G. Asher, Rahul Sen and Sadhana Srivastava

INTRODUCTION

The period since the early 1990s has witnessed a perceptible shift in relations between India and the members of ASEAN.[1] The density of economic and political interactions has increased, and this trend is expected to continue as both sides enhance their capacity and willingness to engage with each other, and establish institutions and mechanisms for wider and deeper linkages. A good beginning has been made, but the relations will require continued nurturing (Asher, 1997).

This paper discusses factors contributing to increased density of economic relations between India and ASEAN, and suggests possible measures and avenues to take advantage of emerging economic opportunities for mutual benefits. In the Post Cold War globalized era, the role of economic diplomacy has increased considerably in relations between nations. It is therefore expected that increased density of economic relations will help provide a more conducive context for cooperation in political and other non-economic areas as well.

India's engagement with ASEAN will need to be at two levels. The first will be to engage ASEAN as an organization. However, because ASEAN as an organization has been intentionally provided by the members with very limited authority and resources to pursue economic cooperation and to acquire expertise or capacity for monitoring developments, India will also need to devise country-specific bilateral strategies and tactics. The bilateral approach is also necessary because the expanded ASEAN is considerably more heterogeneous in its economic structure and level of development, and in its political philosophy and orientation. As a result, it has become increasingly difficult to evolve a common ASEAN view on economic and other issues. The 1997 crisis has considerably reduced Indonesia's capacity and willingness to provide political leadership, while high-income members such as Singapore have focused on economic opportunities with countries beyond the region since the crisis (Lim, 2001; Khanna, 2000).[2] India has been sympathetic to the challenges faced by the ASEAN countries as a result of the 1997 crisis. The negative perceptions of the ASEAN region both internally and externally since the 1997 crisis notwithstanding,[3] the crisis has not altered its determination to engage with the ASEAN countries (Sridharan, 2001; Slater and Dhume, 2001). India thus takes a long-term view of its relations with ASEAN, and has proved to be a reliable partner.

The rest of the paper is organized as follows. A discussion of the major factors that have contributed to a more positive dynamics in economic (and political) relations between India and ASEAN is undertaken, followed by a brief overview of the existing economic relations centering on merchandise trade, investments and tourism. An analysis of the emerging economic opportunities between India and ASEAN as an organization, and between ASEAN and individual ASEAN members bilaterally is then undertaken. The final section provides the concluding observations.

FACTORS CONTRIBUTING TO POSITIVE DYNAMICS

Various factors contributing to a greater density of economic and political relations between India and the ASEAN members may be grouped under political and security environment, globalization and associated technological changes, and institutional foundations. Each is discussed in turn.

POLITICAL AND SECURITY ENVIRONMENT

ASEAN was formed as a Cold War organization aligned with the West. In return, the United States, Japan, and European countries were on the whole willing to integrate ASEAN in the international economic system, and in some cases subordinated their economic and commercial interests for security needs. Since the end of the Cold War, the US in particular has been pursuing its own economic and commercial interests much more vigorously, thus adversely affecting the original ASEAN members.

In the post-Cold War period, much greater mutual understanding of security and strategic interests has marked India's relations with the Western countries, particularly the US. India has demonstrated its willingness, backed up by expanded strategic capability and political engagement, to play a role beyond South Asia to which its adversaries have attempted to confine it.

The political and security environment thus is no longer as lopsided in favour of ASEAN as it was during the Cold War period. ASEAN members do not have any outstanding bilateral or multilateral security or political issues with India (ASEAN Secretariat, 1995). Indeed, in a new post-Cold War environment, greater engagement with India has the potential to enhance leverage of ASEAN with the rest of the world, as well as of each ASEAN member with respect to others in the organization. Attempts by some countries in ASEAN to confine India to South Asia are therefore not consistent with the broader interests of these countries or of ASEAN as an organization. Deeper and broader engagement between India and ASEAN is an essential element in Asia's attempts to enhance its role in the world.

Globalization and Associated Technological Changes

The unfolding globalization process has centered on vastly expanded cross-border production and distribution networks, and on financial institutions, products, and transactions. Adjusting to globalization while attempting to maintain social cohesion and internal political stability, has become a vital preoccupation of most countries around the world.

Globalization has been aided by the technological revolutions in communications, life sciences, including biotechnology, micro-electromechanical systems (MEMS), and information processing and dissemination. These have profoundly altered the requirements for participating meaningfully in the global economy and sustaining economic growth and employment. The importance of developing appropriate institutions, and of transparency and meaningful participation in social and political spheres has also increased. The role of individual initiative and entrepreneurship has also increased.

During the Cold War period, ASEAN countries grew rapidly, and were able to considerably improve their ranking in human development indicators including poverty reduction. Their integration with the international economy provided substantial benefits in terms of markets, investments, technology, manpower flows, and bilateral and multilateral loans and assistance, while they experienced little pressure for institutional reforms in political and economic spheres. India, on the other hand, chose not to be integrated with the international economy, with detrimental effects on its economic performance, and poverty reduction, though in many significant ways it remained a much more open society than most developing countries. It also devoted considerable energies to developing institutions, including those mediating between the centre and the states; and in laying foundations for democratic participation.

Globalization and associated technological changes ushered in a new era of economic uncertainty. ASEAN countries had greater integration with the world economy but were ill-equipped to suddenly deal with the new uncertainties. The 1997 East Asian economic crisis, whose proximate cause was the devaluation of the Thai baht on 2 July 1997 has considerably reduced ASEAN's earlier dynamism and adversely affected its medium term growth prospects. It is now clear that most ASEAN countries will need to devote considerable energies in developing political and other institutions, including for mediating centre-state issues (Lim, 2001). The 1997 crisis thus had an adverse impact on ASEAN's capacity to act as an economic partner. This has reduced the attention paid by the high-income countries, including those from the region such as Singapore, to the ASEAN members. Thus, they need to diversify their economic partners. ASEAN's limited domestic market has also increased the need to find economic partners with large markets, such as India. As India is not a direct competitor for ASEAN's export-led economies, particularly in the manufacturing sector, the opportunities for mutual gain are considerable (Khanna, 2000).

India experienced a major economic crisis in 1991 which was a result of overvaluation of the exchange rate, persistent and relatively large current account deficits, and loss of investor confidence (Cerra and Saxena, 2000). While the crisis did coincide with the Gulf War, the root causes lay much deeper in India's lack of emphasis on economic efficiency and limited integration with the world economy. The crisis clearly demonstrated the urgent need for a fundamental re-think of its economic philosophy, strategy, and tactics. Since 1991, India has embarked on wide ranging reforms that will significantly enhance the role of the markets and integrate it with the international economy.[4]

India's real GDP grew at an annual rate of 6.4 per cent between 1992-3 and 2000-1. India aims to increase the annual growth rate to about 7.0 per cent. This should provide ample opportunities to its economic partners, including those in ASEAN. India thus now has both greater willingness and capacity to engage with the outside world.

Unlike ASEAN, India clearly did not take sufficient advantage of the growth in international trade and investments since the 1960s. But its cautious approach to reforms, and nurturing of professional and technical human resources, and indigenous companies in pharmaceuticals and other knowledge-intensive sectors, are likely to positively contribute to its ability to compete in the twenty-first century. New activities, particularly the Internet, are beneficial when there is pluralism and contestability in not just economic but also in socio-political spheres. Indians are accustomed to operating in such an environment, and India's complex, multi-ethnic society and polity, and its social networks provide advantages in operating globally in new economy activities (Tschang, 2001).

Its systems of governance and institutions, while in need of reform, are consistent with evolving international norms, and more importantly elicit widespread acceptance and internalization by the Indian population. Thus, in a real sense, India's political and social systems have stability and resilience.[5] This is the main contributory factor in rapid acceptance of the reforms, even though consensus building process for introducing reform measures has been slow. India also needs to considerably enhance economic and technological sophistication of its policy-makers and bureaucracy. For both India and ASEAN, the only realistic choice is to participate in shaping the globalization process in a manner that makes them less unequal partners in relation to the high-income countries; and to address social realities at home. Thus, globalization has increased the need for greater engagement between the two, particularly as both face challenges in areas such as environment, drug trafficking, across-the-border terrorism, food security, designing effective social safety nets, applying technology to a diverse set of activities, and energy security.[6]

Institutional Foundations

The 1990s have also witnessed strengthening of the institutional foundations for engagement between India and ASEAN. India enunciated a 'Look East' Policy in 1991 with a view to deepening economic and political relations with the East Asian countries, and drawing lessons from them for managing its economy. In 1992, India became a sectoral dialogue partner of ASEAN on trade, investment, tourism, and science and technology. At the fifth ASEAN summit in Bangkok in December 1995, India was invited to be a full dialogue partner. This was followed by India becoming a member of the ASEAN Regional Forum (ARF) where regional security issues are discussed. India' s participation in these two fora has been low-key but confident and constructive. India's evolving economic cooperation with the United States has positively impacted on the environment in which India participates in the ARF. Participation of India in ASEAN working groups and in various committees as an observer could help deepen the understanding among the officials and private sector participants from both sides.

India and the ASEAN countries also have opportunities for cooperation and discussion in other fora such as G-15 (Group of 15 developing countries which included India, Indonesia, and Malaysia); Indian Ocean Rim Association for Regional Cooperation (IOR-ARC), which includes Indonesia, Malaysia, Singapore and Thailand as members; the Mekong-Ganga Cooperation (MGC), which includes Cambodia, India, Laos, and Vietnam; and the BIMST-EC (which includes India, Myanmar, and Thailand).

In addition, India has been especially active in forging bilateral relations with individual ASEAN countries, particularly, Indonesia, Myanmar, Singapore, and Vietnam. This is reflected in a recent series of visits by India's President, Prime Minister and External Affairs Minister, along with large business delegations, to these countries. The frequency of bilateral visits to India by the ASEAN leaders and their business delegations has also increased in recent months. The Indian Prime Minister's State visit to Malaysia in May 2001 which had considerable business and technological as well as political and strategic objectives was designed to extend such bilateral relations to more countries.

India's private sector has also been active in establishing institutional presence in ASEAN. This is exemplified by the establishment in Singapore in the mid-1990s of a South-East Asian regional office of the Confederation of Indian Industry (CII), a broad-based, pro-reform organization representing industry throughout the country. The CII is set to open its second overseas office in ASEAN in Kuala Lumpur some time in 2001. This will permit businesses in ASEAN to reduce their transaction costs in finding suitable and reliable business partners in India, and vice-versa. There is, however, no comparable private sector presence from the ASEAN side in India, a gap which ASEAN countries may consider addressing.

Before analysing the emerging economic opportunities, it may be useful to gain an understanding of recent trends in economic relations between ASEAN and India.

AN OVERVIEW OF EXISTING ECONOMIC RELATIONS

Existing economic relations between India and ASEAN cover a wide range, involving merchandise trade, trade in service transactions, investments, tourism, and manpower flows. Before discussing each in turn, some observations based on selected indicators provided in Table 1 may be useful. Because of data limitation, only six ASEAN countries are included in Table 1.[7]

(i) India's population of one billion is more than twice that of ASEAN. The most populous country in ASEAN, Indonesia, has about one-fifth of India's population.

TABLE 1: INDIA AND ASEAN: SELECTED MACRO-ECONOMIC INDICATORS

Country	*Population*	*GNP (1999)*		*GNP Per Capita (1999)*		*FDI (1998)*	*External Debt*		*ODA**	
	Million (1999)	*US $ billion current value*	*PPP*	*US $ current value*[a]	*PPP*	*US $ billion*	*US $ billion*	*% of GNP*	*$ per capita*	*% of GNP*
India	998.0	442.2	2,144.1	450.0	2,149.0	2.6	98.2	20.0	2.0	0.4
ASEAN[b]	450.0	519.4	1,547.3	1,154.2	3,438.4	19.0	352.0	67.8	8.3[c]	1.3
Indonesia	207.0	119.5	505.0	580.0	2,439.0	-0.4	150.9	126.0	6.0	1.5
Malaysia	23.0	77.3	180.8	3,400.0	7,963.0	2.3	44.8	69.0	9.0	0.3
Philippines	77.0	78.0	292.9	1,020.0	3,815.0	1.7	47.8	66.0	8.0	0.9
Singapore	3.0	95.4	87.1	29,610.0	27,024.0	7.2	-	-	1.0	0.0
Thailand	62.0	121.0	345.4	1,960.0	5,599.0	6.9	86.2	79.0	11.0	0.6
Vietnam	78.0	28.2	136.1	370.0	1,755.0	1.2	22.4	76.0	15.0	4.3

NOTES: - Nil or negligible

[a] World Bank estimates based on the World Bank Atlas method.

[b] Excludes Brunei, Cambodia, Laos, and Myanmar as complete data are not available.

[c] Calculated as simple average of the six countries.

SOURCE: *World Bank, World Development Report, 2000/2001.*

(ii) In contrast, ASEAN's per capita income in 1999 (US $1,154.2) is about two and a half times that of India at current exchange rates, and 1.6 times that of India in PPP terms.

(iii) In absolute terms, ASEAN's GNP in 1999 of US $519.4 billion at current exchange rates is nearly one-fifth higher than that of India. However, in PPP terms, India's GNP of US $2144.1 billion exceeds ASEAN's by more than a third. The gap in GNP at current exchange rates between India and ASEAN has been narrowing during the 1990s, particularly since the 1997 crisis. If India sustains its current growth rate, which is higher than that for ASEAN as a group for another decade, this gap could narrow further or even reverse. ASEAN, however, will continue to enjoy higher per capita income for the foreseeable future.

(iv) ASEAN's greater integration in the world economy is indicated by its Foreign Direct Investment (FDI) inflow in 1998 of US $19.0 billion as compared to only US $2.6 billion for India; by Official Development Assistance (ODA) per capita of more than four times (US $8) as compared to India (US $2.0); and by external debt of US $352 billion (68 per cent of GNP), as compared to US $98 billion (20 per cent of GNP) for India.

MERCHANDISE TRADE

The data for aggregate merchandise trade for the 1991-2 to 2000-1 (April-September) period is summarized in Tables 2-4. The source for the data is the Centre for Monitoring Indian Economy (CMIE), an independent economic research organization. It should be noted that the CMIE data might not necessarily be consistent with the data from ASEAN country sources. This is because the CMIE data are on the basis of fiscal rather than calendar year; the data reflect as far as possible the country of origin for recording India's imports, and country of destination for India's exports, thus excluding re-exports; and reflect values recorded by the Indian authorities.

The following observations may be made concerning the trends in merchandise trade between India and ASEAN during the 1990s:

(i) India's merchandise exports to ASEAN-6 nearly tripled from about US $1.0 billion (5.7 per cent of its world exports) in 1991-2 to US $2.9 billion in 1996-7 (8.5 per cent of its world exports), before declining sharply to only US $1.6 billion in 1998-9 as a result of the Asian crisis (Table 2). There has been a recovery since then, but the pre-

TABLE 2: TRENDS IN INDIA'S MERCHANDISE EXPORTS TO ASEAN, 1991-2 TO 1999-2000

(*million US $*)

		1991-2	*1992-3*	*1993-4*	*1994-5*	*1995-6*	*1996-7*	*1997-8*	*1998-9*	*1999-2000*	*2000 (Apr.-Sep.)*
World	Amount (US $ mn.)	17,998.29	18,538.76	22,213.01	26,337.5	31,842.32	33,497.98	34,020.95	33,651.03	37,644.39	21,373.4
	Growth rate (%)	n.a.	(3.0)	(19.8)	(18.6)	(20.9)	(5.2)	(1.6)	-(1.1)	(11.9)	(21.1)
ASEAN-6	Amount (US $ mn.)	1,022.27	1,242.94	1,675.12	1,899.58	2,672.83	2,851.64	2,353.07	1,585.38	2,199.37	1,251.7
	Growth rate (%)	n.a.	(21.6)	(34.8)	(13.4)	(40.7)	(6.7)	-(17.5)	-(32.6)	(38.7)	(23.7)
	Share in ASEAN (%)	(100.00)	(100.00)	(100.00)	(100.00)	(100.00)	(100.00)	(100.00)	(100.00)	(100.00)	(100.00)
	Share in India's Total Exports (%)	(5.7)	(6.7)	(7.5)	(7.2)	(8.4)	(8.5)	(6.9)	(4.7)	(5.8)	(5.9)
Indonesia	Amount (US $ mn.)	149.54	138.51	234.68	277.77	663.4	592.34	435.9	186.68	326.83	189.1
	Growth rate (%)	n.a.	-(7.4)	(69.4)	(18.4)	(138.8)	-(10.7)	-(26.4)	-(57.2)	(75.1)	(45.9)
	Share in ASEAN (%)	(14.6)	(11.1)	(14.0)	(14.6)	(24.8)	(20.8)	(18.5)	(11.8)	(14.9)	(15.1)
	Share in India's Total Exports (%)	(0.8)	(0.8)	(1.1)	(1.1)	(2.1)	(1.8)	(1.3)	(0.6)	(0.9)	(0.9)
Malaysia	Amount (US $ mn.)	203.9	189.85	247.03	286.57	393.75	531.58	481.82	317.69	435.52	254.5
	Growth rate (%)	n.a.	-(6.9)	(30.1)	(16.0)	(37.4)	(35.0)	-(9.4)	-(34.1)	(37.1)	(15.4)
	Share in ASEAN (%)	(19.9)	(15.3)	(14.7)	(15.1)	(14.7)	(18.6)	(20.5)	(20.0)	(19.8)	(20.3)
	Share in India's Total Exports (%)	(1.1)	(1.0)	(1.1)	(1.1)	(1.2)	(1.6)	(1.4)	(0.9)	(1.2)	(1.2)
Philippines	Amount (US $ mn.)	64.73	54.65	58.18	99.45	144.45	183.80	236.07	116.38	143.76	83.40
	Growth rate (%)	n.a.	-(15.6)	(6.5)	(70.9)	(45.2)	(27.2)	(28.4)	-(50.7)	(23.5)	(17.1)
	Share in ASEAN (%)	(6.3)	(4.4)	(3.5)	(5.2)	(5.4)	(6.4)	(10.0)	(7.3)	(6.5)	(6.7)
	Share in India's Total Exports (%)	(0.4)	(0.3)	(0.3)	(0.4)	(0.5)	(0.5)	(0.7)	(0.3)	(0.4)	(0.4)

(Contd.)

TABLE 2 (Contd.)

		1991-2	1992-3	1993-4	1994-5	1995-6	1996-7	1997-8	1998-9	1999-2000	2000 (Apr.-Sep.)
Singapore	Amount (US $ mn.)	391.00	589.90	751.16	770.50	902.99	978.29	739.80	519.92	692.01	400.00
	Growth rate (%)	n.a.	(50.6)	(27.6)	(2.6)	(17.2)	(8.3)	-(24.4)	-(29.7)	(33.1)	(21.2)
	Share in ASEAN (%)	(38.2)	(47.4)	(44.8)	(40.6)	(33.8)	(34.3)	(31.4)	(32.8)	(31.5)	(32.0)
	Share in India's Total Exports (%)	(2.2)	(3.2)	(3.4)	(2.9)	(2.8)	(2.9)	(2.2)	(1.5)	(1.8)	(1.9)
Thailand	Amount (US $ mn.)	200.0	253.66	356.09	406.71	473.63	447.45	338.00	319.68	457.26	234.70
	Growth rate (%)	n.a.	(26.8)	(40.4)	(14.2)	(16.5)	-(5.5)	-(24.5)	-(5.4)	(43.0)	(23.1)
	Share in ASEAN (%)	(19.6)	(20.4)	(21.3)	(21.4)	(17.7)	(15.7)	(14.4)	(20.2)	(20.8)	(18.8)
	Share in India's Total Exports (%)	(1.1)	(1.4)	(1.6)	(1.5)	(1.5)	(1.3)	(1.0)	(0.9)	(1.2)	(1.1)
Vietnam	Amount (US $ mn.)	13.01	17.36	27.98	58.59	94.61	118.17	121.48	125.03	143.99	99.00
	Growth rate (%)	n.a.	(33.4)	(61.2)	(109.4)	(61.5)	(24.9)	(2.8)	(2.9)	(15.2)	(28.6)
	Share in ASEAN (%)	(1.3)	(1.4)	(1.7)	(3.1)	(3.5)	(4.1)	(5.2)	(7.9)	(6.5)	(7.2)
	Share in India's Total Exports (%)	(0.1)	(0.1)	(0.1)	(0.2)	(0.3)	(0.4)	(0.4)	(0.4)	(0.4)	(0.4)

SOURCES: Calculated from CMIE, *Foreign Trade*, various issues; CMIE, *Monthly Review of the Indian Economy*, January 2001.

TABLE 3: TRENDS IN INDIA'S MERCHANDISE IMPORTS FROM ASEAN, 1991-2 TO 1999-2000

		1991-2	*1992-3*	*1993-4*	*1994-5*	*1995-6*	*1996-7*	*1997-8*	*1998-9*	*1999-2000*	*2000 (Apr.-Sep.)*
World	Amount (US $ mn.)	19,554.9	21,883.47	23,304.89	28,662.22	36,729.98	39,165.46	41,534.56	42,379.20	47,269.56	25,647.7
	Growth Rate (%)	n.a.	(11.9)	(6.5)	(22.9)	(28.1)	(6.6)	(6.1)	(2.0)	(11.5)	(11.7)
ASEAN-6	Amount (US $ mn.)	1,274.59	1,227	1,101.67	1,939.98	2,688.02	2,921.13	3,382.27	4,142.59	4,949.29	2,040.70
Growth Rate (%)		n.a.	-3.8	-10.2	76.1	38.6	8.7	15.8	22.5	19.5	-(16.0)
	Share in ASEAN (%)	(100.0)	(100.0)	(100.0)	(100.0)	(100.0)	(100.0)	(100.0)	(100.0)	(100.0)	(100.0)
	Share in India's total imports (%)	(6.5)	(5.6)	(4.7)	(6.8)	(7.3)	(7.5)	(8.1)	(9.8)	(10.5)	(8.0)
Indonesia	Amount (US $ mn.)	67.40	59.97	119.52	322.31	461.83	599.16	732.51	828.92	991.97	511.10
	Growth Rate (%)	n.a.	-11.0	99.3	169.7	43.3	29.7	22.3	13.2	19.7	(18.3)
	Share in ASEAN (%)	(5.3)	(4.9)	(10.9)	(16.6)	(17.2)	(20.5)	(21.7)	(20.0)	(20.0)	(25.0)
	Share in India's total imports (%)	(0.3)	(0.3)	(0.5)	(1.1)	(1.3)	(1.5)	(1.8)	(2.0)	(2.1)	(2.0)
Malaysia	Amount (US $ mn.)	391.97	405.83	249.16	490.21	904.08	1,042.24	1,180.32	1,610.38	2,059.34	592.70
	Growth Rate (%)	n.a.	(3.5)	-(38.6)	(96.7)	(84.4)	(15.3)	(13.2)	(36.4)	(27.9)	-(43.5)
	Share in ASEAN (%)	(30.8)	(33.1)	(22.6)	(25.3)	(33.6)	(35.7)	(34.9)	(38.9)	(41.6)	(29.0)
	Share in India's total imports (%)	(2.0)	(1.9)	(1.1)	(1.7)	(2.5)	(2.7)	(2.8)	(3.8)	(4.4)	(2.3)
Philippines	Amount (US $ mn.)	31.54	9.78	5.94	11.78	21.50	16.46	27.77	37.25	56.67	22.00
	Growth Rate (%)	n.a.	-(69.0)	-(39.3)	(98.3)	(82.5)	-(23.4)	(68.7)	(34.1)	(52.1)	(5.3)
	Share in ASEAN (%)	(2.5)	(0.8)	(0.5)	(0.6)	(0.8)	(0.6)	(0.8)	(0.9)	(1.2)	(1.08)
	Share in India's total imports (%)	(0.2)	(0.0)	(0.0)	(0.0)	(0.1)	(0.0)	(0.1)	(0.1)	(0.1)	(0.09)

(Contd.)

TABLE 3 (Contd.)

		1991-2	*1992-3*	*1993-4*	*1994-5*	*1995-6*	*1996-7*	*1997-8*	*1998-9*	*1999-2000*	*2000 (Apr.-Sep.)*
Singapore	Amount (US $ mn.)	696.28	632.14	626.11	899.95	1,115.15	1,064.21	1,199.33	1,383.85	1,508.28	745.50
	Growth Rate (%)	n.a.	-(9.2)	-(1.0)	(43.7)	(23.9)	-(4.6)	(12.7)	(15.4)	(9.0)	-(1.5)
	Share in ASEAN (%)	(54.6)	(51.5)	(56.8)	(46.4)	(41.5)	(36.4)	(35.5)	(33.4)	(30.5)	(36.5)
	Share in India's total imports (%)	(3.6)	(2.9)	(2.7)	(3.1)	(3.0)	(2.7)	(2.9)	(3.3)	(3.2)	(2.91)
Thailand	Amount (US $ mn.)	48.86	58.32	57.15	171.65	169.95	197.36	233.60	273.05	321.34	162.90
	Growth Rate (%)	n.a.	(19.4)	-(2.0)	(200.3)	-(1.0)	(16.1)	(18.4)	(16.9)	(17.7)	-(1.97)
	Share in ASEAN (%)	(3.8)	(4.8)	(5.2)	(8.9)	(6.3)	(6.8)	(6.9)	(6.6)	(6.5)	(7.98)
	Share in India's total imports (%)	(0.2)	(0.3)	(0.2)	(0.6)	(0.5)	(0.5)	(0.6)	(0.6)	(0.7)	(0.64)
Vietnam	Amount (US $ mn.)	38.54	60.62	43.79	44.08	15.51	1.70	8.74	9.14	11.69	6.50
	Growth Rate (%)	n.a.	(57.3)	-(27.8)	(0.7)	-(64.8)	-(89.0)	(414.1)	(4.6)	(27.9)	(61.1)
	Share in ASEAN (%)	(3.0)	(4.9)	(4.0)	(2.3)	(0.6)	(0.1)	(0.3)	(0.2)	(0.2)	(0.3)
	Share in India's total imports (%)	(0.2)	(0.3)	(0.2)	(0.2)	(0.0)	(0.0)	(0.0)	(0.0)	(0.0)	(0.0)

SOURCE: Calculated from Centre for Mointoring Indian Economy, *Foreign Trade*, various issues.

TABLE 4: INDIA'S BILATERAL BALANCE OF MERCHANDISE TRADE WITH ASEAN 6, 1991-2 TO 1999-2000

(million US$)

Year	*Indonesia*	*Malaysia*	*Philippines*	*Singapore*	*Thailand*	*Vietnam*	*ASEAN 6*	*India/World* *
1991-2	82.1	-188.1	33.2	-305.3	151.2	-25.5	-252.3	-1,556.6
1992-3	78.5	-216.0	44.9	-43.2	195.3	-43.3	16.3	-3,344.7
1993-4	115.2	-2.1	52.2	125.1	298.9	-15.8	573.5	-1,091.9
1994-5	-44.5	-203.6	87.7	-129.5	235.1	14.5	-40.4	-2,324.7
1995-6	201.6	-510.3	123.0	-212.2	303.7	79.1	-15.2	-4,887.7
1996-7	-6.8	-510.7	167.3	-85.9	250.1	116.5	-69.5	-5,667.5
1997-8	-296.6	-698.5	208.3	-459.5	104.4	112.7	-1,029.2	-7,513.6
1998-9	-642.2	-1,292.7	79.1	-863.9	46.6	115.9	-2,557.2	-8,728.2
1999-2000	-665.1	-1,623.8	87.1	-816.3	135.9	132.3	-2,749.9	-9,625.2
2000 (Apr.-Sep.)	-322.0	-338.2	61.4	-345.5	71.8	63.5	-809.0	-4,274.3

NOTE: *India's overall Balance of Trade

SOURCE: Calculated from Centre for Monitoring Indian Economy, *Foreign Trade*, various issues.

crisis peak has not yet been reached. Nevertheless, in 1999-2000, India's exports to ASEAN exceeded its exports to Japan (US $1.7 billion), and to Germany (US $1.8 billion).

(ii) There has, however, been considerable shift in the share of total Indian exports to ASEAN among the individual members during the 1990s. In general, the share of India's exports to Indonesia (particularly until the 1997 crisis), and Vietnam increased significantly, while the share of Singapore declined during the decade. In absolute terms, however, Singapore remains the largest market in ASEAN for India's goods, followed by Malaysia, Thailand, Indonesia, Vietnam, and the Philippines.

(iii) India's imports from ASEAN have increased nearly four times, from US $1.3 billion in 1991-2 to US $4.9 billion in 1999-2000 (Table 3). Indeed, in 1999-2000, ASEAN accounted for 10.5 per cent of India's imports from the world (Table 3). Thus, there is an asymmetry. ASEAN is much more important to India as a source of imports (particularly electronic goods, cooking oil, forest products and petroleum products) than it is as a market for its exports. India thus has been able to contribute positively to ASEAN's export-led recovery.

(iv) During the 1990s, the relative importance of ASEAN countries in India's imports has changed considerably (Table 3). In 1991-2, Singapore's share was 54.6 per cent, but by 1999-2000, its share had dropped to only 30.5 per cent (Table 3). Correspondingly, the share of Malaysia increased from 30.8 per cent to 41.6 per cent; and Indonesia from 5.3 per cent to 20.0 per cent (Table 3). Thus, in relative terms, Singapore's importance has been declining.

(v) India-ASEAN merchandise trade has more than tripled from US $2.3 billion in 1991-2 to US $7.1 billion in 1999-2000. As India's imports from ASEAN have grown much faster than its imports, the balance of trade has shifted sharply in favour of ASEAN (Table 4). During the 1990s, in only two years did India exhibit a surplus with ASEAN. India's trade deficit with ASEAN increased quite sharply after the 1997 crisis, reaching US $2.7 billion in 1999-2000, more than a quarter of its total deficit with the world[8] (Table 4). In 1999-2000, India had the highest bilateral deficit with Malaysia (US $1.6 billion), followed by Singapore (US $0.8 billion), and Indonesia (US $0.7 billion). As noted below, India is also likely to experience adverse balance of trade in services, particularly in tourism, logistics and transportation services, with ASEAN. Precise data however are not available.

As India continues its reforms and good macroeconomic performance, ASEAN countries will find further economic opportunities with it. This could in part counterbalance the adverse impact of China's entry into the World Trade Organization on ASEAN's exports and investment flows (Thornhill, 2001).

INVESTMENT RELATIONS

Existing investment relations between India and ASEAN are limited. Among the ASEAN countries, only Singapore is a net lender abroad. Singapore-based MNCs, and Singapore's government-linked-companies (GLCs) such as Singapore Telecom, Port of Singapore Authority, and Singapore Technologies have made investments in India. There have also been some investments by Singapore's private sector companies in health care, real estate, and tourism.

Because of the significant presence of the MNCs in Singapore; the use of Mauritius to route investments because of its favourable double taxation treaty with India; and the recording of investment flows by the Non-Resident Indians (NRIs) from around the world as a separate category, it is not possible to accurately quantify approved or actual investment flows from Singapore to India. Singapore's role as a financial centre has also been important in India's transactions with the rest of the world.

Large companies, particularly conglomerates from other ASEAN countries such as Malaysia, Indonesia and Thailand, have made occasional investments in India. But the 1997 economic crisis has affected them adversely, and many of their investments in India have undergone ownership and other changes.[9]

The Indian diaspora in ASEAN countries has not played a significant role in expanding economic relations with India, including in investment. In part this reflects weak economic and political position of the citizens of Indian origin, who are a minority. In part, it reflects the lack of effective recognition on the part of the Indian political and business elites in ASEAN countries that, without a strong and resurgent India, their own position will become even more marginalized than it is today. Indeed, Malaysia and Singapore are perhaps the only two significant economies in the world where the socio-economic status of their citizens of Indian origin is lower than that of the population as a whole. Prospects for reversing this situation in the near future are not favourable, as these are rooted in entrenched public policies and in the mindset of the Indian leaders which have internalized the rationale for the current status of the Indian communities, and therefore are unwilling to take concerted action. As a result, the emigration rate of Indian professionals from these two countries is quite large, though no precise data are available. In the case of Singapore, inward flow of Indian technical and professional personnel does counterbalance the above trend, but it changes the character and the dynamics of the Singapore Indian community.

A recent study by Yogarajah (2000) based on 75 interviews with firms from Malaysia and Singapore who have invested in India found a high-level of satisfaction with their decision to invest in India, and most were considering expansion or diversification. The favourable experience and profitability of Singapore's Technology Park in Bangalore has also created a positive environment for investments in India.

The Indian companies had limited capacity until recently to invest abroad, including in ASEAN. There have been limited Indian investments in ASEAN countries, dating back to the 1960s. Their presence, however, is insignificant in aggregate terms. Businesses of the Indian diaspora, particularly trading companies, were quite adversely affected by the 1997 East Asian crisis. Many are yet to fully recover.

However, as the reform process gathers momentum, and as the regulations permitting foreign investments by the Indian companies, particularly by those in the Information and Communication Technology (ICT) sector, become more and more liberal (the 2001-2 Budget substantially liberalizes such investments), the presence of Indian companies in ASEAN is likely to grow. Unlike in the earlier period, their presence will be motivated by economic efficiency and profitability criteria and not by the desire to escape a restrictive business environment at home. The Indian business environment (in such areas as taxation, regulations) is now at least comparable to most ASEAN countries, while its market potential is considerably greater than in ASEAN countries.

Tourism Services

In ASEAN, Indonesia, Malaysia, the Philippines, and Singapore have developed considerable expertise and competitive advantage in tourism services. In recent years, Vietnam is also developing into an important tourist destination.

India on the other hand has only very recently realized the need to implement an integrated tourism industry which will induce not only substantially larger number of international visitors than the current 2.2 million per year,[10] but also provide a conducive atmosphere and value-for-money services to increase their expenditure per day. India has a substantial domestic tourism sector, and this could be leveraged for the above purpose.

In 1996, the year before the East Asian crisis, tourism receipts were highest for Thailand (US $8.7 billion), followed by Singapore (US $8.0 billion), Indonesia (US $6.1 billion), Malaysia (US $4.1 billion), India (US $3.0 billion), and the Philippines (US $2.7 billion) (Table 5).

Trends in visitor arrivals from India to ASEAN-5 indicate that the total number of visitors have increased from 421.4 thousand (2 per cent of total visitors) in 1992 to 578.6 thousand (2.1 per cent of total visitors) in 1999 (Table 6). In 1999, Singapore attracted nearly half of all Indian visitors to ASEAN-5, followed by Thailand (31.3 per cent), Malaysia and Indonesia about 8 per cent each, and Philippines accounted for about 3.2 per cent (Table 6). Malaysia has recently been taking aggressive steps to make up for the missed opportunities in developing the Indian tourism market. Thus, in 2000, Indian visitors to Malaysia increased by 217 per cent as compared to the previous year, reaching to 140 thousand (*Business Standard*, New Delhi, 6 February 2001). (http://www.business-standard.com)

The flow of ASEAN visitors to India is quite small. While data are not available for ASEAN countries, in 1998, visitors from Singapore to India numbered only 54 thousand (Sen et al., 2000, p. 22). As similar imbalance in tourism flows is likely to prevail with respect to other ASEAN countries, the balance of trade in tourism services is likely to significantly favour ASEAN countries.

Manpower Flows

ASEAN's rapid economic growth has led to manpower shortages at all skill levels, particularly in Singapore, Malaysia, and Thailand. The 1997 crisis did affect the demand for foreign talent in ASEAN for a limited period. However, their recovery from the crisis has once again revived the need for foreign talent. In India on the other hand, supply of manpower has exceeded demand. There are therefore complementarities between the two in this area. The worldwide shortage of talent, particularly in the ICT sector, has also increased the demand for talent from India as its manpower is internationally competitive, English speaking, and accustomed to operating in a multicultural environment (Tschang, 2001). The increasing presence of the some western MNCs in both ASEAN and India has also been a contributory factor in augmenting manpower flows from India. Unfortunately, no data are available on the manpower flows to undertake a more detailed analysis.

TABLE 5: TOURISM RECEIPTS OF ASEAN-5 AND INDIA: 1988-97

(US $ million)

	Thailand			*Philippines*			*Singapore*			*Malaysia*			*Indonesia*			*ASEAN-5*		*India*	
	Amount	*% Gr.*	*Share in ASEAN-5*	*Amount*	*% Gr.*	*Share in ASEAN-5*	*Amount*	*% Gr.*	*Share in ASEAN-5*	*Amount*	*% Gr.*	*Share in ASEAN-5*	*Amount*	*% Gr.*	*Share in ASEAN-5*	*Amount*	*% Gr.*	*Amount*	*% Gr.*
1988	3121		28.2	1301		11.8	2622		23.7	745		6.7	1283		01.2	11060		1500	
1989	3753	20.2	29.2	1465	12.6	11.4	3307	26.1	25.8	1038	39.3	8.1	1285	0.2	01.0	12837	16.1	1535	2.3
1990	4326	15.3	27.1	1306	-10.9	8.2	4596	39.0	28.7	1667	60.6	10.4	2105	63.8	01.3	15990	24.6	1513	-1.4
1991	3923	-9.3	24.8	1281	-1.9	8.1	4560	-0.8	28.8	1530	-8.2	9.7	2522	19.8	01.6	15807	-1.1	1757	16.1
1992	4829	23.1	25.4	1674	30.7	8.8	5499	20.6	28.9	1768	15.6	9.3	3278	30.0	01.7	19040	20.5	2120	20.7
1993	5013	3.8	22.6	2122	26.8	9.6	6998	27.3	31.6	2050	16.0	9.2	3988	21.7	01.8	22164	16.4	2001	-5.6
1994	5762	14.9	22.5	2283	7.6	8.9	7396	5.7	28.8	3440	67.8	13.4	4785	20.0	01.9	25660	15.8	2265	13.2
1995	7664	33.0	26.2	2454	7.5	8.4	8337	12.7	28.5	3607	4.9	12.3	5228	9.3	01.8	29285	14.1	2609	15.2
1996	8664	13.0	27.5	2701	10.1	8.6	7958	-4.5	25.3	4093	13.5	13.0	6087	16.4	01.9	31499	7.6	2963	13.6
1997	7048	-18.7	33.2	2831	4.8	13.3	6843	-14.0	32.3	2497	-39.0	11.8	n.a	n.a	n.a	21216	-32.6	3152	6.4

SOURCE: UN-ESCAP, *Statistical Yearbook for Asia and the Pacific*, 1999.

TABLE 6: TRENDS IN VISITOR ARRIVALS FROM INDIA IN ASEAN-5

(Number in thousands)

Countries	1992				1993				1994			
	Total Visitors Number	*Share of Indian visitors to ASEAN-5*	*Visitors from India Number*	*Share in total visitors*	*Total Visitors Number*	*Share of Indian visitors to ASEAN-5*	*Visitors from India Number*	*Share in total visitors*	*Total Visitors Number*	*Share of Indian visitors to ASEAN-5*	*Visitors from India Number*	*Share in total visitors*
Singapore	5,989.9	58.2	245.3	4.1	6,425.8	61.8	233.7	3.6	6,899.0	58.2	225.0	3.3
Indonesia	3,064.2	3.7	15.6	0.5	3,403.1	3.9	14.8	0.4	4,006.3	5.4	21.0	0.5
Malaysia	6,016.2	11.3	47.5	0.8	6,503.9	4.1	15.4	0.2	7,197.2	5.7	21.9	0.3
Thailand	5,136.4	25.0	105.2	2.0	5,760.5	27.9	105.4	1.8	6,166.5	27.9	107.8	1.7
Philippines	1,153.0	1.9	7.9	0.7	1,372.1	2.4	9.0	0.7	1,573.8	2.8	10.8	0.7
ASEAN-5	21,359.7	100.0	421.4	2.0	23,465.4	100.0	378.1	1.6	25,842.8	100.0	386.6	1.5

Countries	1995				1996				1997			
	Total Visitors Number	*Share of Indian visitors to ASEAN-5*	*Visitors from India Number*	*Share in total visitors*	*Total Visitors Number*	*Share of Indian visitors to ASEAN-5*	*Visitors from India Number*	*Share in total visitors*	*Total Visitors Number*	*Share of Indian visitors to ASEAN-5*	*Visitors from India Number*	*Share in total visitors*
Singapore	7,137.3	54.9	238.2	3.3	7,292.5	55.3	253.2	3.5	7,198.0	48.7	226.6	3.1
Indonesia	4,324.2	7.4	32.0	0.7	5,034.5	5.9	26.9	0.5	5,185.2	9.7	44.9	0.9
Malaysia	7,468.7	6.4	27.7	0.4	7,138.5	7.0	32.0	0.4	6,210.9	6.2	28.9	0.5
Thailand	6,451.6	28.5	123.7	1.9	7,192.1	28.3	129.8	1.8	7,294.0	31.6	147.3	2.0
Philippines	1,760.1	2.9	12.4	0.7	2,049.4	3.5	16.1	0.8	1,171.6	3.8	17.7	1.5
ASEAN-5	27,141.9	100.0	434.0	1.6	28,707.0	100.0	458.0	1.6	27,059.7	100.0	465.5	1.7

(Contd.)

TABLE 6 (Contd.)

Countries	1998				1999			
	Total Visitors Number	*Share of Indian visitors to ASEAN-5*	*Visitors from India Number*	*Share in total visitors*	*Total Visitors Number*	*Share of Indian visitors to ASEAN-5*	*Visitors from India Number*	*Share in total visitors*
Singapore	6,242.0	48.4	243.6	3.9	6,958.0	49.8	288.4	4.1
Indonesia	4,606.4	8.5	42.9	0.9	4,727.5	7.6	44.1	0.9
Malaysia	5,550.7	6.7	33.7	0.6	7,317.6	8.0	46.5	0.6
Thailand	7,842.7	32.2	162.1	2.1	8,651.3	31.3	181.0	2.1
Philippines	2,149.4	4.2	20.9	1.0	n.a	3.2	18.6	n.a
ASEAN-5	26,391.2	100.0	503.2	1.9	27,654.4	100.0	578.6	2.1

SOURCES: *Yearbook of Tourism Statistics*, World Tourism Organization (WTO), various issues; WTO. *Tourism Market Trends 1999*; *Statistik Indonesia*, 1999; *Philippines Statistical Yearbook*, 1999; *Statistical Yearbook of Thailand*, 1999 and Pacific Asia Travel Association (PATA), *Annual Statistical Report*, 1999.

EMERGING ECONOMIC OPPORTUNITIES BETWEEN ASEAN AND INDIA

The discussion in the previous sections has provided an overview of the growing economic linkages between India and ASEAN, and the basis for increasing density of economic relations. We now examine specific areas and prospects for India's future economic opportunities with ASEAN as a regional organization and explore emerging economic opportunities on a bilateral basis with each ASEAN country.

ASEAN-India Interactions

ASEAN as an organization has an important role to play in facilitating trade and investments. The ASEAN Free Trade Area (AFTA), and the ASEAN Investment Area (AIA) have laid the foundation for greater cooperation among members. ASEAN holds a large number of technical meetings on a wide range of subjects relating to trade facilitation, technology, particularly IT, and industry standards. ASEAN may consider permitting India to participate as an observer in selected technical meetings related to trade facilitation and standards. ASEAN and India could also use their dialogue partner relationships to expand technological cooperation, educational exchanges, and rules governing movement of natural persons, and E-commerce.

To further strengthen the institutional base for deeper engagement, and to forge Asia-wide cooperation, India's participation in the ASEAN plus Three (China, Japan, and South Korea) annual meeting; or alternatively, holding of ASEAN-India annual summit merits serious consideration.

India does engage in fruitful annual dialogue with the European Union at the summit level. Its relations with the US have also become deeper and wide-ranging. If East Asia in general and ASEAN in particular continue with their unwillingness to take the relationship at a higher level, economic and broader human security options for both will unfortunately narrow at the time when other regions such as the Americas and Europe are expanding their options.

Indonesia-India

Emerging opportunities between Indonesia and India exist in a wide range of areas from food and energy security to infrastructure and human resource development. India is seeking to diversify its conventional energy sources, and significantly increase exploration of oil in its territory. Indonesia possesses enough expertise in this area as well as in the nuclear power sector, providing considerable scope for energy cooperation.

For both countries, food security is an important concern. This will require application of biotechnology, and other knowledge-intensive activities to improve productivity in the agricultural sector. Both countries also need to encourage food-processing industries. India also has considerable shortages of cooking oil, while Indonesia is emerging as a major palm-oil producer. Thus, there exist significant avenues to enhance the cooperation in food security. Besides, India is also a major importer of forest products while Indonesia is a major exporter, which indicates another potential area of expansion of bilateral trade.

India could also cooperate with Indonesia in pharmaceutical and health care sectors. Indonesia is heavily dependent on imported drugs and health care equipment. Indian pharmaceutical companies are internationally competitive in certain areas, particularly in generic drugs that are much cheaper than branded drugs.

Another important area of economic cooperation between the two countries could be in the area of infrastructure development, particularly in railways and aviation, and in commercialization of space activities in which India is emerging as a competitor.

Given the recent developments in the ICT sector in India, the two countries also benefit from cooperation particularly in the area of development of human resources and in that of software programmes in Bahasa Indonesia. Another area of cooperation that holds promise concerns the entertainment and media sector. Firms from the two countries could consider joint production of films, television programmes, and Internet content for both domestic and international audiences, particularly those whose main language is Malay. India and Indonesia may also consider cooperating in the area of telecommunications, particularly in expanding rural connectivity. The Indian technology in this area has been found to be cost-effective, and cooperation could benefit both sides.

As Indonesia continues its recovery from the 1997 crisis, there are prospects for the emergence of an Indian diaspora in Indonesia, centred on professional and technical personnel. This development will also have a positive impact on economic relations between the two countries. Indonesia's public support at the highest levels for India's bid for a permanent seat on the UN Security Council has created a favourable atmosphere for deeper economic engagement between the two countries (Baruah, 2001e).

MALAYSIA-INDIA

In recent months, the two countries have shown renewed interest in exploring substantial complementarities existing between them.

The Indian Prime Minister's state visit to Malaysia in May 2001, accompanied by a large business delegation, has given impetus to bilateral economic relations (Baruah, 2001d). The aim is to triple the current bilateral trade of US $2.5 billion in the next few years by broadening and deepening the economic linkages.

The decision of India's CII to set up its second office in ASEAN in Kuala Lumpur has provided an institutional basis for private sector interactions between the two countries. It is hoped that the Malaysian business organizations will consider setting up a similar representative office in India. Malaysia has permitted one of India's state-controlled but partly privatized banks to operate in Malaysia. This should reduce transactions costs for bilateral business and individual customers.

Malaysia has in recent years, particularly before the 1997 crisis, made substantial investments in expanding capacities in selected infrastructural areas such as airports, seaports, highways, and information technology. It is also aiming to reduce its dependence on the infrastructural facilities in Singapore in its international trade. The large capacities which it has built up require large volumes to be economically viable. India could be one of the trading partners to assist Malaysia in this respect. Encouragement of direct linkages between the two countries could be one such measure. India has granted permission for Malaysia's national carrier to fly to Mumbai, Bangalore, and Hyderabad.

Malaysia aims to be an important centre for information technology. It has invested heavily in requisite infrastructure facilities, but lacks a critical mass of talent in the ICT sector. India is an internationally recognized source of such talent (Tschang, 2001). Malaysia needs to augment its current talent pool if it is to realize its objectives. The Indian talent could also be leveraged to develop software and E-commerce services in the Malay language, and to take advantage of the opportunities in entertainment and multimedia activities. In particular, Media Development Corporation, in charge of developing Malaysia's ambitious multimedia super-corridor, may consider being more deeply engaged with India's IT training and development institutions and firms.

An impediment to Indian companies setting up operations in the Malaysia's multimedia super-corridor is that these companies undertake work for Malaysian entities indirectly, through subcontracting from the US and

European firms. If the Malaysian entities were willing to provide direct contracts to the Indian companies, there would be mutual benefits, including a more sustainable business model for Indian information technology companies to set up operations in Malaysia's multimedia super-corridor.

India is currently a centre of medical education for Malaysian students. The cooperation between the two countries in the education sector could be widened to other areas, such as management and information technology. Given the rapidly rising health care costs in Malaysia, opportunities exist in health care activities, and in generic and other drugs, including for the HIV-AIDS. Indian Ayurvedic medicines also have potential to be culturally more compatible and affordable to a wider population in Malaysia. Joint efforts in this area thus could be beneficial to both sides. Some Indian companies from the health and pharmaceutical sectors already have presence in Malaysia, but the two countries could consider strengthening it.

India and Malaysia have undertaken joint ventures to facilitate satellite launches by Malaysia from Indian facilities on globally competitive terms (Baruah, 2001d). This cooperation in space has the potential to open up new avenues for economic linkages as India is intent on commercial spin-offs from its investments in space research and development (*Business India*, 1997). Malaysia is among the first set of countries with which India is sharing its space technology.

Malaysia for its part is in a strong position to assist India in providing infrastructure expertise and investments; and in the energy sector. The Indian government has recently signed a MoU with the Malaysian government for roads (*Business Standard*, 15 January 2001). The Malaysian government will bring in equity for this project.

The Malaysian companies have won over a dozen tenders for road and highway projects in India in open international competition. This testifies to their international competitiveness and to their acceptability in India. The potential for their participation in India is much greater, and they may consider setting up a consortium office in India. The energy sector companies from the two countries could also cooperate with each other in oil and gas exploration and in downstream processing activities.

Malaysia possesses considerable strength in the plantations sector, particularly in research on rubber. India's need and low level of development in this sector therefore could provide opportunities for mutually beneficial cooperation, particularly as Malaysia's wage levels require it to restructure more labour intensive aspects of the value chain of its plantations sector.

A key issue of concern to Malaysia is the high import duties levied on refined palm oil by India to protect its farmers and industry. The permitted maximum tariffs under the WTO vary depending on the type of crop. Thus, for soya beans, the maximum tariff rate is 45 per cent, while for palm oil it is 300 per cent. India already levies duties on soya beans at the maximum rate, but for palm oil, its duties of 45 per cent are considerably below the maximum rate.

India has however agreed to consider the current level of palm oil tariffs in view of the importance attached to it by the Malaysian side. The palm oil has a limited market due to perceived health concerns, and India is among the largest buyer of palm oil. During the Indian Prime Minister's visit in May 2001, Malaysia offered a barter deal worth US $1.5 billion involving palm oil for railway lines contract. Both sides need to find a satisfactory solution to the palm oil, perhaps through an agreement on division of labour in palm oil value chain.

MYANMAR-INDIA

Myanmar and India have only recently begun to lay a foundation for closer economic relations. This has been achieved through a series of recent bilateral visits. The two share a 1600 km long border; and Myanmar's strategic location as a gateway to ASEAN from India's North-East, an area India wants to develop for both economic and security reasons, have provided an impetus for cooperation. Currently, the main emphasis is in developing road and banking links.

In 1999-2000, the two-way trade was US $217 million, with Myanmar's exports being US $141 million. Indeed, India is now Myanmar's largest export market. Its exports are mainly forest products, and agricultural commodities such as pulses. Given Myanmar's isolation from the Western world, it can reap significant benefits from economic cooperation with India.

There are emerging bilateral opportunities in infrastructure sector such as roads and ports; hydroelectric and hydrocarbon sectors, particularly in natural gas; and in technological cooperation in such areas as agriculture and natural resource monitoring. Indeed, in February 2001, a Myanmar-India friendship centre for Remotes Sensing and Data Processing was inaugurated. The centre has capabilities of weather forecasting, determination of forest cover and other land-use delineations, ground water survey, etc. The two countries should also consider re-establishing banking and other financial institutional linkages.

PHILIPPINES-INDIA

The existing economic relations between the two countries are rather limited (Tables 2-4). The end of the Cold War has not significantly altered the world view of the policy-makers and the elite in the Philippines, traditionally indifferent towards India. This is the only ASEAN country with which high level contacts have not taken place in recent months, or is being currently contemplated. Both sides need to address this gap in bilateral relationship.

There are however, indications that in select areas, greater cooperation between the two countries may emerge. Thus, the government of the Philippines has used importation of selected drugs from India to enhance contestability in the sector and thus reduced the pricing power of the domestic manufacturers. This shift at the margin from nearly exclusive concentration on producers to consumer interests holds promise as Indian pharmaceutical companies are internationally competitive, particularly in generic drugs which are cheaper. Whether this shift will be retained by the Philippines government however remains to be seen. But if it does, many drugs, including those needed to treat HIV-AIDS could be sourced from India at affordable prices.

The Philippines and India are internationally competitive in selective niches in the ICT sector. The business concept of competition through cooperation could be applied by the ICT firms from both countries to pursue mutually beneficial opportunities. As an example, one of India's leading software companies is exploring the feasibility of opening a major software development centre in the Philippines that will eventually employ about 2000 people.

Indian companies are also exploring cooperation in the agricultural sector, including research. Some of the Indian companies have been accredited to export meat to the Philippines.

The potential network of the Indian alumni of the Asian Institute of Management (AIM), many of whom are now in responsible positions in business in India, has also not been fully tapped. This network may be an important avenue for further economic linkages. The AIM, based in Manila, may consider taking the lead in this regard, and strengthen its links with management institutes in India.

An internationally well-known brand of Philippine beer (San Miguel) is being produced in India under an exclusive manufacturing and marketing license. There are plans to expand its availability nationwide. This appears to be the only significant involvement of a major Philippine corporation in India.

SINGAPORE-INDIA

While Singapore's manufacturing base centring on electronics and petrochemicals, and its role as an entrepot will continue to sustain the merchandise trade, the emerging opportunities are largely in the services sector, particularly in ICT, logistics services, business and financial services, tourism, and health services (Sen et al., 2000). This is more so as Singapore plans to develop into a service hub and improve its capabilities in areas where there exist considerable complementarities with India. The opportunities are not only in trade in services transactions (such as used by Singapore Airlines of India as a base for some of its IT-enabled services),[11] but also in investments (presence of Indian ICT, Pharmaceutical, and trading companies in Singapore, and Singapore's investments in India's ICT, tourism and health services, besides in port development and logistics). The probable involvement of Singapore's polytechnics in technical education in Tamil Nadu, and perhaps other states, could further strengthen bilateral linkages.

The Info-Comm Development Authority of Singapore (IDA) has signed an MoU with India's premier IT training company, the National Institute of Information Technology (NIIT), to persuade IT professionals to locate in Singapore from anywhere in the world (Jayanth, 2000). As Indian professionals are internationally competitive and culturally compatible, India is among the largest sources of IT manpower in the world and a significant proportion is likely to be sourced from India. This could create a dynamic Indian diaspora with positive externalities for both countries. The investments by Singapore Telecom (SingTel) in India's telecom sector in partnership with India's Bharti Televentures to take advantage of India's huge potential domestic telecom and Internet market is also another example in this sector.

In the tourism sector, opportunities are emerging rapidly for Singapore as Indian tourists have become the highest spenders and the fourth largest revenue generating market in 1999, with growing affluence among the Indian middle class. Singapore tourism authorities has also been actively involved in promoting select areas in India as a tourism destination for Singaporeans, through a joint marketing by the Government of India tourism office already established in Singapore.

Indeed, Singapore's two airlines, Singapore Airlines and Silk Air have quite liberal rights to fly to several destinations in India. They could however take greater advantage of India's open sky policies concerning air cargo. These carriers may be permitted by the Indian authorities to lease unused bilaterals of Air-India, as the national carrier is unlikely to be able to utilize them. These airlines may also consider new destinations in India to expand the air traffic volume between the two countries.

In the logistics sector, the Port of Singapore Authority (PSA) has been involved in port development and management in Tuticorin in Tamil Nadu and Pipavav in Gujarat. These have the potential to lead to major investment opportunities for other Singapore firms in the logistics sector. Negotiations between Singapore's largest supermarket operator, NTUC Fairprice which has close links with the government, and India's Apollo Group, one of Asia's largest hospital and healthcare management companies, to set up a pharmacy and retail chain of convenience stores numbering in the hundreds in petrol stations run by the Indian oil corporation also hold promise for greater economic linkages (Saywell, 2001). It would contribute to Singapore's food security, and to its supply chain for other essential household goods.

Indian IT companies have recognized the importance of Singapore as a marketing and development centre, and their presence is growing. As Indian businesses have been given much greater freedom to invest abroad, presence of Indian companies from other sectors in Singapore is also increasing. This should also have a positive impact on Singapore's importance as a business hub, and on trade in business services.

Singapore intends to increasingly rely at the margin on investment income from abroad. Its rather large reserves, conservatively estimated to be about US $90 billion, are mostly invested abroad through holding companies of the Singapore government. It is suggested that these holding companies consider passive investments in infrastructure projects in India. Setting up of a physical presence in India by the Singapore Government Investment Corporation (SGIC), and other such Singapore government investment companies merits serious consideration. Currently, these holding companies do act in a limited way as venture capitalists for Indian IT companies. However, there is much greater scope in not only the IT sector but also in biotechnology, life sciences, and other areas. For these purposes also, physical presence in India would be beneficial.

THAILAND-INDIA

The 1997 East Asian Crisis, which originated in Thailand, has severely impacted the Thailand economy and its growth prospects. Several Thai companies which had invested in India, had to restructure their operations. The bilateral trade has also been affected adversely though it is beginning to recover (Tables 2-4). Thailand also traditionally had weak institutional linkages with India: Thailand's business and tourism promotion agencies have not set up offices in India and the frequency of business delegations between two countries has been rather low. The decision by CII to set up a representative office in Kuala Lumpur and deepen engagement with the Federation of Malaysian Manufactures could adversely impact these businesses in Thailand that compete with Malaysia.

There are several areas where Thailand and India could cooperate for mutual gain. As Thailand aims to develop knowledge-based economic activities, it need to augment professional and technical manpower, particularly in the IT sector, have become more evident (Janviroj, 2000). There is a global competition for IT talent. India is internationally recognized as a major source for such talent (Tschang, 2001). Thailand's realization of its higher technology objectives rests on attracting foreign, including Indian talent (Einhorn, 2001, p. 21). It therefore needs to give more positive signals to India and to Indians on economic cooperation. By fostering the formation of the Indian diaspora, Thailand can address one of the challenges in regaining economic growth and dynamism, namely the need to augment the pool of professional and technical personnel comfortable with the new economy activities.[12]

Thailand is experiencing rapid individual and population ageing as reflected in increased life expectancy, and an increasing proportion of the population above 60 years of age. Its health care costs are expected to increase significantly due to population and individual ageing and due to sexually transmitted HIV-AIDS. Thailand has undertaken many innovative measures to address this issue, and greater cooperation between Thailand and Indian pharmaceutical industry could be an element in containing health care costs. This is because there is now an increased recognition that generic drugs are cheaper and more than commensurately effective, and in this area, Indian firms have a degree of international competitiveness. The catalytic role of Indian firms such as Cipla, in putting competitive pressures towards reducing prices of HIV-AIDS drugs worldwide has also been recognized (Harris, 2001). This should benefit not only Thailand, but other ASEAN countries as well.

Another area for potential cooperation is the gems and jewellery sector. Both Thailand and India have thriving industries in gems and jewellery. Greater cooperation between the two could provide each with competitive advantages in the international arena.

Thailand's expertise in the food-processing industry, particularly in deep-sea fishing and other marine related activities represent another area where cooperation is likely to be fruitful.

The balance of bilateral transactions is currently in favour of Thailand (Table 6). Bangkok is an important tourism destination and hub for Indian visitors. Thailand's facilities for issuing visa to Indian passport holders at reasonable cost on arrival at the airport holds particular lessons for other ASEAN countries if they desire to increase visitors from India. There is, however, much further scope for expanding tourism services in both directions. India, for example, could facilitate more entry points and frequency of flights by the national air carrier of Thailand, just as it has permitted airlines from Malaysia and Singapore. The Thai carrier could consider taking greater advantage of India's open sky regime for air cargo and for chartered flights. The two countries have also not adequately explored the opportunities of heritage tourism; given that the major Buddhist pilgrimage centres are located in India, while Thailand is a predominantly Buddhist country. Thus, the Thai national carrier may consider Bhubaneswar in the state of Orissa as a destination to develop Buddhist heritage tourism.

A deeper and more broad-based economic engagement between India and Thailand would require appropriate signals from the high level political and economic policy-makers. Thailand may consider appropriate signals to alter widespread perception in India that it is indifferent at best to the objectives of India's 'Look East' Policy in economic and security spheres.[13] As India forges ahead, with deeper engagement with other countries in East Asia, Thailand may be faced with narrower set of opportunities to sustain its growth.

VIETNAM-INDIA

The main challenge for Vietnam and India is to develop a substantial economic and commercial content to their traditionally close political relationship. Economic reforms being pursued by the two countries, and an increasing capacity of Indian companies to invest abroad, provides a conducive context in which to undertake this task.

India's national oil company is already involved in a joint venture to explore oil and natural gas in Vietnam. Thus, the two countries are already cooperating in the energy sector, but there is scope for strengthening it. Cooperation in the civilian nuclear power sector for energy is also feasible and desirable. Mineral exploration and processing is another area which is being actively explored by the two sides.

For both the countries, food security is an important pre-occupation. While in some commodities, such as rice, tea, pepper, and cashews, the two countries are in competition, there are several other areas, particularly those relating to agricultural research, and biotechnology where the scientists from the two countries could fruitfully cooperate. Facilitating trade and investments in agro-chemicals and fertilizers also merit serious consideration.

As Vietnam aims to develop its ICT sector, cooperation between the companies from the two countries, particularly in human resource development, and in the development of software in Vietnamese language represents another avenue of emerging opportunities. The two countries could also cooperate in the area of pharmaceuticals and health care, particularly in the area of sourcing drugs for diseases like HIV-AIDS.

The previous sections have analysed the factors that have contributed to the positive dynamics in India-ASEAN relations. During the 1990s, ASEAN as an organization, and many of its members demonstrated greater willingness to enhance economic and political relations with India. There are no contentious issues between the two sides as was the case during the Cold War period. India now has greater capacity and economic and technological momentum to sustain its growth. Encouraging acceptance of Indian capabilities in the ICT sector in particular has perceptibly altered the environment in which India's relations with major powers, particularly the United States, the European Union and Japan are being conducted. This has had a positive impact on India-ASEAN relations as well.

The previous sections have also indicated the emerging economic opportunities between India and ASEAN in merchandise trade, in services, and in investments and manpower flows. These are primarily in the ICT sector; biotechnology, and life sciences; agricultural products; infrastructure; logistics; tourism services; the energy sector; educational services; and in commercial use of nuclear and space technologies.

This paper has stressed that while the general areas of emerging opportunities overlap, to realize these opportunities, India will need to evolve strategies and tactics both with ASEAN as an organization, and bilaterally with each individual country. Both sides have much to gain from cooperating with each other. The potential of some bilateral relationships however, will not be realized unless high-level political commitment is made to do so. This applies particularly to Thailand and the Philippines.

India is determined to accelerate its integration with the world economy. Its first Special Economic Zone (SEZ) at Positra in Gujarat costing US $1.3 billion has achieved financial closure and another 2 to 3 such SEZs will do so in the near future. The SEZ is a specially delineated duty free enclave, for undertaking manufacturing, assembling, trading and various other services. It will have a public utility status, and a single point clearance for exports and imports. The private sector has taken the lead in establishing the Positra SEZ and similar ownership is expected in the other SEZs.

Several US and European MNCs have evinced keen interest in operating from the Positra SEZ. If ASEAN companies (or those MNCs based in ASEAN) similarly take advantage of the opportunities in India's SEZs in selected areas, greater impetus to bilateral relationship could be achieved.

Cooperation between ASEAN and India in various multilateral fora, such as the WTO, particularly on issues relating to the workings of Intellectual Property Rights regime involving access to life-saving drugs at affordable prices could bring mutual benefits. Greater convergence of views on economic management and similar developmental challenges faced by the two sides should help in this regard.

India needs to vigorously pursue its Look East Policy, and continue its efforts to engage each and every ASEAN member in a mutually beneficial manner. It would therefore need to considerably strengthen its emphasis on commercial diplomacy, and coordination between business associations and diplomatic missions.

Indian missions in ASEAN need to set goals and benchmarks, and assess strategies and tactics on an ongoing basis. 'Software' skills being a global and regional economic player is important in commercial diplomacy as perceptions and 'Brand Image' become increasingly important. ASEAN on the other hand, is strongly urged to facilitate India's participation in all regional fora in which it has considerable leverage. Some ASEAN countries, particularly Malaysia, Singapore, and Thailand, need to enhance the presence of their commercial and promotional agencies in India to build on the existing bilateral relations. ASEAN countries may also consider further measures to attract professional and technical talent from India, and to better utilize the possibilities provided by the presence of the Indian diaspora, the way United States has done. Continued nurturing of the relations along these lines by the two sides is essential to translate the emerging economic opportunities into reality.

NOTES

* We would like to thank Dr Ramkishan Rajan and Dr Shashanka Bhide for helpful comments. The usual caveat applies.

1. ASEAN was founded in 1967 as a cold war organization by Indonesia, Malaysia, Philippines, Singapore, and Thailand. Since then it has doubled its membership to all ten countries in South-East Asia. Brunei joined ASEAN in 1984, Vietnam in 1995, Laos and Myanmar in 1997, and Cambodia in 1999.
2. ASEAN members, particularly Malaysia, have expressed strong reservations about Singapore's aggressive perusal of the bilateral free trade agreements with major trading partners such as the US, Japan, Australia, and New Zealand (see Rajan, Sen and Siregar, 2001).

3. Indeed, some commentators such as Morgan Stanley's Lian (2001) have already begun to suggest that the East Asian Economic Model (EAEM) may be in the early stages of being dismantled, though the alternative model is not yet in sight. The main attributes of the EAEM model are high savings and investment, and outward orientation in trade, and high reliance on direct and portfolio foreign investment. This suggests a certain lack of confidence and focus for the ASEAN countries which have followed this model.
4. For a report card on the reforms in different sectors and the tasks ahead, see Parikh (1999). The 2000-1 Economic Survey published in February 2001 by the Ministry of Finance; and the FY 2001-2 budget speech of the Finance Minister presented on 28 February 2001, are other authoritative sources on India's performance and reform plans. Both these may be accessed on http://www.indiabudget.nic.in. India's 2001-2 Budget has drawn nearly universal approval for its vision and specific measures designed to accelerate market-oriented reforms (Nageshwaran, 2001; *The Economist*, 2001; Slater, 2001). The budget has laid a blueprint for higher growth, and tackled many difficult reform issues such as labour market reform, pension reform, and infrastructure. The budget and India's 2001 Export-import (EXIM) Policy demonstrated refreshing willingness to draw relevant lessons from other countries, particularly China. Please see details of the EXIM Policy on http://dgftcom.nic.in/exim/2000. India's second-generation reforms will involve, privatization, labour market reforms and deeper and more extensive depoliticization of economic decisions, and will involve legislative changes designed to bring India's policy framework in line with International best practices.
5. Therefore, perceptions in some ASEAN circles that change in governments are indications of political instability in India are grossly oversimplified. They also ignore recent history in South-East Asia where one person or one party rule has provided only superficial stability followed by considerable flux in the absence of necessary institutional foundations for participation and conflict mediation. In both ASEAN and India there is considerable room for improving governance and delivery of government services.
6. These themes were stressed by the Indian Prime Minister A.B. Vajpayee in an address entitled 'India and ASEAN-Shared Perspectives' to the Institute of Diplomatic and Foreign Relations in Kuala Lumpur during his state visit to Malaysia in May 2001 (Baruah, 2001c).
7. Brunei, Cambodia, Laos, and Myanmar are excluded because of the lack of comparable data in not only Table 1 but also in other tables in this paper.
8. A combination of factors is responsible, though rigorous empirical studies assessing relative importance of each of the factors are not available. The factors include, depreciation of currency of most ASEAN countries increasing their relative export competitiveness, lower economic growth in ASEAN which has dampened demand; higher economic growth in India which has stimulated imports; and random factors such as weather-induced need for cooking oil imports by India.
9. As an example, in May 2001 an Indian firm acquired a 100 per cent stake in Sinar Mas Pulp and Paper India Limited, a two-step removed subsidiary of Singapore-based but Indonesian controlled Asia Pulp and Paper Co. Ltd for US $136.5 million. A similar buy-out of some of Indian investments of Thai firms has also occurred since the crisis.
10. The average length of stay per visitor is about 29 days, considerably higher than the average for the ASEAN countries. Thus, in Singapore, the average length of stay in 2000 was 3.16 days (http://www.cybraary.com.sg/pages/archive2000/fact1200.html).

11. Singapore Airlines has also bid with India's Tata group for 26 per cent stake in Air-India, currently a government owned national carrier.
12. The economic contribution that the Indian diaspora can make to Thailand's economic dynamism is indicated by the computer animation company founded by an Indian, Mr. S.R. Ramanna, which is headquartered in Bangkok, and which has the ambition to make blockbuster digital animated movies that will contest for a share of the global market (Seno and Mitton, 2001, pp. 39-46).
13. A possible signal would be a visit by Thailand's Prime Minister to India, which has substantive business as well as political content.

REFERENCES

ASEAN Secretariat, 1995. *Report of the ASEAN-India Experts Group on Trade and Investment Cooperation*, Jakarta, ASEAN Secretariat, February.

Asher, M. 1997. 'ASEAN-India Economic Relations: A Good Beginning but Continued Nurturing Need', in M.L. Aranal-Sereno and J.S. Santiago (eds.), *The ASEAN: Thirty Years and Beyond.* Quezon City: Institute of International Legal Studies, University of the Philippines Law Center, pp. 223-43.

Baruah, A. 2001a. 'India-ASEAN engagement will come about: Mahathir', *The Hindu*, 2 February. http://www.the-hindu.com/stories/0506134a.htm

———, 2001b. 'India steps up efforts towards engaging Myanmar', *The Hindu*, 12 February. http://www.the-hindu.com/stories/03120005.htm

———, 2001c. 'Talks with ASEAN will Ease Tensions : PM', *The Hindu*, 17 May. http://www.thehindu.com/stories/01117006.htm

———, 2001d. 'Building Bridges Through Business', *The Hindu*, 14 May. http://www.thehindu.com/stories/03140004.htm

———, 2001e. 'Jakarta Backs India's Case for UN Security Council Seat', *The Hindu*, 11 January. http://www.thehindu.com/stories/01110003.htm

Business India, 1997. 'Space: the New Business Frontier', 21 April-4 May 1997, pp. 53-9.

Center for Strategic and International Studies (CSIS), 2000. 'India Looks East', *CSIS South Asia Monitor*, no. 23, 6 July. http://www.csis.org/saprog/sam23.html

Cerra, V. and S.C. Saxena, 2000. 'What Caused the 1991 Currency Crisis in India?', Washington, D.C., *International Monetary Fund Working Paper*, no. 157.

Einhorn, B., 2001. 'Can Thai Tech Go High-Tech?', *Business Week* (Asian Edition), 21 May, pp. 20-1.

Harris, G., 2001. 'AIDS Gaffes Abroad Come Back to Haunt Drug Firms at Home', *The Asian Wall Street Journal*, 24 April, pp. 1 and 7.

Janviroj, P., 2000. 'Thailand must join global battle for IT staff', *The Nation*, (Bangkok), 29 March.

———, 2000. 'Nasscom signs MoU with Singapore', *The Hindu*, 12 November, http://www.the-hindu.com/stories/06120006.htm

Joshi, M. 2001. 'Vajpayee woos Vietnam with infotech', *The Times of India*, 9 January.

Khanna, V. 2000. 'India and East Asia: Huge Synergies to tap', *Business Times*, (Singapore), 5 May.

Lim, S.B. 2001. 'Political Instability hinders growth of ASEAN economies', *The Straits Times*, Singapore, 1 January.

Lian, D. 2001. 'Asia-Pacific: First Steps in Dismantling the East Asia Economic Model', http://www.morganstanley.com/gefi

Nageswaran, V.A. 2001. 'A thumbs-up for Mr. Sinha', *The Business Line* (India), 1 March.

Parikh, K. 1999. 'India Development Report 1999-2000', New Delhi, Oxford University Press.

Rajan, R., R. Sen and R. Siregar, 2001. 'Singapore and the New Regionalism: Bilateral Economic Relations with Japan and the U.S.', mimeo.

Saywell, T. 2001. 'Singapore's New India Play', *Far Eastern Economic Review*, 25 January, pp. 49-50.

Sen, R., M.G. Asher and C. Rajam, 2000. 'India and Singapore: Emerging Trade Opportunities and Challenges', Singapore: Centre for Advanced Studies, National University of Singapore, Research Paper, no. 19.

Seno, A.A. and R. Mitton, 2001. 'Toy Story Too ?', *Asiaweek*, 27 April, pp. 39-46.

Slater, J. 2001. 'India: Pleasant Surprises', *Far Eastern Economic Review*, 15 March, p. 62.

Slater, J. and S. Dhume, 2001. 'Gazing East', *Far Eastern Economic Review*, 1 March, p. 61.

Sridharan, K., 2001. 'Regional Perceptions of India', unpublished.

The Economist (London), 2001. 'India's Breakthrough Budget', 3 March, pp. 27-8.

Thornhill, J. 2001. 'Enter the Dragon', *The Financial Times* (London), 20 February.

Tschang, T 2001. 'The Basic Characteristics of Skills and Organizational Capabilities in the Indian Software Industry', Tokyo: Asian Development Bank Institute, Working Paper, no. 13.

World Bank, 2001. *World Development Report, 2000/2001*, Washington, D.C., The World Bank.

Yogarajah, A. 2001. 'Liberalization and its Impact on Foreign Direct Investment in India', Ph.D. thesis submitted to Nanyang Business School, Nanyang Technological University, Singapore.

Indo-ASEAN Trade Prospects: A Study of Trade Complementarity

Atul Sarma and Pradeep Kumar Mehta

Recognizing the importance of economic cooperation among developing countries, India articulated a Look East Policy in the 1990s. Several factors contributed to the choice of ASEAN as India's potential partner for closer economic cooperation. Apart from geographical proximity and the presence of a large Indian origin population, the fast growing ASEAN market[1] of half a billion population with a $737-billion income,[2] their greater openness[3] and larger role in the global market[4] provided a rationale for the new policy thrust. Indian entrepreneurs in the new economic environment at home have sought a closer association and strategic alliance with their ASEAN counterparts for mutual benefit.

Under the Look East Policy, India initiated several measures for promoting trade and economic cooperation with ASEAN states. The latter have reciprocated with encouraging responses, granting India an ASEAN dialogue partner status, allowing it to join the Ganga-Mekong Suvannaphoom programme, identifying India as a priority market, and forming a new regional grouping by two ASEAN and three SAARC states.[5] There is also a growing dialogue at official and non-official levels, as evident from the visits of five ASEAN heads to India in 1999 alone. At another level, several joint committees both at bilateral[6] and ASEAN[7] levels were constituted to suggest ways to strengthen economic ties. Some Indian trade and commerce associations such as CII have also set up their offices in ASEAN states.

All this has yielded positive results. For example, the volume of trade between India and ASEAN-5 rose to $6 billion in 1997-8 from $2.9 billion in 1993 and just $77 million in 1971 even if it formed only 6 per cent of India's global trade and a mere two per cent that of ASEAN's. ASEAN investment in India also rose by $2.54 billion during 1991-7. By December 1999, Indian entrepreneurs sought approvals for 169 joint ventures and

130 wholly owned subsidiaries involving Rs. 6.02 and Rs. 5.2 billion respectively.[8] Many of them are already in operation.

It is against this background that this paper attempts to identify trade possibilities between India and the ASEAN-5 states based on their existing trading patterns both at the global and bilateral levels. The prospect of trade between them would essentially depend on the extent to which their production and demand structures are mutually supportive or complementary. The goods that are traded between them broadly indicate the level of realization of such complementarity. This, however, does not necessarily reflect the level of trade potential, for historical factors and several rigidities might stand as impediments to fuller trade realization. Yet a clearer understanding of trade potential would lead to conscious efforts to promote trade.

To start with, we examine the extent to which India's global trade corresponds with the individual ASEAN states at the aggregate level. To take a view on this, we have used two measures of trade complementarity, the *coefficient of complementarity (EICI & IECI) and rank correlation coefficients (RCC-1 & RCC-2)* between export pattern of a country and import pattern of its partner.[9]

At the disaggrgate level, an understanding of the nature of complementarity by types of product groups will have much larger implications on future strength of bilateral trade. We may mention here that trade complementarity or correspondence essentially relates the revealed comparative advantage (RCA) of a country's export under a particular product group to the revealed import dependence (RID) of the partner country under the same product group. This measure of complementarity takes into account the inter-temporal change of RCA and RID estimates in terms of the cut-off value of 100. On the basis of inter-temporal movement of RCA and RID and the corresponding values, complementary product groups are classified into three categories:

(i) Product groups with high and growing complementarity,
(ii) Product groups expected to exhibit high complementarity in the near term, and
(iii) Product groups exhibiting declining complementarity.

The required data are collected from the UN *International Trade Statistics Yearbook* and bilateral trade statistics from the UN *Commodity Trade Statistics.*

This paper primarily deals with the period 1985-94, extending over the era of liberalization and economic reforms in India. The post-1994 years were not included in the study mainly because the East Asian financial and currency crisis of 1997 had its origin in the functioning of the affected economies during the preceding two years or so. As such, growth and composition of trade of the ASEAN states between 1995 through 1997 were significantly distorted.

After analysis of trade complementarity at the aggregate level we discuss the Indo-ASEAN trade prospects based on disaggregate complementarity.

AGGREGATE TRADE CORRESPONDENCE

Both the indices of complementarity at the aggregate level suggest that Indian exports did not enjoy complementarity with imports of ASEAN states to any significant degree (Table 1). But rank correlation coefficients bring out that India's trade complementarity clearly improved with most ASEAN states over time, though they are still around 0.3. Interestingly, ASEAN exports revealed a far higher degree of correspondence with Indian imports.

TABLE 1: TRADE COMPLEMENTARITY AT AGGREGATE LEVEL

Measure	*Year*	*Indonesia*	*Malaysia*	*Philippines*	*Singapore*	*Thailand*
Indian Exports and ASEAN imports						
6. EICI	1985	0.30	0.36	0.31	0.32	–
(cosine)	1988	0.19	0.26	0.28	0.22	0.31
	1991	0.28	0.24	0.37	0.28	0.42
	1994	0.30	0.18	0.31	0.21	0.31
7. RCC (1)	1985	0.08	0.27	0.14	0.21	–
(rank-correlation)	1988	0.14	0.32	0.30	0.29	0.34
	1991	0.24	0.20	0.32	0.21	0.28
	1994	0.29	0.24	0.31	0.29	0.33
ASEAN exports and Indian imports						
8. IECI	1985	0.86	0.76	0.24	0.85	–
(cosine)	1988	0.63	0.52	0.36	0.54	0.29
	1991	0.76	0.49	0.16	0.60	0.16
	1994	0.62	0.23	0.33	0.40	0.22
9. RCC (2)	1985	0.03	0.00	0.30	-0.05	–
(rank-correlation)	1988	-0.06	0.30	0.20	0.27	-0.01
	1991	0.46	0.66	0.95	0.65	0.76
	1994	0.63	0.69	0.69	0.74	0.47

More important, this trade complementarity improved considerably over time as rising rank correlation in the range of 0.47 to 0 .74 indicated.

The growth of bilateral trade between India and ASEAN-5 states during 1971-95 was in alignment with the above findings. Just to illustrate, India's exports to ASEAN-5 witnessed a growth of 13.1 per cent per annum during 1971-95 while the latter's exports to the former at the rate of 20.9 per cent per annum during the same period.

PROSPECTS FOR INDO-ASEAN TRADE

ASEAN states imported only under 33 to 40 product groups out of a large number of product groups that India exported (Table 2). But these products accounted for more than half (55.8 per cent) to one-third (34.7 per cent) of India's global exports and a little less than half (47.1 per cent) to around one-fourth (24.0 per cent) of total imports of the ASEAN states. This meant that despite being fewer in number, the complementary products were important in the global trade of respective countries. Further, more than half to three-fourth of Indian exports to these countries, except Malaysia (42.7 per cent), related to those product groups. It shows that complementary products played an important role even at the bilateral level.

Viewed from the angle of ASEAN exports, the number of product groups that were complementary with Indian imports in the global market was smaller: they were in the range of 21 to 34. But they accounted for as much as 53.1 to 65.7 per cent of total exports of Singapore, Malaysia and the Philippines and a little less than 40 per cent in Indonesia and Thailand. India imported these very products from the world market to the extent of 35.1 to 41.2 per cent of its total imports. At the bilateral level, Malaysia, Singapore and the Philippines exported these products to India to the tune of 62.1, 48.7 and 44.8 per cent of their respective total exports to India. Indonesia and Thailand did so to a lesser extent at 27.2 and 60.3 per cent respectively.

The point to note, however, is that there were several product groups in respect of which complementarity declined. At the same time, some product groups were expected to emerge as those enjoying high complementarity.

With these broad observations on the extent and inter temporal behaviour of complementary products, we move to the nature and characteristics of complementary products that shaped the bilateral trade between India on the one side and ASEAN states on the other. Tables 3 and 4 present the sectoral overview of the complementary products while Tables 5 and 6 relate to India's pairing with each of the ASEAN-5.

TABLE 2: COMPLEMENTARITY AT A DISAGGREGATE LEVEL: OVERVIEW

Nature of Complementarity	*Indonesia*	*Malaysia*	*Philippines*	*Singapore*	*Thailand*
Indian Export vs. *ASEAN Imports*					
High and Growing complementarity	23 (23.0, 22.0, 52.8)	5 (6.2, 3.4, 19.3)	8 (11.0, 9.1, 8.2)	7 (13.3, 2.3, 8.0)	15 (28.2, 15.8, 57.2)
Expected to be high complementarity	2 (0.9, 0.5, 0.04)	3 (16.6, 1.2, 4.2)	3 (2.7, 0.9, 0.3)	4 (16.9, 0.8, 10.1)	1 (0.9, 0.03, 0)
Declining complementarity	15 (10.8, 19.4, 24.0)	26 (23.5, 19.4, 19.3)	25 (21.4, 37.1, 56.9)	23 (25.6, 22.2, 34.2)	17 (18.8, 22.0, 12.6)
Total	40 (34.7, 41.9, 76.9)	34 (46.2, 24.0, 42.7)	36 (35.1, 47.1, 65.4)	34 (55.8, 25.2, 52.3)	33 (47.9, 37.7, 69.8)
ASEAN Export vs. *Indian Imports*					
High and Growing complementarity	7 (28.0, 16.6, 3.1)	2 (0.4, 1.3, 15.1)	4 (5.1, 6.1, 5.0)	5 (10.8, 13.4, 9.5)	2 (3.4, 8.3, 4.7)
Expected to be high complementarity	1 (0.2, 0.3, 0)	4 (2.5, 11.1, 0.8)	3 (2.3, 1.7, 0)	4 (2.4, 2.6, 2.3)	6 (3.1, 12.6, 2.1)
Declining complementarity	13 (11.7, 19.3, 24.1)	19 (50.3, 28.3, 46.3)	15 (58.3, 27.2, 39.8)	25 (57.1, 25.2, 36.9)	14 (24.7, 15.8, 9.2)
Total	21 (39.9, 36.2, 27.2)	25 (53.1, 40.7, 62.1)	22 (65.7, 35.1, 44.8)	34 (69.5, 41.2, 48.7)	22 (31.2, 36.7, 16.0)

NOTE: Brackets: share in exporting country, share in importing country, share in bilateral export.

SOURCE: Complimenatry estimated from UN: International Trade Statistics, various issues. Bilateral Trade Statistics is from UN, Commodity Trade Statistics, various volumes (print).

INDIA AND INDONESIA

Indian Exports to Indonesia

A wide range of Indian global exports was such that they corresponded to Indonesia's imports from the world market. These complementary product groups were 40 in number and contributed to 34.7 per cent of India's exports and 41.9 per cent of Indonesia's imports (Table 3). Among them, intermediate goods of heavy and chemical industry (K1) numbering 11 product groups, were the most prominent, making up 6.2 per cent of Indian exports and 11.1 per cent of Indonesia's imports. Next in importance were another 11 product groups of light manufactures (L1, L2 and L3) accounting for 16.4 per cent of India's exports and 7.0 per cent of Indonesia's imports. Other product categories that were significant for both were food and beverages (A1) and capital goods (K2) contributing 4.5 and 2.9 per cent of Indian exports and 4.4 and 11.4 per cent of Indonesian imports respectively.

There was, however, a qualitative difference in between the first three categories and the last one: the former group was characterized by the dominance of high and growing complementarity, the latter by declining complementarity.

At the product group level, complementary product groups under K1 largely related to iron and steel and chemical products (Table 5). Only other K1 product group that showed complementarity was aluminium. But the important point to note is that most iron and steel product groups, India exported to Indonesia were semi-processed items such as pig iron and primary forms, together constituting 16.3 of the total bilateral exports. The former cornered almost one-third of its total Indonesian imports and the latter around 4 per cent. Interestingly, iron-ore concentrate that comes under non-fuel minerals (N1) was also one of the important Indian exports to Indonesia, capturing 6.8 per cent of its total imports.

As for chemicals, Indian exports under four of the complementary product groups had some presence in Indonesian market but none of them claimed more than 4 per cent of market share.

Indian exports under K1 were diverse and varied and had correspondence to Indonesian imports. But not all of them figured in bilateral trade. Even those which did, were not significant in most cases. On the other hand, Indonesian import of some of them constituted a significant proportion of its total imports. In such cases, it can be argued, there did exist a sizeable market for Indian exports. Its realization would, however, critically depend on supply elasticity as well as international competitiveness.

TABLE 3: SECTORAL PATTERN OF COMPLEMENTARY PRODUCT GROUPS: INDIAN EXPORTS Vs. ASEAN IMPORTS

Exporting country →	*India*										
Partner (importing) country ↓	*A1*	*A2*	*N1*	*N2*	*L1*	*L2*	*L3*	*K1*	*K2*	*O*	*Total*
Indonesia											
High Complementarity	5 (4.4, 4.23)	2 (0.45, 3.24)	1 (1.57, 0.27)		4 (6.24, 1.97)	1 (0.34, 0.33)	2 (5.45, 1.95)	7 (4.13, 7.79)	1 (0.41, 2.24)		23 (22.99, 22.02)
Expected Complementarity	1 (0.08, 0.18)				1 (0.83, 0.32)						2 (0.91, 0.5)
Declining Complementarity		1 (0.48, 0.26)	1 (0.56, 0.23)	1 (1.59, 4.03)		3 (3.66, 2.4)		4 (2.04, 3.32)	5 (2.44, 9.14)		15 (10.77, 19.38)
Total	6 (4.48, 4.41)	3 (0.93, 3.50)	2 (2.13, 0.50)	1 (1.59, 4.03)	5 (7.07, 2.29)	4 (4.00, 2.73)	2 (5.45, 1.95)	11 (6.17, 11.11)	6 (2.85, 11.38)		40 (34.67, 41.9)
Malaysia											
High Complementarity	2 (1.10, 0.6)						1 (4.00, 0.55)	2 (1.11, 2.22)			5 (6.21, 3.37)
Expected Complementarity					1 (0.49, 0.42)		1 (15.43, 0.29)	1 (0.64, 0.52)			3 (16.56, 1.23)
Declining Complementarity	4 (3.81, 1.35)	1 (0.28, 0.27)	1 (0.56, 0.3)	1 (1.59, 1.93)	4 (5.92, 2.3)	4 (4.00, 1.95)		4 (1.28, 3.21)	6 (2.84, 6.73)	1 (3.16, 1.37)	26 (23.45, 19.41)
Total	6 (4.91, 1.95)	1 (0.28, 0.27)	1 (0.56, 0.3)	1 (1.59, 1.93)	5 (6.41, 2.72)	4 (4.00, 1.95)	2 (19.43, 0.84)	7 (3.03, 5.95)	6 (2.84, 6.73)	1 (3.16, 1.37)	34 (46.22, 24.01)

(Contd.)

TABLE 3 (Contd.)

Exporting country →					*India*						
Partner (importing) country ↓	*A1*	*A2*	*N1*	*N2*	*L1*	*L2*	*L3*	*K1*	*K2*	*O*	*Total*
Philippines											
High Complementarity	1 (0.05, 1.62)				1 (3.47, 0.73)		1 (4.00, 0.54)	3 (2.55, 2.52)	2 (0.96, 3.67)		8 (11.02, 9.08)
Expected Complementarity			1 (1.57, 0.00)		1 (0.83, 0.52)			1 (0.29, 0.40)			3 (2.69, 0.92)
Declining Complementarity	3 (3.09, 1.65)	1 (0.17, 0.5)	1 (0.56, 1.37)	2 (1.80, 3.28)	3 (2.53, 1.92)	3 (3.66, 2.1)	1 (1.45, 0.3)	6 (3.09, 4.94)	4 (1.89, 2.94)	1 (3.16, 18.12)	25 (21.40, 37.12)
Total (3.14, 3.27)	4 (0.17, 0.5)	1 (2.13, 1.37)	2 (1.80, 3.28)	2 (6.83, 3.17)	5 (3.66, 2.1)	3 (5.45, 0.74)	2 (5.93, 7.86)	10 (2.85, 6.61)	6 (3.16, 18.12)	1 (35.11, 47.12)	36 Singapore
High Complementarity					6 (6.41, 3.79)			1 (0.88, 0.29)			7 (13.32, 2.27)
Expected Complementarity	1 (0.66, 0.23)	1 (0.48, 0.12)					1 (15.43, 0.25)	1 (0.31, 0.15)			4 (16.88, 0.75)
Declining Complementarity	1 (1.75, 0.35)			1 (1.59, 3.1)	5 (6.41, 3.08)	4 (4.00, 1.76)	1 (4.00,0.22)	6 (2.71, 3.56)	4 (2.01, 8.95)	1 (3.16, 1.17)	23 (25.63, 22.19)
Total	2 (2.41, 0.58)	1 (0.48, 0.12)		(1.59, 3.1)	1 (18.85, 5.06)	11 (4.00, 1.76)	4 (19.43, 0.47)	2 (2.90, 4.00)	8 (2.01, 8.95)	4 (3.16, 1.17)	1 34 (55.83, 25.51)

Thailand											
High Complementarity	1 (2.21, 0.89)				5 (6.41, 3.79)		2 (16.89, 2.13)	6 (4.34, 7.01)	1 (0.55, 2.82)		15 (28.18, 15.75)
Expected Complementarity								1 (0.88, 0.03)			1 (0.88, 0.03)
Declining Complementarity	1 (0.66, 1.02)	1 (0.17, 1.04)		1 (1.59, 2.62)		4 (4.00, 3.11)	1 (4.00, 0.38)	4 (3.25, 4.66)	4 (2.01, 7.74)	1 (3.16, 1.38)	17 (18.84, 21.95)
Total	2 (2.87, 1.91)	1 (0.17, 1.04)		1 (1.59, 2.62)	5 (6.41, 3.79)	4 (4.00, 3.11)	3 (20.89, 2.51)	11 (8.47, 11.7)	5 (2.56, 10.56)	1 (3.16, 1.38)	33 (47.9, 37.73)

NOTE: Brackets: share in exporting country, share in importing country.
Name of the product groups:
A1: Food and Beverages
A2: Crude Agricultural Raw Materials
N1: Metals and Minerals (excluding fuels)
N2: Mineral fuels and lubricants
L1: Light manufacturing, final products with relatively low skill requirements
L2: Light manufacturing, final products with relatively high skill requirements
L3: Light manufacturing intermediate products
K1: Intermediate goods of heavy and chemical industry
K2: Heavy machines and transport equipment
O: Residual

SOURCE: For details on product classification, see, S. Naya (1967), 'The Commodity Pattern and Export Performance of Developing Asian Countries to the Developed Countries', *Economic Development and Cultural Change*, vol. 15, no. 4, July, pp. 433-4.

TABLE 4: SECTORAL PATTERN OF COMPLEMENTARY PRODUCT GROUPS: INDIAN IMPORTS *vs* ASEAN EXPORTS

Importing country →	India										
Partner (exporting) country ↓	*A1*	*A2*	*N1*	*N2*	*L1*	*L2*	*L3*	*K1*	*K2*	*O*	*Total*
Indonesia											
High Complementarity		1		3				3			7
		(2.78, 0.59)		(23.92, 14.03)				(1.28, 1.96)			(27.98,16.58)
Expected Complementarity								1			1
								(0.15, 0.34)			(0.15, 0.34)
Declining Complementarity			1	2	1		1	2	5	1	13
			(2.83, 0.26)	(2.31, 9.6)	(1.21, 0.76)		(1.69, 0.56)	(0.77, 3.76)	(2.54, 2.72)	(0.37, 1.64)	(11.72, 19.93)
Total		1	1	5	1		1	6	5	1	21
		(2.78, 0.59)	(2.83, 0.26)	(26.23, 23.63)	(1.21, 0.76)		(1.69, 0.56)	(2.20, 6.06)	(2.54, 2.72)	(0.37, 1.64)	(39.85, 36.22)
Malaysia											
High Complementarity								1	1		2
								(0.38, 1.3)	(2.65, 2.56)		(0.38, 1.30)
Expected Complementarity				1				1	2		4
				(1.14, 9.27)				(0.43, 0.58)	(0.89, 1.2)		(2.46, 11.05)
Declining Complementarity		2		2		1	1	3	9	1	19
		(6.95, 1.3)		(6.1, 11.77)		(0.43, 0.30)	(0.56, 0.56)	(1.12, 2.67)	(34.46, 5.10)	(0.67, 6.65)	(50.29, 28.34)
Total		2		3		1	1	5	12	1	25
		(6.95, 1.3)		(7.24, 21.04)		(0.43, 0.30)	(0.56, 0.56)	(1.93, 4.55)	(38.00, 8.86)	(0.67, 6.65)	(53.13, 40.69)

Philippines											
High Complementarity	1 (2.58, 1.12)							2 (0.98, 3.38)		1 (1.57, 1.64)	4 (5.13, 6.14)
Expected Complementarity				1 (0.71, 0.3)			1 (0.32, 0.56)		1 (1.23, 0.85)		3 (2.26, 1.71)
Declining Complementarity	1 (0.56, 2.55)	1 (3.53, 0.59)	1 (1.01, 0.26)	1 (0.75, 9.27)				4 (6.39, 4.49)	6 (14.65, 4.01)	1 (34.91, 6.65)	15 (58.27, 27.23)
Total	2 (3.14, 3.67)	1 (3.53, 0.59)	1 (1.01, 0.26)	2 (1.46, 9.57)			1 (0.32, 0.56)	6 (7.37, 8.87)	7 (15.88, 4.86)	2 (36.48, 8.29)	22 (65.66, 35.08)
Singapore											
High Complementarity				1 (9.21, 9.27)		2 (1.01, 1.53)		1 (0.31, 2.05)	1 (0.23, 0.50)		5 (10.76, 13.35)
Expected Complementarity								2 (1.07, 1.00)	2 (1.34, 1.59)		4 (2.41, 2.60)
Declining Complementarity					2 (0.82, 1.01)	2 (1.21, 1.27)	1 (0.28, 0.56)	4 (2.4, 3.91)	15 (51.34, 11.83)	1 (1.05, 6.65)	25 (56.8, 26.53)
Total				1 (9.21, 9.27)	2 (0.82, 1.01)	4 (2.22, 2.80)	1 (0.28, 0.56)	7 (3.78, 6.96)	18 (52.91, 13.92)	1 (1.05, 6.65)	34 (69.97, 42.48)
Thailand											
High Complementarity							1 (2.35, 5.7)		1 (1.08, 2.56)		2 (3.43, 8.26)
Expected Complementarity				1 (0.49, 9.27)		1 (0.19, 1.04)	1 (0.5, 0.25)		3 (1.9, 2.05)		6 (3.08, 12.61)
Declining Complementarity	2 (3.25, 2.97)			1 (0.29, 0.3)		1 (0.42, 0.30)	1 (1.12, 0.56)	2 (1.19, 2.23)	8 (21, 5.76)	1 (0.69, 6.65)	16 (24.71, 15.8)
Total	2 (3.25, 2.97)			2 (0.78, 9.57)		2 (0.61, 1.34)	3 (3.97, 6.50)	2 (1.19, 2.23)	12 (23.98, 10.37)	1 (0.69, 6.65)	24 (34.47, 39.64)

NOTE: Same as Table 3.

TABLE 5: COMPLEMENTARITY AT THE LEVEL OF PRODUCT-GROUPS BETWEEN INDIAN EXPORTS AND IMPORTS OF ASEAN STATES

				Indian export		*Indonesian Import*				*Malaysia's Import*				*Philippines Import*				*Singapore's Import*				*Thai Import*			
Sr. No.	*Gr-oup*	*SITC*	*Commodity*	*Cate-gory*	*Share*	*Cla-ss*	*Cate-gory*	*Imp. Share*	*Mkt. Share*	*Cla-ss*	*Cate-gory*	*Imp. Share*	*Mkt. Share*	*Cla-ss*	*Cate-gory*	*Imp. Share*	*Mkt. Share*	*Cla-ss*	*Cate-gory*	*Imp. Share*	*Mkt. Share*	*Cla-ss*	*Cate-gory*	*Imp. Share*	*Mkt. Share*
1	A1	034	Fish fresh, chilled frozen	X2	0.66					C1	M2	0.30	3.87	D2	M5	0.24	0.00	C2	M3	0.23	5.13	D2	M4	1.02	1.28
2	A1	041	Wheat etc. unmilled	X1	0.05	C1	M1	1.81	0.00	D2	M5	0.36	0.00	C1	M1	1.62	0.00								
3	A1	042	Rice	X1	1.46	C1	M2	0.49	0.00	D2	M4	0.19	0.00												
4	A1	054	Veg etc. fresh smply prsrvd	X2	0.45	C1	M2	0.32	0.00	C1	M1	0.30	16.91												
5	A1	057	Fruit, nuts, fresh dried	X1	1.75													D2	M4	0.35	2.79				
6	A1	061	Sugar & honey	X3	0.08	C2	M3	0.18	0.00	D2	M5	0.45	0.63												
7	A1	081	Feeding stuff for anml	X1	2.21	C1	M1	1.30	25.75	D2	M5	0.35	17.87	D2	M4	1.00	30.63					C1	M1	0.89	18.97
8	A1	121	Tobacco & unmfgd refuse	X1	0.22	C1	M2	0.31	0.00					D2	M4	0.41	0.00								
			Sub-Total - A1		6.88			4.41				1.95								0.58				1.91	
1	A2	222	Seeds for soft fixed oil	X2	0.28	C1	M1	1.05	3.73	D2	M4	0.27	0.88												
2	A2	263	Cotton	X1	0.17	C1	M1	2.19	2.72					D2	M5	0.50	1.62					D2	M4	1.04	2.14
3	A2	424	Fixed veg oil non-soft	X3	0.48	D2	M4	0.26	0.00									C2	M3	0.12	0.00				
			Sub-Total - A2		0.93			3.50				0.27				0.50				0.12				1.04	
1	K1	513	Carboxylic acids etc.	X2	0.32	C1	M1	1.09	0.98					D2	M5	0.42	0.78					C1	M1	0.8	0.52
2	K1	514	Nitrogen-fnctn compounds	X4	0.72	D1	M1	0.77	2.40					D1	M2	0.35	0.83					D1	M2	0.37	5.97
3	K1	516	Other organic chemicals	X2	0.39	C1	M1	0.40	0.30																
4	K1	531	Syntic dye, nat indigo lakes	X1	1.34	C1	M1	0.67	3.97					C1	M1	0.24	6.27					D2	M4	0.3	5.17
5	K1	553	Perfumery, cosmetics etc.	X4	0.34					D3	M4	0.27	2.20					D1	M1	0.45	0.50				
6	K1	583	Polymerization etc. prods	X2	0.34	C1	M1	2.36	0.00	D2	M5	1.26	0.00	C1	M1	2.12	0.00	D2	M6	0.85	0.59	C1	M2	1.64	0.00
7	K1	591	Pesticides disinfectants	X1	0.32																	C1	M1	0.232	0.49
8	K1	661	Lime, cement bldng prods	X2	0.88									C1	M2	0.16	4.98	C1	M1	0.29	4.98	C2	M3	0.03	0.00

9	K1	671	Pig iron etc.	X4	0.72	D1	M2	0.36	32.48																
10	K1	672	Iron steel primary forms	X2	0.31	D2	M4	1.20	3.81	D2	M6	0.91	0.00	D2	M4	1.93	0.00	C2	M3	0.15	0.00	C1	M1	2.14	0.54
11	K1	673	Iron steel shapes etc.	X2	0.64	C1	M1	0.64	0.20	C2	M3	0.52	2.22	D2	M5	0.49	1.09	D2	M6	0.54	0.46	D2	M4	1.45	0.11
12	K1	674	Iron stl univ plate sheet	X2	0.56	C1	M1	1.83	0.00	C1	M2	1.57	0.00	D2	M5	1.28	0.00	D2	M6	0.76	0.10	D2	M4	2.54	0.00
13	K1	678	Iron, stl tubes, pipes etc.	X2	0.29	D2	M4	0.99	0.00	D2	M4	0.77	0.00	C2	M3	0.40	0.29	D2	M5	0.51	0.11	C1	M2	0.46	0.52
14	K1	684	Aluminium	X2	0.55	C1	M2	0.80	1.62	C1	M2	0.65	5.45	D2	M6	0.47	1.25	D2	M5	0.45	13.12	C1	M1	0.85	1.78
			Sub-Total - K1		7.70			11.11				5.95				7.86				4.00				10.81	
1	K2	713	Intrnl combus pstn engin	X1	0.41	C1	M1	2.24	0.09	D2	M5	0.71	0.39	C1	M2	1.29	0.66	D2	M6	0.8	0.66	D2	M5	1.07	0.29
2	K2	724	Textile leather machinery	X1	0.28	D2	M4	2.62	1.31	D2	M6	0.46	1.05	D2	M4	0.72	0.32								
3	K2	781	Pass motor vehic excl buses	X2	0.55	D2	M5	0.27	0.00	D2	M4	1.81	0.00	C1	M1	2.38	0.18					C1	M1	2.82	0.11
4	K2	784	Motor vhcls pts, access NES	X4	0.96	D1	M1	4.79	0.17	D3	M6	0.39	0.43	D3	M5	0.89	0.08	D3	M6	0.74	0.56	D3	M4	3.63	0.05
5	K2	752	Automatic data proc equip	X5	0.32	D3	M6	0.29	0.00	D3	M6	0.69	0.02	D3	M6	0.51	0.00	D1	M1	4.96	0.27	D1	M3	0.94	0.00
6	K2	778	Electrical machnry NES	X6	0.34	D3	M6	1.17	0.34	D1	M1	2.67	0.10	D1	M3	0.82	0.67	D3	M4	2.45	0.18	D1	M2	2.1	0.08
			Sub-Total - K2		2.84			11.38				6.73				6.61				8.95				10.56	
1	L1	612	Leather etc manufactures	X1	1.15	C1	M2	0.38	0.00																
2	L1	625	Rubber manufactures NES	X4	0.90									D3	M5	0.36	3.47								
3	L1	652	Cotton fabrics woven	X1	3.47	C1	M2	0.35	0.66	D2	M4	0.43	2.46	C1	M1	0.73	3.66	D2	M5	0.27	3.66	C1	M2	0.39	5.17
4	L1	653	Wovn man-made fib fabric	X2	1.35	C1	M2	0.74	0.12	D2	M5	0.51	2.08	D2	M5	0.69	0.00	D2	M4	0.64	4.11	C1	M2	0.77	0.18
5	L1	655	Knitted etc. fabrics	X2	0.28	C1	M2	0.50	0.14	D2	M4	0.39	0.07	D2	M4	0.87	0.00	D2	M5	0.28	0.28	C1	M2	0.34	0.00
6	L1	831	Travel goods handbags	X1	0.96													C1	M1	0.27	0.41				
7	L1	843	Womens outwear non knit	X1	5.36													C1	M1	0.32	0.27				
8	L1	845	Outwear knit non elastic	X2	1.29													C1	M1	0.42	4.27				
9	L1	846	Under garments knitted	X1	1.83													C1	M2	0.31	1.25				
10	L1	851	Footwear	X1	1.31													C1	M1	0.25	1.37				
11	L1	893	Articles of plastic NES	X2	0.83	C2	M3	0.32	0.12	D2	M4	0.97	0.11	C2	M3	0.52	0.10	D2	M5	0.73	6.82	C1	M1	1.37	0.11
12	L1	897	Gold, silver ware jewelry	X2	1.70													C1	M2	0.41	4.96				
13	L1	898	Musical instruments pts	X2	0.49					C2	M3	0.42	0.07					D2	M4	1.16	0.81	C1	M2	0.92	0.00
			Sub-Total - L1		20.91			2.29				2.72				3.17				5.06				3.79	

(Contd.)

TABLE 5 (Contd.)

Sr. No.	Gr-oup	SITC	Commodity	Indian export		Indonesian Import				Malaysia's Import				Philippines Import				Singapore's Import				Thai Import			
				Cate-gory	Share	Cla-ss	Cate-gory	Imp. Share	Mkt. Share	Cla-ss	Cate-gory	Imp. Share	Mkt. Share	Cla-ss	Cate-gory	Imp. Share	Mkt. Share	Cla-ss	Cate-gory	Imp. Share	Mkt. Share	Cla-ss	Cate-gory	Imp. Share	Mkt. Share
1	L2	541	Medicinal, pharm prod	X4	2.23	D3	M5	0.60	0.56	D3	M5	0.46	1.05	D3	M4	1.18	0.48	D1	M3	0.51	0.63	D1	M2	0.71	1.04
2	L2	695	Tools	X1	0.34	C1	M1	0.33	0.42	D2	M4	0.34	0.61					D2	M5	0.34	1.13	D2	M4	0.5	0.90
3	L2	699	Base metal mfrs NES	X4	0.56	D1	M3	0.54	0.15	D3	M4	0.90	0.55	D3	M6	0.42	0.35	D3	M5	0.64	1.09	D1	M1	1.37	0.17
4	L2	785	Cycles etc. motorzd or not	X4	0.87	D3	M4	1.26	0.61	D3	M6	0.25	2.01	D1	M2	0.50	0.18	D1	M3	0.27	2.00	D3	M4	0.53	0.95
			Sub-Total - L2		4.00			2.73				1.95				2.10				1.76				3.11	
1	L3	611	Leather	X1	1.45	C1	M2	1.08	0.54					D2	M6	0.30	0.25					C1	M2	0.5	0.00
2	L3	651	Textile yarn	X1	4.00	C1	M1	0.87	0.85	C1	M1	0.55	7.08	C1	M2	0.54	10.35	D2	M6	0.22	10.35	D2	M5	0.38	2.36
3	L3	667	Pearl, prec semi-p stone	X1	15.43					C2	M3	0.29	6.16					C2	M3	0.25	26.08	C1	M2	1.63	19.73
			Sub-Total - L3		20.88			1.95				0.84				0.84				0.47				2.51	
1	N1	281	Iron ore concentrates	X1	1.57	C1	M1	0.27	6.84					C2	M3	0.00	0.00								
2	N1	287	Base metal ores, conc NES	X4	0.56	D3	M5	0.23	0.00	D3	M4	0.30	0.00	D3	M4	1.37	0.00								
			Sub-Total - N1		2.14			0.50				0.30				1.37				0.00				0.00	
1	N2	334	Petroleum products, refin	X6	1.59	D1	M2	4.03	0.00	D3	M6	1.93	0.13	D1	M3	2.49	0.00	D3	M5	3.10	0.54	D3	M6	2.62	0.38
2	N2	341	Gas, natural & manufactr	X2	0.21									D2	M4	0.79	0.00								
			Sub-Total - N2		1.80			4.03				1.93				3.28				3.10				2.62	
1	O	931	Special transactions	X4	3.16					D1	M3	1.37	0.67	D1	M1	18.12	0.05	D1	M3	1.17	0.20	D3	M6	1.38	0.20
			Sub-Total - O		3.16			0.00				1.37				18.12				1.17				1.38	
			Grand total		142.48			41.90				24.01				47.12				25.21				37.73	

Another supply related point that can be made in this context is that given the importance of iron and steel products in Indian exports to Indonesia, a shift towards export of more processed (in place of raw and less processed) ones would yield larger value addition.

Light manufactures comprising final products with low (L1) and high skill (L2) requirement and intermediates (L3) was another complementary category. Indian world export of light manufactures were far larger in proportion to total exports than their Indonesian import in its total world imports. This could be attributed to the fact of both the countries being competitive under this product range. Given the smaller market, the Indian export of light manufactures to Indonesia was understandably limited. Even within the limited domain, India's presence was nominal, not reaching up to one per cent of Indonesia's import under any of the categories. This indicates that so far as light manufactures are concerned, India could improve its trade prospects, to an extent, by appropriately diversifying its light manufactures in alignment with Indonesia's demand structure.

The global Indian exports as well as Indonesia's imports under food and beverages (A1) were diverse. Even so, the bilateral exports constituted only one group, animal feed. The Indian export under this group was, however, large, cornering one-fourth of its Indonesian import. But the Indonesian import under different product groups belonging to this category ranged from 0.2 to 1.8 per cent of its total and Indian global export under A1 product groups other than animal feed varied from 0.1 to 1.5 per cent. Among them, Indonesian import of wheat was considerable. Given India's bulging stock of wheat year after year, Indonesia could provide a market outlet.

Indian global export and Indonesian world import enjoyed complementarity in regard to six product groups under capital goods (K2). Indonesian imports under four of them were fairly high but Indian exports were small and marked by declining complementarity. Given these characteristics, the bilateral exports, if at all, were understandably small and their market presence in Indonesia nominal. This means that India would be able to partake in a part of the large Indonesian market for capital goods only if its product mix is right and the price competitive.

Of the remaining product groups, cotton and seeds for soft fixed vegetable oils, both belonging to crude agricultural raw materials (A2), were important in terms of nature of complementarity, which was high and growing. Both of them were among the Indonesia's significant imports accounting for 2.2 and 1.2 per cent of its global imports respectively. What is more, India exported to Indonesia under both, and captured 3-4 per cent of the Indonesian import market. Given the size of Indonesian import, India should be able to enhance its market share further. That would, of course, depend on its competitiveness.

Another group that needs mention is refined petroleum products, under the fuel minerals (N2), in which India's global exports were 1.6 per cent and Indonesia's imports from the world as much as 4.0 per cent of their respective totals. But there was no export from India to Indonesia. This indicates the scope for bilateral export.

Indonesian Exports to India

Indonesian exports enjoyed trade complementarity with Indian imports in only half the number of product groups in which Indian exports did with Indonesian imports. Complementary products accounted for less than two-fifths of both Indonesia's global exports and India's global imports (Table 4). What is noteworthy is that a little more that a quarter of total Indonesian exports to India relate to complementary products. This means that the bilateral export from Indonesia to India grew fast in the post-liberalization period (1985 onwards) but not did expand to make full use of the existing potential. The point will be clear from the following discussion.

Among the product categories, mineral fuels (N2) was one in which the share of Indonesian exports and Indian imports in their respective totals was the highest, and their correspondence was very close (Table 6). Five groups thereunder—three with high and growing complementarity—together accounted for around one-fourth of both Indonesian exports and Indian imports. From amongst them, crude petroleum alone claimed around 12 per cent of both Indonesia's total export and India's total import. But even with such close correspondence, there was no export from Indonesia to India. Similar was the case with coal that contributed around 2 per cent of both Indonesian global export and Indian total import from the world. In the case of refined petroleum products, Indonesia exported to earn 2.3 per cent of its total export earnings while India imported the same product from the global market to the tune of 9.3 per cent of its total import. Although the bilateral export of refined petroleum products was as much as 10.5 per cent of the total Indonesian exports to India, it only formed 1.3 per cent of India's total import. This analysis shows the bright prospects of Indonesian export to India under various product groups under this product category.

Similarly, though at a far lower scale, two categories of processed development inputs (K1 & K2), with as many as 11 product groups,

TABLE 6: COMPLEMENTARITY AT THE LEVEL OF PRODUCT-GROUPS BETWEEN EXPORTS OF ASEAN STATES AND INDIAN IMPORTS

			Indian import		*Indonesian export*				*Malaysia's export*				*Philippines export*				*Singapore's export*				*Thai export*			
Sr. No.	*Gr-oup*	*SITC Commodity*	*Cate-gory*	*Share*	*Cla-ss*	*Cate-gory*	*Exp. Share*	*Mkt. share*	*Cla-ss*	*Cate-gory*	*Exp. Share*	*Mkt. share*	*Cla-ss*	*Cate-gory*	*Exp. Share*	*Mkt. share*	*Cla-ss*	*Cate-gory*	*Exp. Share*	*Mkt. share*	*Cla-ss*	*Cate-gory*	*Exp. Share*	*Mkt. share*
1	A1	057 Fruit, nuts, fresh dried	M1	1.12									C1	X1	2.58	0.19								
2	A1	061 Sugar & honey	M2	2.55									D1	X4	0.56	0.43								
		Sub-Total - A1		3.67											3.14									
1	A2	247 Oth wood rough squared	M4	0.71					D3	X4	1.66	32.85												
2	A2	424 Fixed veg oil non-soft	M1	0.59	C1	X1	2.78	0.00	D1	X4	5.29	0.00	D1	X4	3.53	0.00								
		Sub-Total - A2		1.30			2.78				6.95				3.53									
1	K1	251 Pulp & waste paper	M1	0.71	C1	X2	0.34	4.82					C1	X2	0.23	0.00								
2	K1	511 Hydrocarbons NES, derivs	M1	2.05													C1	X1	0.31	8.98				
3	K1	512 Alcohols, phenols etc.	M4	0.43					D2	X1	0.49	2.80	D3	X4	0.29	1.27								
4	K1	514 Nitrogen-fnctn compounds	M1	0.65	C1	X2	0.35	0.00																
5	K1	515 Org-inorg compounds etc	M4	0.37													D2	X1	0.78	1.38				
6	K1	562 Fertilizers manufacture	M1	2.67	D1	X4	0.45	2.13					C1	X1	0.75	0.00								
7	K1	582 Prod of condensation etc.	M3	0.42														X2	0.41	2.39				
8	K1	583 Polymerization etc. prods	M5	1.59					D2	X2	0.44	0.00	D3	X6	0.21	0.00	D3	X4	0.91	0.00	D2	X2	0.73	0.00
9	K1	598 Misc. chemical products	M3	0.58					C2	X1	0.43	10.99	D1	X6	0.24	0.00	C2	X1	0.66	2.41				
10	K1	672 Iron steel primary forms	M1	1.09	D1	X4	0.32	0.00																
11	K1	673 Iron steel shapes etc.	M3	0.34	C2	X2	0.15	0.00																
12	K1	678 Iron, stl tubes, pipes etc.	M4	0.64					D2	X3	0.19	0.00					D3	X4	0.26	0.00	D3	X4	0.46	0.00
13	K1	682 Copper exc cement copper	M1	1.30					C1	X2	0.38	1.11	D1	X4	2.12	0.00	D1	X4	0.45	1.85				
14	K1	684 Aluminium	M2	0.60	C1	X1	0.59	0.09																
		Sub-Total - K1		13.46			2.20				1.93				3.84				3.78				1.19	

(Contd.)

TABLE 6: (Contd.)

Sr. No.	Gr-oup	SITC	Commodity	Indian import Cate-gory	Indian import Share	Indonesian export Cla-ss	Indonesian export Cate-gory	Indonesian export Exp. Share	Indonesian export Mkt. share	Malaysia's export Cla-ss	Malaysia's export Cate-gory	Malaysia's export Exp. Share	Malaysia's export Mkt. share	Philippines export Cla-ss	Philippines export Cate-gory	Philippines export Exp. Share	Philippines export Mkt. share	Singapore's export Cla-ss	Singapore's export Cate-gory	Singapore's export Exp. Share	Singapore's export Mkt. share	Thai export Cla-ss	Thai export Cate-gory	Thai export Exp. Share	Thai export Mkt. share
1	K2	713	Intrnl combus pstn engin	M3	0.42					D1	X4	0.3	0.00					C2	X1	0.45	2.15				
2	K2	714	Engines and motors NES	M2	0.50													C1	X2	0.23	1.20				
3	K2	716	Rotating electric plant	M3	0.77					C2	X2	0.57	0.06					D1	X4	0.93	1.63	C2	X2	0.68	0.00
4	K2	728	Oth machy for spcl indus	M3	1.17													C2	X1	0.89	2.08				
5	K2	736	Metal working mach-tools	M6	0.64													D2	X1	0.30	0.00				
6	K2	741	Heating, cooling equipment	M6	0.41					D3	X4	1.40	0.11					D3	X5	0.66	0.91	D2	X2	1.32	0.70
7	K2	743	Pumps NES, centrfuges etc.	M3	0.43					C2	X3	0.32	0.33					D1	X4	0.70	3.15	C2	X2	0.37	0.44
8	K2	744	Mechanical handling equip	M5	0.57													D2	X1	0.56	4.33				
9	K2	749	Nonelect mach pts, acc NES	M6	1.34													D2	X1	1.10	1.31	D2	X1	0.82	0.06
10	K2	752	Automatic data proc equip	M6	0.44	D3	X6	0.24	0.23	D2	X2	2.49	1.15	D2	X3	1.33	0.00	D3	X4	15.15	28.08	D2	X2	4.68	0.22
11	K2	759	Office adp mach pts, acces.	M6	0.50	D2	X2	0.34	0.22	D2	X2	5.73	0.14	D2	X3	0.40	0.00	D3	X4	7.62	19.69	D3	X5	3.53	1.06
12	K2	764	Telecomm eqpt, pts, acc NES	M6	0.87	D3	X6	1.00	0.06	D2	X1	5.38	0.00	D2	X3	3.71	0.06	D3	X4	6.29	6.66	D2	X3	2.73	1.21
13	K2	772	Switch gear etc. pts NES	M6	0.60					D3	X5	1.51	0.00	D2	X3	0.70	0.00	D3	X4	2.15	12.59	D2	X2	1.40	0.53
14	K2	776	Transistor, valves etc.	M6	0.94					D3	X4	16.17	2.80	D3	X6	8.16	0.07	D2	X1	12.45	20.69	D3	X5	4.96	0.85
15	K2	778	Electrical machnry NES	M6	0.66	D3	X6	0.79	0.00	D2	X3	1.00	0.40	D2	X3	0.35	0.00	D2	X1	1.99	10.60	D3	X4	1.56	0.29
16	K2	784	Motor vhcls pts, access NES	M3	0.85									C2	X2	1.23	0.00	D1	X4	0.30	0.35	C2	X2	0.85	0.00
17	K2	792	Aircraft etc.	M1	2.56					C1	X1	2.65	9.77					D1	X5	0.24	1.30	C1	X2	1.08	0.04
18	K2	793	Ships and boats etc.	M6	0.25	D3	X6	0.17	0.00	D2	X3	0.48	0.00					D2	X1	0.90	11.87				
		Sub-Total - K2			13.91			2.54				38.00				15.88				52.91				23.98	
1	L1	641	Paper and paperboard	M6	0.76	D3	X4	1.21	1.96									D3	X5	0.32	0.64				
2	L1	892	Printed matter	M4	0.25													D2	X1	0.50	11.36				
		Sub-Total - L1			1.01			1.21				0.00				0.00				0.82				0.00	

1	L2	541	Medicinal, pharm prod	M1	1.04													C1	X1	0.51	0.51	C2	X3	0.19	0.35
2	L2	699	Base metal mfrs NES	M6	0.30					D2	X2	0.43	0.13					D3	X4	0.46	3.45	D2	X2	0.42	0.00
3	L2	874	Measurng, controlng instr	M5	0.97													D2	X1	0.75	2.74				
4	L2	882	Photo cinema supplies	M1	0.49													C1	X1	0.50	1.08				
			Sub-Total - L2		2.80			0.00				0.43				0.00				2.22				0.61	
1	L3	611	Leather	M3	0.25																	C2	X1	0.50	0.37
2	L3	651	Textile yarn	M2	0.56	D1	X4	1.69	13.57	D1	X6	0.56	0.00	C2	X3	0.32	0.00	D1	X6	0.28	3.24	D1	X4	1.12	3.52
3	L3	667	Pearl, prec semi-p stone	M1	5.70																		X2	2.35	0.47
			Sub-Total - L3		6.51			1.69				0.56				0.32				0.28				3.97	
1	N1	287	Base metal ores, conc NES	M4	0.26	D2	X1	2.83	0.00					D3	X4	1.01	0.00								
			Sub-Total - N1		0.26			2.83				0.00				1.01				0.00				0.00	
1	N2	322	Coal, lignite & peat	M1	2.26	C1	X2	2.05	0.00																
2	N2	333	Crude petroleum	M1	11.47	C1	X1	12.66	0.00	D1	X4	4.33	3.56												
3	N2	334	Petroleum products, refin	M1	9.27	D1	X5	2.31	1.25	C2	X3	1.14	0.07	D1	X5	0.75	0.00	C1	X1	9.21	0.36	C2	X3	0.49	0.07
4	N2	335	Residual petrlm prod NES	M2	0.33	D1	X5	0.00	0.00																
5	N2	341	Gas, natural & manufactr	M2	0.30	C1	X1	9.21	0.00	D1	X5	1.77	0.00	C2	X3	0.71	0.00					D1	X6	0.29	0.00
			Sub-Total - N2		23.63			26.23				7.24				1.46				9.21				0.78	
1	O	931	Special transactions	M4	6.65					D2	X3	0.67	0.55	D2	X1	34.91	0.05	D3	X6	1.05	0.52	D3	X6	0.69	0.02
2	O	971	Gold non-monetary NES	M2	1.64	D1	X4	0.37	0.00					C1	X2	1.57	0.00								
			Sub-Total - O		8.29			0.37				0.67				36.48				1.05				0.69	
			Grand Total		74.84			39.85				55.78				65.66				70.27				31.22	

together accounted for almost 5 per cent of Indonesian export and 9 per cent of Indian import. But Indonesian export to India was significant only under two product-groups, fertilizers and pulp and waste paper. Even these two groups had marginal market presence, 2.1 and 4.8 per cent respectively. For the rest of the groups under K1 and K2, Indonesian export to India was nil or negligible.

At a still lower scale, only one product group from among the remaining categories, textile yarn (under light manufacturing intermediates) qualifies for special mention. For the Indonesian export constituted 6.8 per cent of India's total imports from that country and claimed a market share of 13.6 per cent in India.

To sum up, the bilateral trade between India and Indonesia that flourished was somewhat asymmetrical: Indian exports covering more than three-fourths of the bilateral trade were anchored on complementary products, while only a little more than one-fourth of Indonesian exports to India related to such products.[10] If the extent of correspondence between Indian export and Indonesian imports at the product level are viewed together with the realized level of bilateral trade, one can easily see a huge unrealized potential as reflected in a complete absence or marginal market presence in a large number of groups. Such potential is still larger in respect of Indonesian export to India. This is implicit in the low base of realized bilateral trade in complementary products. We have indicated only the broad contour of Indo-Indonesian trade prospects. The actual realization would call for larger promotional efforts, keeping in view the domestic supply conditions.

India and Malaysia

Indian Exports to Malaysia

Almost half of the Indian exports (46.2 per cent), numbering 34 SITC groups, showed complementarity with Malaysian imports (Table 3). But such products claimed a smaller share, less than a quarter (24.0 per cent), in the total imports of Malaysia. What is more, such Malaysian imports, both in terms of number (26) and share (19.4 per cent), are mostly characterized by declining complementarity. This meant that trade promotion on the basis of identified complementary groups might be good for the short to medium term but in the longer run India would require to identify more promising product groups amongst the Malaysian imports for a better and growing presence in the Malaysian market.

Further, more than half of the complementary product groups, 19 out of 34, originated from only three product categories, intermediate goods of heavy and chemical industry (K1), capital goods (K2) and food and beverages (A1) (Table 3). But they together accounted for only 10.8 and 14.6 per cent of Indian exports and Malaysian imports respectively.

The important point to note is that Indian exports were not in close alignment with the Malaysian demand structure as reflected in its import pattern. This explains the reason why the share of Malaysia in the Indian export to ASEAN-5 slumped over time from 30.1 per cent in 1971 to 15 per cent in 1994. In other words, Indian exports to Malaysia failed to keep pace with exports to ASEAN-5. But the significant feature is that even with lower share, complementary products claimed a little more than two-fifths (42.7 per cent) of Indian exports to Malaysia. This means that Indian exports made inroads into whatever limited market was available in some of complementary product range. The point may be elaborated further at the product group level.

The Malaysian import of animal feed, vegetables, textile yarn, pearls and aluminium, for example, claimed less than 1 per cent of its global import, which indicates smaller market for these products (Table 5). But these very products accounted for more than two-thirds of the bilateral share (28.9 per cent out of 42.7 per cent) of the complementary products that India exported to Malaysia. Understandably, all of them captured a high market share ranging from 17.9 per cent (feed for animals) to 5.5 (aluminium) of the respective Malaysian imports.

On the other hand, five product groups (excluding special transactions), each accounting for more than 1 per cent of Malaysian imports, did not figure among significant exports from India to Malaysia. In fact, four from amongst them did not appear at all in the bilateral trade.

In short, India did not explore the relatively large market that Malaysia offered. What it did was only in respect of those that provided a narrow market within the complementary product range.

Malaysian Exports to India

Malaysian exports that were complementary to Indian imports were fewer in number than those observed earlier in respect of India's exports versus Malaysian imports. But then these fewer product groups covered a larger share in their respective totals. Such 25 complementary groups accounted for 53.1 per cent of Malaysia's exports and 40.7 per cent of India's imports (Table 4).

Almost half (12) of the complementary product groups came under capital goods (K2) contributing 38.0 per cent of Malaysia's exports but only 8.9 per cent of India's imports (Table 6). Similarly, two groups of crude agricultural raw materials (A2) accounted for 7.0 per cent of the former's exports but only 1.3 per cent of the latter's imports. On the other hand, three groups under mineral fuels (N2) and five groups under the intermediate group of heavy and chemical industry (K1) contributed respectively 7.2 and 1.9 per cent of Malaysia's export but 21.0 and 4.6 per cent of India's imports.

Malaysian exports to India thrive on the strength of complementarity to the tune of 62.1 per cent of its total. But its predominant global exports played a relatively insignificant part in the bilateral export. For example, Malaysian export under the most predominant category, viz., K2 contributed 19.7 per cent of its total exports to India while a much less significant category, N2, did as much as 24.3 per cent.

The point becomes sharper at the product group level. Malaysian exports under K2 were both dominant and diverse. But these products were far less prominent in the bilateral export. For example, transistor valves, etc., contributed as much as 16.2 per cent of its global exports but only 1.1 per cent of the bilateral export. The contrast was also true: aircraft which accounted for just 2.7 per cent of Malaysian global exports formed as much as 14.7 per cent of the bilateral export.

Such contrasting cases went far beyond the K2 category. In fact, much larger Malaysian export to India took place in product groups which were not among the more prominent export groups. To illustrate, wood rough with a 1.7 per cent share in Malaysian global exports contributed 13.7 per cent of its export to India and captured 32.9 per cent of the India's import market. Similarly, crude petroleum that formed only 4.3 per cent of Malaysian global exports contributed to one-fourth of the bilateral export.

All this suggests that Malaysian export structure and Indian import pattern were not in alignment. This probably contributed to a high degree of fluctuation in the bilateral trade volume, resulting in an unstable growth. As in the case of India's export to Malaysia, the latter's exports to the former as percentage of the total ASEAN-5 declined from 44.8 in 1985 to 26.0 in 1994. This implies that the Malaysian exports did not keep pace with the rise in the total exports by ASEAN-5 together.

In a situation such as this, the most relevant question that arises is: What are India's trade prospects with Malaysia? While it is difficult to provide an unequivocal answer, one should recognize the following facts. First, historically, Malaysia is India's most important trade partner after Singapore among the ASEAN states. Second, both Indian exports to Malaysia as well as exports from the latter to the former reveal a considerable degree of complementarity. In other words, the export from and import of both the countries bear correspondence to a significant extent. This clearly indicates a fair trade potential. Third, they enjoy geographical proximity that warrants lower transport costs. Fourth, a large population of Indian origin in Malaysia provides an environment of stronger trade ties. The fact that the number of Indian joint ventures in Malaysia is the largest among ASEAN states lends support to the above observation.

All this suggests that the mismatch between demand structure and supply conditions as observed could perhaps be corrected by adopting the right set of trade promotional initiatives on both sides. Its success would essentially hold the key to further trade prospects between the two countries.

India and the Philippines

Indian Exports to the Philippines

Trade ties between India and the Philippines were the weakest among the ASEAN states. Nevertheless, a large number of Indian exports (35 product groups excluding special transaction covered under residual category) showed complementarity with the Philippines' imports. But they contributed one-third of Indian exports and 29.0 per cent of the Philippines' import (Table 3). The majority of them, 24 out of 35 groups, again, were characterized by declining complementarity.

Indian global exports bore correspondence with Filipino imports under all the product categories but did so more significantly in respect of light manufactures (L1, L2 & L3), intermediate goods of heavy and chemical industry (K1) and food and beverages (A1) (Table 3).

Indian exports to the Philippines at the product level also followed more or less the same pattern within the broad band of complementary product groups. As such, almost two-thirds of India's export to the Philippines (65.4 per cent) covered complementary goods. However, one single product group, animal feed, contributed 47 per cent of India's total exports to the Philippines. This implied that less than one-fifth (18.4 per cent) of India's exports to the Philippines spread over diverse groups of complementary products.

Among the other product groups, only two light manufactures and one intermediate goods of heavy and chemical industry were noteworthy both on account of their size of share and market presence. Cotton woven fabrics contributed 4.0 per cent of India's exports to the Philippines and captured a market share of 3.7 per cent. Similarly, textile yarn, another light manufacture group, accounted for only 1.5 per cent of India's exports to the Philippines, but formed 10.4 per cent of its total Filipino imports. Again, synthetic dyes, a K1 product group, with 1.6 per cent of India's exports to the Philippines, claimed 6.3 per cent market share.

The important point to note is that all these product groups claiming a respectable market share related to those product groups under which Filipino imports from the world formed less than 1 per cent of it total imports. On the other hand, several products that the Philippines imported from the world in significant proportion contributed nothing or only a marginal part of Indian exports to the Philippines. For example, refined petroleum products and polymer products, constituting each more than 2 per cent of the Filipino total imports, did not figure in India's exports to the Philippines.

Given the size of Indo-Philippines trade, the number of complementary products was large, though their share in the respective totals was on the lower side. Second, almost two-thirds of Indian exports to the Philippines came within the range of complementary products. But just one single product group claimed slightly less than half of India's exports to the Philippines. Third, less than one-fifth of India's exports was dispersed over a wide variety of complementary product groups but without any significant market presence barring a few. Fourth, those few that had considerable market presence were greatly constrained by the very size of import market. On the other hand, Indian exports had no or marginal presence in respect of the products with relatively larger market. These basic features suggest that Indian exports would fare better in the Filipino market only if trade promotion moves towards bringing about better alignment with its demand structure, assuming Indian exports are competitive.

Philippines Export to India

The Filipino global exports in contrast to its import of Indian goods witnessed a much higher degree of correspondence with India's global imports. Such complementary exports contributed 65.7 per cent of its total exports but only 35.1 per cent of India's total imports (Table 4). If special transactions are excluded, as was done earlier, the corresponding proportion of complementary products slumped to 30.8 and 28.4 respectively. In either case, however, an overwhelmingly large proportion of these products revealed declining complementarity for both the countries.

Among the complementary product categories, capital goods (K2) and intermediate goods of heavy and chemical industry (K1) were the two most significant categories at least as far as Filipino exports go (Table 4). As for Indian imports that were complementary to Filipino exports, mineral fuels (N2) stood out as the most significant category followed by food and beverages (A1).

When it comes to bilateral trade, complementary products excluding special transactions contributed only 41.7 per cent of the Filipino exports to India. These bilateral exports concentrated in just five product groups. Among these five product groups, one, sugar and honey, contributed more than one-fourth (26.9 per cent) of the total Filipino exports to India. The remaining product groups were transistors, etc. (5.9 per cent), fruit (5.0), alcohol, etc. (2.5), and telecom equipment (1.3). But none of them captured any significant market share.

The above discussion highlights a few important points. First, the Filipino global export basket revealed a fair degree of correspondence with Indian world import pattern. It is far higher if special transactions are not taken into account. Second, even with such correspondence, complementary products contributed only a little more than two-fifths of the Filipino exports to India. Third, these Filipino exports to India solely concentrated in just five product groups but none of them enjoyed any significant market presence in India.

What does this add up to? One has to recall that the Philippines among the ASEAN states is India's weakest trade partner, involving no more than $ 100 million, only 10 per cent of which were the Filipino exports to India in 1994. But the fact is that the Filipino global exports did enjoy complementarity with India's imports over a wide spectrum of products, but this was not reflected in the realized bilateral trade. Its implication is that better matching of Filipino product specialization with India's demand structure would contribute to enlarging trade between them. The Look East Policy that the Government of India adopted in recent years should yield a desirable outcome even though the financial crisis of 1997 was a setback.

INDIA AND SINGAPORE

Indian Exports to Singapore

With $1.5 billion trade volume, Singapore was India's strongest trade partner within the ASEAN region. The destination of more than two-fifths (42.7 per cent) of India's export to ASEAN-5 and the origin of almost half (48.4 per cent) of its imports from the region was Singapore.

34 product groups with more than half of India's global exports (55.8 per cent) enjoyed complementarity with Singapore's import from world (Table 3). Such complementary products accounted for one-quarter of Singapore's global imports. But then the majority of them with the share of 22.2 per cent in Singapore's world import revealed declining complementary.

Complementary products under light manufactures from among all categories were the most dominant, accounting for 42.3 per cent of India's global exports (Table 5). But they constituted only 7.3 per cent of Singapore's imports.

All complementary products together claimed more than half of India's exports (52.3 per cent) to Singapore. More important, almost all complementary product groups figured in the bilateral export with a market presence ranging from 26.1 per cent to 0.1 per cent. From this angle, Singapore among ASEAN states was uniquely positioned in its bilateral trade with India.

One remarkable feature of the bilateral export is as follows 3 product groups, pearls, aluminium and plastic articles, each contributing more than 5 per cent of India's exports to Singapore, were such that each of its import from the world by the latter constituted less than 1 per cent of the total. For example, India's exports of pearls to Singapore was 8.6 per cent of the bilateral total but its import by the latter was mere 0.3 per cent of its global imports. What is noteworthy is that India's export under these very product groups captured considerably large market shares ranging from 26.1 to 6.8 per cent.

On the other hand, India's bilateral export of products with much larger market size as reflected in their share in Singapore's global imports was low with a marginal market presence. To illustrate, automatic data processing equipment accounted for almost 5 per cent of Singapore's global imports but India's export under this was just 1.7 per cent of the bilateral total and claimed only 0.3 per cent of its total market.

What follows from the above analysis is that so far as Singapore is concerned, the basic issue for Indian exports is not how to penetrate the market, but how to enlarge its market share.

The other important feature is that the bilateral exports have not flourished on the strength of complementary products, their share in Singapore's global import being not much in excess of a quarter. On the other hand, as observed earlier, India's product specialization widely differed from Singapore's import pattern, signifying its demand structure, which is what led to a large chunk of mutually exclusive exports/imports or a low share of whatever India exported to Singapore.

All this suggests that India's export prospect in Singapore would brighten as its pace of development quickens thus bringing closer both its production and demand structure to the latter's.

Singapore's Export to India

Singapore's exports revealed correspondence with India's imports in an equal number of groups as observed in the case of its imports. These complementary product groups accounted for as much as 70.0 per cent of Singapore's global exports and more than 42.5 per cent of India's imports from world (Table 3). The point to note is that among the five ASEAN states, Singapore enjoyed highest level of complementarity with Indian imports both in terms of number of product groups as well as their respective shares.

However, similar to Indian exports, most of these exports of Singapore witnessed a declining complementary. Such product groups, 25 in number, claimed a large share—as much as 56.8 per cent of Singapore's global exports and 26.5 per cent of India's import. This feature of complementarity could weaken the trade prospects.

The single most dominating complementary product category was capital goods (K2) alone claiming more than half (52.9 per cent) of Singapore's total export. Their contribution in Indian imports was, however, only 13.9 per cent of its total. Next in importance was mineral fuels (N2) accounting for around nine per cent of both Singapore's and India's global export and import respectively. Intermediate goods of heavy and chemical industry (K1) were also somewhat important at 3.8 per cent of Singapore's exports and 7.0 per cent of India's imports. It means that India holds out larger prospects for Singapore's export of development inputs, processed or otherwise.

Singapore's export to India under complementary goods constituted close to one-half of its bilateral export. While its export to India was diverse encompassing almost all the different product groups, capital goods dominated the most accounting for two-thirds of its bilateral exports (Table 6). More important, several amongst them captured a high market share. In fact, five of them formed more than one-tenth of India's total import under the concerned group. Three commodity groups out of them, automatic data processing equipment, transistor valves, and office machinery claimed one-fifth or more of India's global import of the respective groups.

As for N2, however, Singapore's exports to India were solely concentrated in refined petroleum products—that too claiming a small share of 1.4 per cent of the total bilateral exports and market share of just 0.4 per cent.

However, one related group though clubbed under intermediate goods of heavy and chemical industry (K1), hydrocarbons, claimed not only a high share at 7.5 per cent in Singapore's bilateral export but also a tidy market presence at 9.0 per cent of its total import in India. Equally noteworthy is that this product group occupied its place among the few groups enjoying high and growing complementarity.

Outside these three predominant categories, one product group deserves a special mention. It is printed matter under light manufactures (L1) which captured a market share of 11.4 per cent with its small share of 1.1 per cent in Singapore's total exports to India.

Singapore's export to India and vice versa under complementary products showed both similar and dissimilar features. Similarity was striking in regard to a wide spread of diverse complementary products that figured in the bilateral trade. So was the case in regard to the share of complementary products in the bilateral trade. But dissimilar features were more marked in some sense. For example, Indian exports had market presence but were significant only in a fewer product groups while Singapore's exports had much wider market visibility. Similarly, Singapore's export of capital goods had both wider and deeper market penetrations in India. No parallel category exports were observable among Indian exports to Singapore. Despite such dissimilarities, the bilateral trade between Singapore and India thrived largely on the strength of complementarity. It could do so more as India moves to a higher growth trajectory.

India and Thailand

Indian Exports to Thailand

Indian exports under 33 product groups showed complementarity with Thai imports, though almost half of them were of declining type. Such product groups covered close to half (47.9 per cent) of India's global exports and close to two-fifths (37.7 per cent) of Thai imports from world (Table 3).

At the level of product categories, light manufactures inclusive of final products (L1 & L2) and intermediates (L3) together contributed 31.3 per cent of India's exports but only 9.4 per cent of Thai imports (Table 5). Between them, intermediates were more dominant with 20.9 per cent share in India's exports though only 2.5 per cent of Thai imports.

Next in importance was the category related to intermediates of heavy and chemical industry (K1) contributing 8.5 per cent of the total Indian exports but 11.7 per cent of Thai imports from world. Capital goods (K2) also contributed more than one-tenth (10.7 per cent) of Thai imports but its contribution in Indian exports was merely 2.6 per cent.

The pattern of Indian exports and Thai imports as observed above highlights one important feature: the Thai import market was far larger for K1 and K2 products than that for light manufactures while the Indian exports catered more to the latter than the former.

Complementary products contributed 69.8 per cent of India's export to Thailand. As to their distribution across product groups it broadly followed the relative order of India's global export basket. For example, L3 exports, which was the most predominant category among light manufactures contributed to more than one-third (34.5 per cent) of India's exports to Thailand. Within L3 product groups, however, pearls contributed the most (33.1 per cent) and captured almost one-fifth (19.7 per cent) of its total Thai imports. The issue to flag is whether India can retain this high market share in the face of growing pearl industry in Thailand.

As mentioned above, the Thai import demand for K1 and K2 products were high in comparison. Yet Indian exports of K1 products though spread over eight groups formed only 7.6 per cent of its total exports to Thailand. Two of them, nitrogen function compound and synthetic dyes had, however, a market share of around 5 per cent even though their import demand was substantially low, less than 0.4 per cent of the total Thai imports. On the other hand, India exported marginally or not at all the products with much larger import demand. For example, four iron and steel product groups accounted for 6.6 per cent of the total Thai imports. Three of them contributed just 1.3 per cent of India's exports to Thailand while the most predominant one with 2.5 per cent share in Thai imports did not figure in India's export basket to Thailand.

As for K2 with a large import demand, India's export under four product groups claimed only 1 per cent of its total export to Thailand. None of them had any significant market share.

Outside these prominent categories, there was one group, animal feed, which contributed 17.4 per cent of India's exports to Thailand and captured a market share of 19.0 per cent. The point to stress is that this significant product group among India's exports to Thailand was also one with very low import demand at 0.9 per cent of the total Thai import.

Thai Exports to India

Thai export groups that showed correspondence with Indian imports were fewer in number, 24 in all. Such complementary products contributed 39.9 per cent of Thai exports and 34.2 per cent of India's imports

(Table 4). But more than two-thirds of them revealed declining complementary with a little less than one-fifth (19.1 per cent) of Thai exports and more than one-fourth (27.7 per cent) of Indian imports.

The only prominent complementary product category was capital goods (K2) contributing 24.0 per cent of Thai exports and 10.4 per cent of India's imports (Table 6). Most of the K2 product groups were among the significant Thai exports, each accounting for more than one per cent of its total exports. But the size of import market for them in India was by and large small. Yet, it is noteworthy that all but two of them figured, though with smaller market share of below 1.3 per cent, in bilateral trade from Thailand to India. They collectively contributed just 6.1 per cent of Thai exports to India but two of them, telecom equipment and transistor valves, claimed a share between 1 and 2 per cent of the total.

The other important categories, which were remote cousins of K2, were light manufacturing intermediates (L3) and food and beverages (A1). Their respective shares were only 4.0 and 3.3 per cent in total Thai exports and 6.5 and 3.0 per cent in total India's imports.

Among the L3 Thai exports, pearls, textile yarn and leather groups together accounted for 8.0 per cent of the bilateral export from Thailand to India. Of them, only textile yarn captured a market share of 3.5 per cent while the other two less than one per cent. In contrast, both the A1 groups claimed a respectable market share in Indian imports. In fact, sugar and honey claimed almost one-tenth of its total import by accounting for as much as two-fifth of Thai export to India.

What is remarkable is that though complementary products contributed less than two-fifth of Thai global exports, they claimed a much larger share (60.3 per cent) in the bilateral export to India. Among the product categories, food and beverages (A1) alone accounted for 44.4 per cent of Thai exports to India and within this sugar and honey claimed 40.2 per cent of the total with 9.4 per cent market share. Leaving this group aside, Thai export under no other group reached 5 per cent mark. But then a variety of complementary products formed a part of bilateral export to India. Pearls and vegetables among them were notable items of Thai exports, each contributing a little more than 4 per cent of the bilateral total but their market presence was not significant.

In sum, what emerges is that the bilateral trade between India and Thailand largely boomed on the strength of complementary products. But India's reach in the Thai market was broadly within light manufactures and food, of which the import demand of Thailand was limited. Similarly, Thai exports to India were mainly restricted to the items under food and beverages.

India failed to expand its export of K1 and K2 products in which Thai import demand was large. Even with these limitations, that India witnessed high export growth of more than 25 per cent per annum during 1985-95 making Thailand its second largest export market among ASEAN states was indeed remarkable. But the sustainability of rapid growth of export as in the past would depend on how soon and how effectively India could realign exports in conformity with Thai import patterns.

On the other hand, Thailand faced a limited Indian market within the range of complementary products. India revealed a considerably large import demand only in refined petroleum products among complementary products in which Thailand was not a major global supplier. This explained lower growth of Thai exports to India (5.2 per cent per annum during 1985-94) as compared to India's booming export growth of 25 per cent plus during the same period.

CONCLUDING REMARKS

Trade played a much larger role in ASEAN states than in India for a far longer period. In the development process, their trade was greatly integrated with the global system. Neither India for its traditional political alignment as well as inward-oriented development strategy, nor the ASEAN states, sought one another as major trade partners. Only in the 1990s, with the policy slant towards globalization and the articulation of the Look East Policy, did India make concrete efforts to strengthen economic ties with ASEAN. So did ASEAN states with the opening up of the Indian economy. In this background the bilateral trade that took place in the long past might not entirely indicate the future possibilities. Even so, a careful analysis of trade patterns since 1980 would not only suggest trade specialization but also the directions of possible cooperation in the newer trade regime.

The bilateral trade as examined in regard to complementary products has brought out several important facts that have great bearing on future trade possibilities between India and ASEAN.

First, the bilateral trade between India and ASEAN partners anchored largely on complementary products, though the extent of their prominence varied from country to country. With the exception of Malaysia, Indian exports to ASEAN states were largely constituted in complementary products. This fact stood in contrast to ASEAN global exports in aggregate being in greater correspondence with India's global imports. This means that a considerable part of bilateral trade did not exactly reflect the global trade pattern, partly of the cut-off point (0.3 per cent) adopted in the data source.

Second, there was realignment of India's trade partners among ASEAN states: Singapore replaced Malaysia in the 1990s as the most important trade partner, and Indonesia overtook Thailand since the mid-1990s as the third important partner. The point to note is that India expanded trade at a rapid pace particularly in the 1990s with the ASEAN-5.

Third, even with the expansion of trade, one important fact stood out: there is a huge scope for restructuring trade in alignment with India and ASEAN trade partners' demand and supply conditions. For several complementary products were not traded at all between them and wherever traded their market presence was mostly insignificant.

Finally, the recent changes in policy regime in India towards market driven system and globalization would facilitate trade on the basis of resource endowments and competitive strength. Some of the recent initiatives both by ASEAN and India would hasten the process.

NOTES

1. This is despite the fact that some of the ASEAN states were badly hit by the East Asian currency and financial crisis of 1997 dampening their medium term growth prospects. In fact, economic recovery in the crisis-ridden ASEAN states have already begun and, they are expected to be again on high growth path.
2. If its dialogue and sectoral partners are also included, the association's reach in economic terms is much wider.
3. The external trade of ASEAN-5 as a proportion of their GDP rose to 128 per cent in 1999 from 75 in 1980 as against 18.4 per cent from 13.5 per cent for India over the corresponding years. It was much higher in Singapore (266 per cent) and Malaysia (201 per cent) as compared to the remaining countries. Incidentally, Singapore was a unique example of re-export activities as reflected in its exports exceeding GDP by almost 35 per cent in 1999.
4. Their combined share in world trade rose to around 6 per cent in the second half of the nineties from 2 per cent in 1970.
5. At the initiative of Thai commerce Minister in April 2000, the BIMST-EC (Bangladesh, India, Myanmar, Sri Lanka and Thailand-Economic Cooperation) was launched with the objective of establishing a free trade area to boost trade and investment in the region. A couple of important decisions in the field transportation, custom procedures, investment, preferential visa regime and a common approach on WTO have been taken in the three ministerial meetings till 2000. A Trans-Asian Highway and a Trans-Asian Railway linking Thailand, Myanmar, Bangladesh and India are the projects that the group is considering actively. In fact, India has already taken the first step in this direction by way of building the road linking Tamu (Manipur) to Kalemyo, a key communication junction in the centre of Myanmar.
6. India has active joint business councils with Thailand, Singapore, Malaysia and the Philippines. It signed an agreement with Malaysia in 1998 to set up an exclusive joint committee to strengthen and develop cooperation in various fields of science and technology.

7. The ASEAN-India joint business council identifies practical ideas regularly to strengthen and develop economic cooperation in various fields.
8. In addition to these, there are several Indian joint ventures and wholly owned subsidiaries set up out of the profits of their established bases are not on the official records, according to Ashok Jha, adviser, Federation of Indian Chambers of Commerce and Industry (FICCI).
9. The methodology is detailed out in a larger study on Indo-ASEAN Trade Prospects that the authors have recently published. See Atul Sarma, and Pradeep Kumar Mehta (2002): *Exploring Indo-ASEAN Economic Partnership in Globalising World*, New Delhi: Bookwell, pp. 439-44.
10. The extent and nature of complementarity in several product groups accounting for as much as 68.9 per cent of total India's import from Indonesia in 1994 could not be estimated because of data limitation. Owing to the high cut-off mark (0.3 per cent of the total), global trade statistics from the selected source did not report the trade volumes of these groups for one or both of the paired countries.

Indian Diaspora in South-East Asia and the Emerging Relations between India and ASEAN: An Economic Perspective

Baladas Ghoshal

It is difficult to give an exact meaning to the concept of diaspora. In one sense, it refers to the traumatic displacement of colonized peoples, their cultural alienation and dislocation across the globe and their interactions in plural settings. Most on diaspora literature focuses on the forces behind displacement of diasporas and natives, the problem of integration, lack of civic loyalties, the tenacity of diasporas to preserve their culture, and the role of colonial powers. There is also a tendency to treat diasporas as not really autonomous entities in the true sense of the word. They are treated as though they have never severed their umbilical cords with the lands of their origins. The governments of their homelands, not due to any sense of cultural affinity but merely to enlist their financial support, have remembered some diasporas. Economic difficulty in terms of securing adequate capital investments from others has propelled these governments to secure the participation of diasporas by granting them various cultural and political concessions.

There also exists another perspective, the plural society thesis, that describes diasporas as ethnic minorities, marginalized groups, sojourners and others. According to this perspective diasporas lead a problematic existence in the countries of their adoption. Their minority status, cultural exclusiveness, their lack of civic consciousness in integrating with the indigenous natives and related features are presented as sources of considerable conflict to other communities. Instances of discrimination and attacks against diasporas stemming from native nationalism are often cited to convey the suggestion that diasporas are themselves responsible for this state of affairs. In the earlier plural society thesis of Furnivall, cultural antagonisms are played up to reveal the incompatibilities between natives and diasporas and hence the justification for the presence of the colonial powers. Then there is the emphasis on identity politics, which suggests maintenance and perpetuation of cultural essentialisms among diasporas.

Conceptualization of modernity is another problematic in the literature on diasporas. Modernity conceived within the nation state focus provides little room for the consideration of alternative modernities. Within the national context, the diaspora form of modernity is a partial one, subject to a variety of controls and domination. Consideration of modernities in the global context might present a somewhat different picture of the alternative modernities available for diasporas. Recent works on the subject have pointed to the way flexible production on a global scale has empowered diasporas, particularly the Chinese, Indian, and Jewish. As argued by some, the making of these alternative modernities cannot be understood independent of the networkings brought on by capitalism's own dynamic with those of the nation state. Capitalist interests and the nation states must understand diasporic modernity as interplay between strategies of accumulation and experiences of dislocation and the different constructions of modernity. Insofar as diasporas are concerned, modernities are not confined to one place, they are multiple sites on a global scale that allows for mobility, identity and subjectivity.

Having stated some of the theoretical problems in rendering precise meaning to the concept of diaspora, we may now turn to the specific case of the Indian diaspora, where they stand in relation to identity, and how they relate to their land of origin. We will focus on their current position and how they are trying to organize themselves into a pressure group not only to promote their own interests within national and global settings, but also promote the interests of their origin country to emphasize the fact that the umbilical cord has still not snapped.

Indians settled abroad in about 136 countries are estimated to be 12 million and the majority are located in Africa, Caribbean and Oceania. During ancient times, they went as merchants from western India to Africa and western Asia. From the eastern part of south India, they emigrated to Burma, Malaysia and other parts of South-East Asia. This group derived its livelihood from international trade and maintained kinship and economic overseas networks. Some south Indian rulers had even sent successful expeditions to South-East Asia. Some migrated to eastern Asia and South-East Asia about the same period to spread the message of Buddhism. The bulk of the Indian migration, however, took place during the colonial period. Large number of Indians migrated as (i) indentured labourers in sugar plantations to the Caribbean, Oceania and Africa; (ii) under *Kangani* system to Malaysia and Sri Lanka; and (iii) free or passenger Indians primarily to

East Africa. In the twentieth century, Indians emigrated as skilled and semi-skilled workers to Europe, North America and Oceania, and very recently to western Asia, even though they are not allowed citizenship in the Gulf countries. Along with them, thousands went on their own to set up small shops, or to take positions as bankers, brokers, agents, clerks and even teachers. The recent years have also witnessed the beginning of what Prahalad has called the 'Indian Global Nomad' who has the professional and technical skills and temperament to contribute to any organization able to provide the requisite challenges and rewards.[1] This group, along with the diaspora from the industrial countries, according to Mukul Asher, could be crucial in accelerating India's integration into the global economy.[2]

The Indian diaspora is not monolithic. Migrants have a wide divergence based on language, religion, and geographical regions from where they emigrated. Further there are differences based on the way they came to different countries, as indentured labour, traders, professionals or businessmen. In a way, they are a microcosm of Indian diversity. Second, though they are diverse, all have the unifying identity of being ethnic Indians. People of Indian Origin (PIO) around the world seemed to possess a feeling of oneness and have the feeling of being a part of greater Indian society. But more than that natives in the countries of their adoption do not give them a choice of feeling anything other than being Indian, and treat them also as such—ethnic Indians. Third, what puts them in a single category is their advancement in the economic field, either as professionals or businessmen. Almost all of them, whether indentured labour, free passenger, semi-skilled or skilled worker or business community have done well economically and professionally. Therefore, PIO as diaspora has the strength of being prosperous, professionally and intellectually advanced and sharing a common identity and attachment to the country of their origin. The policy of successive governments in India has been to encourage full participation and identification with their respective countries of diaspora's citizenship, the linkages of the diaspora with the government of India of the day are much less than with the Indian society with which it had always maintained strong emotional and other bonds. An overwhelming proportion of the Indian diaspora has taken up the citizenship of the countries of migration, and consequently willingness to be identified as being of an Indian origin varies greatly. There are differences also in socio-economic status in the host country. While in general in the industrial countries and in Africa, income and education levels are above average for the population as a whole (or for other groups), in South-East Asia, the reverse is the case. However, in the case of Singapore, even though no precise data are available, it seems that the share of the citizens of Indian origin in those emigrating is roughly three times their share in the population; and many of those emigrating are professionals and skilled personnel who could provide civic leadership.[3]

Though prosperous and confident of their identity, Indians suffer minority status except in Mauritius where they are the majority and enjoy full political and economic power. The prosperous minority faces subtle or overt hostility. The problems gets compounded when the affluent minority also happens to be an immigrant community and not fully integrated with sons of the soil. The Indian diaspora faces this problem practically in all the countries where they have emigrated. As it does not have networks with similar groups in other countries, its global strength does not help it domestically in the countries they have adopted. Jews realized this at an enormous cost, and have now corrected it through worldwide linkages. Besides, the Indian diaspora suffers from two additional factors. First, they are not an organized diaspora as compared to the Chinese or Jewish minority. Because of its domestic positioning, lack of networking and finally the absence of a strong global organization, the Indian diaspora has failed to mobilize its resources and strength during crises, for example in Burma, Fiji or Uganda.

Second, they are also handicapped by the weakened position of India, their origin country, in the global political and economic sphere. Apart from the networking system by which the Chinese diaspora is linked, their strength also is derived from the increasing economic and strategic clout of China. India, though big in population, is not strong in terms of military and economic clout and therefore is not in a position to help overseas Indians when they are in trouble. Nor do the PIOs look towards India for vital support during crises. This is in contrast to Israeli, Chinese or European diasporas who respond aggressively when members are adversely affected. Just as Israel recognizes every Jew's 'right of return', Beijing takes for granted the support of 55 million overseas Chinese. It is common knowledge that Taiwan, Hong Kong, and Singapore rose magnificently to China's rescue after the Tiananmen Square massacre a decade ago, contributing 80 per cent of the foreign investment in China when the West and Japan cut off funds. For precisely this reason, they are suspected of bonding with China to create 'a borderless nation, linked by blood'. Ironically, India might help exorcize this spectre of Greater China, and also profit from it. One reason why Singapore's Prime Minister, Goh Chok Tong had talked of 'a mild India fever' was to demonstrate that the Chinese would put their money wherever the return is highest. It so happens that despite the vital contribution, the host country may not take PIOs as seriously as other diasporas, whose origin countries seemed to wield much greater clout in world affairs. There is, therefore, an increasing recognition among the Indian diaspora that their further success, both in the contexts of their position within their adopted country and their possible contribution to India, requires an economically resurgent, strong and resilient India. Without a strong India, both economically and militarily, the Indian diaspora will feel neither comfortable nor secure in their own country, or the incentives to lend their hand in India's economic development. A strong India would provide further economic opportunities and positive externalities for the diaspora leading to increased per-unit value of its activities. That is why one witnessed a sudden change in the perception of India among the diaspora after 1991 when it decided to open its economy to global competition; and more so after 1998 when India joined the select nuclear club. On its part, India is aware that the diaspora is in a position to assist in providing necessary ideas, contacts, technology, and finance, marketing and Western management know-how. The diaspora may also be able to assist in creating a mindset in India more appropriate to wealth creation.

Now diasporas are being recognized as an international force. The race for globalization has created an environment to look beyond rigid national boundaries for economic and other aspiration of people. With the globalization of goods and services, the national economic boundaries are slowly disappearing. Efforts are made to minimize controls on trade in goods and services across the boundaries. While those efforts are being continued and enforced by nations, businesses everywhere are looking for opportunities for expansion so that the foundations of their respective business ventures remain sound in the long run. Global networking, interaction and use of complementarity at global level provide emerging opportunities for a diaspora to network and come together. The breathtaking development in science and technology has reduced distances and costs and has broken communication barriers. If there is potentiality and strong will for the diasporic community to come together for fostering the common good and an identity, there is now an ideal global environment for promoting such an objective. There are other reasons for the Indian diaspora to feel the need for networking and coming closer to each other—the uncertainty and insecurity of the post-Cold War period resulting from accelerated technological change, rapid globalization of economic activities and the worldwide debate on Samuel Huntington's 'Clash of Civilization' thesis and finally the assertiveness of a rising China necessitating adjustments in the global balance of power. Modernization and technological change have also brought about an erosion of cultural roots and values, creating an identity crisis, which in turn contributed to an urgent need for enhanced pan-Indian consciousness among the diaspora. Increased interaction among them is now facilitated by revolutions in information and communication, making it possible and cost-effective. As a result, in almost all the countries of the world where Indians have settled, one witnesses a sudden awareness of a community feeling sometimes reinforced by religious rituals and practices. The increased pan-Indian consciousness, to quote Mukul Asher, himself an NRI,

> requires that different elements of the diaspora cooperate to pursue certain common interests and goals. It is entirely consistent with greater identification with and participation in the entire gamut of activities in the respective countries of citizenship. Thus, enhanced pan-Indian consciousness should not be confused with the goals and aspirations of the respective countries of citizenship. Indeed, the diaspora needs to integrate further, particularly in the social sphere, with other communities in the respective countries of citizenship.[4]

The formation of the GOPIO (Global Organisation for People of Indian Origin) to create new linkages or expand the existing ones across international boundaries is therefore an important development as far as the Indian diaspora is concerned. It however needs yet to formulate a plan of action as to how the business community in one country, for example in Malaysia, can have access to knowledge, market information, various sources of finance available, modern management techniques of Indian businesses anywhere in the world, so that a world network of GOPIO businesses can be established. For the Indian diaspora to have the necessary clout, they must strengthen their existing community-based trade networks, which until now are mostly family-owned. Introduction of professional management practices is necessary to transform these firms to more efficient and competitive business ventures. More importantly, rising per capita income and globalization of economic activities have opened up new areas of economic activities, particularly in services, namely health care, entertainment, media, tourism, etc., and in which the growth opportunities are better. In their effort to strengthen community-based trade networks, it would help the Indian diaspora to diversify into these new areas of economic activities. Malaysian Indians, for example, have historically been dominant in the legal and medical fields. Now education is another field where they can excel, particularly with the help of Indians in India. GOPIO members can excel and develop business opportunities if they can devise a mechanism to tie the Indians in the countries where they have made their mark, for example in Indonesia, Thailand and Singapore in South-East Asia. Efforts made by some members of the diaspora to diversify from trading to manufacturing in conjunction with India-based firms are in the right direction. As an example, some of the Indian businesses based in the Philippines have formed the Chariot Holdings Corporation with a paid-up capital of nearly US $10 million. This is an investment company, which proposes to co-invest with Indian firms wishing to start industries in the Philippines, in India, or elsewhere.[5] The main shareholders were in trading, and they initially aimed to be passive industrialists. It seems Indian businesses in Singapore have similarly set up a passive-investment company called Parameswara Holdings with the equity capital of S $ 25 million (US $ 1 = S $1.78). The company has already taken a small stake in the information technology park in Bangalore and in some other projects in India.[6]

Despite favourable opportunities, the Indian diaspora faces dangers as well. In most countries PIOs are a minority and any visible attempt to foster external loyalties, however, innocuous for domestic political system, invite suspicion and hostility if done without taking the local leaders into confidence. Confident and organised PIOs will prove a better asset for the country of their adoption than isolated, sulking and vulnerable PIOs. Another danger would be for the diaspora to reduce itself to a business network. Business should be a propelling force for people to come together and not a sole end in itself.

Much of the interest in the role of diaspora in India's economic development and in promoting India abroad arose out of the unique contribution the Chinese diaspora made in People's Republic of China's spectacular economic progress, as well as the success of the Indian NRIs in Britain and the United States. In the case of the latter, the Indian-Americans have organized themselves and emerged as a powerful lobby in American politics and foreign policy. As Indian troops fought to repel a Pakistani incursion in Kargil, key staff members were bombarded with demands from Indian immigrants—many in the computer and software industries—for a resolution condemning Pakistan's 'aggression'. US lawmakers eventually complied, and a few days later, according to two senior American administration officials with direct knowledge of the conversation[7] in a White House meeting on 4 July 1999, the President cited Congressional pressure in urging the now ousted Pakistani Prime Minister Nawaz Sharif, to withdraw his forces. 'It was gratifying for many of us to see a clear pro-India tilt sweep this city', Congressman Gary Ackerman, Democrat of New York, told a gathering of Indian Americans on 20 July, after Pakistan had withdrawn its forces. 'And this unique phenomenon was made possible in no small measure because of the political activism of the Indian-American community.'[8]

The rise of Indian-Americans as a powerful and effective domestic lobby—one that aspires to the level of influence that American Jews have exerted on behalf of Israel—coincides with the emergence in India of a stable and increasingly self-confident government. The victory by the strongly nationalist Bhartiya Janata Party (BJP) has strengthened the hand of its prime minister Atal Behari Vajpayee at a time of high tension with Pakistan and continued diplomatic fallout in Washington over the 1998 Indian and Pakistani nuclear tests. Since the tests, which triggered US sanctions against India and Pakistan, the Indian government has held a high-level dialogue with Washington aimed at repairing relations. Indian-Americans have figured prominently in that effort, giving generously to political campaigns and meeting with lawmakers and administration officials to explain the security rationale behind the Indian tests.

According to a 1990 census data, Indian-Americans have the highest average household income—US $60,903—of any Asia-Pacific ethnic group, a category that includes Chinese Americans and Japanese-Americans. Indian entrepreneurial skills have had a spectacular impact in the Internet and software industries, where India-Americans have begun to organize themselves into groups such as the Indus Entrepreneurs and the Indian CEO High Tech Council. The latter boasts a membership near Washington, D.C., of 165 Indian-American chief executives, whose companies employ nearly 20,000 people. These software engineers and start-up specialists have not been shy about translating their economic success into political clout. In September 1996, Indian-American executives and professionals held a fund-raiser for President Clinton at the Mayflower hotel that raised a reported US $4,00,000. Even the current Republican president, George W. Bush, has already benefited from the largesse of Indian-Americans. Looking at their social position in the American society, Indian-Americans should have been a more powerful lobby, but then they have their weaknesses as well, like Indian diaspora elsewhere. An Indian student born in the United States puts it aptly:

> Indian Americans will achieve political and cultural power only when we learn to acknowledge our weaknesses and build upon our strengths. Our weaknesses include inability to move beyond petty regional and religious divisions and unwillingness to accept that though many Indians are doctors and architects, many also drive taxis and wait on tables. Our strength lie in our relative affluence, strong cultural ties, educational achievements, geographical concentration, rapidly growing numbers and large representation in key sectors of the American economy such as software and medicine.[9]

Literature on the Indian diaspora has until now remained focused on micro socio-political and economic issues, as that were the main concerns of the marginalized immigrants. However, with the changed positioning of the PIOs, there is the need for new perspective on issues like (i) Indian diaspora as a player in world identity politics, and (ii) Indian diaspora as an international force in world system. An attempt has been done to explore some of those issues in the context of the role played by Indians in South-East Asia in facilitating India's interactions with ASEAN and the role India accords to them in its diplomacy and foreign relations. More, however, needs to be done to be able to get better appreciation of the role of diaspora.

New Delhi's attempts to attract the capital and technology of NRIs have just begun. We have mentioned earlier about the Chinese diaspora whose commonality of culture and commitment stretches across whole swathes of the Asia-Pacific. In South-East Asia alone, it is estimated that the overseas Chinese community controls over three-fifths of the regional economy. In comparison, Indian diaspora's control over the economy would be roughly one to two per cent. In the case of China, most of its overseas immigrants were businessmen, who went in search of trade opportunities abroad. They made substantial profits and chose to invest much of it in China when the process of economic reforms began two decades ago. The Indian diaspora, on the contrary, consists of disparate groups who migrated in different stages for different reasons. Though some of them were businessmen and have taken the earliest opportunity to invest in India, when the liberalization process began in 1991-2, a majority of them are unskilled or semi-skilled labour and professionals. Ethnic Chinese multinationals have already shown their mettle in overseas investments. FDI from Hong Kong and Taiwan has been the major source of regional FDI flows, of which China was one host, albeit a major one, as was Thailand. In addition, many ethnic Chinese multinational companies are also owned by the Chinese living in Singapore or across the rest of the South-East Asian countries. Business deals over the last two decades in China by these overseas ethnic Chinese multinationals have strengthened their ties with their counterparts in the mainland and have already yielded dividends to the latter. Chinese state-owned enterprises used these contacts to first establish their presence in Hong Kong and later in the South-East Asian markets. Such contacts would also prove an advantage when it comes to investment expansion in the more demanding western markets.

Indians in South-East Asia are fairly small in number. As per the last statistics available, there are about 3 million Indians living in 10 countries of South-East Asia, the largest being in Malaysia—nearly 2 million—

followed by Singapore where Indians constitute about 8 per cent of the total population of nearly 4 million. In both these countries, Indians are not affluent compared with the other ethnic groups. In Malaysia, a significant section of them are from the lower middle class or poorer sections. A few of them, however, have done well in professions like law and medicine and live quite well. Only a handful are entrepreneurs, and that too, small-time players. The only big name is Ananda Rajah, a Sri Lankan Tamil, who owns a few conglomerates and is an influential figure on the Malaysian economic scene. While Indians are only 8 per cent of the population, they make up half of the 102 gangs involved in criminal activities. Indians control only 0.9 per cent of total corporate equity in Malaysia. In Singapore too, the picture is not very different, even though their economic conditions are slightly better than their counterparts in Malaysia. In the past, Burma had the second largest Indian population in the region—3,30,000 out of a total population of 44 million in the 1970s, but their numbers have dwindled over the years as the military government initiated economic and social policies detrimental to the interests of the minority overseas population, leading to their influx back to India. In other countries of South-East Asia, their numbers are quite insignificant but economically better off since they comprise mostly traders and businessmen. Indonesia has about 40,000; Thailand 25,000; the Philippines 3,000; Vietnam 1,500; Laos and Cambodia together 3,000; and Brunei 2,200.

Not being collectively as prosperous or as high profile as the Chinese in Indonesia, Malaysia, Vietnam, Thailand or the Philippines, Indians no longer provoke the resentment that they once did in Burma or old Malaya when they held positions of influence under the British. Today's Indians are circumspect enough not to attract too much attention. Narasimha Rao was the first Prime Minister to acknowledge the role the overseas Indians can play in the development of India when he quietly coaxed the community to invest in India, and invoked the sentiment that just as India has a stake in their prosperity, they had a stake in India's development. India is now trying to make up for decades of neglect of the Indian diaspora by establishing a separate section in the Ministry of External Affairs in the form of a NRI cell and by offering a card for the NRIs. As the Indian government can take a cue from the Chinese government in providing a supportive link which inspires immigrants with a sense of security, similarly Indian businessmen who have to operate outside the country should also learn from the Chinese the art of networking with their counterparts in South-East Asia. The businessmen of Indian origin obviously cannot match the overseas Chinese in their economic clout; they can still be valuable partners. In any event, the exercise of networking need not be restricted to links with the ethnic Indians alone, but should include the Chinese businesses as well for the requisite access to finance, technology, markets and political connections. Such networking may involve strategic alliances with others, and help develop increasingly vital skills in simultaneously engaging in competition and cooperation with its business rivals.

As pointed out earlier, compared to the overseas Chinese, the Indians are an affluent community. There is also a basic difference in their attitudes towards China and India. I.G. Patel, former Governor of the Reserve Bank, was not very wrong when he once wrote: 'The non-resident Indians may have their heart in the homeland, but prefer to keep their cash elsewhere.' With India's new economic environment, that attitude may have changed now. During the era of 'closed economy', NRIs were happy to keep out of India, but when the economic opportunities opened up at 'home', they did not want to miss the bus. During the 1990s, some NRIs acquired clout with the successive governments in New Delhi, while many others have generated controversies through their actions. New Delhi has now introduced a new system of entry permits for 'Persons of Indian Origin' (PIO). Instead of having to apply for multiple visas they can get a PIO card which will also be a passport for other concessions and clearances in the matter of setting up business or industry in India. This scheme has received a 'fair response', but certainly not to the extent that New Delhi had expected.

At the same time, one cannot ignore the fact that some of the 20 per cent of actual FDI inflow of US $10 billion, since the launch of economic reforms in India, has come from NRIs. Better still, their rate of 'conversion' of approved FDI into actual inflow of capital is 100 per cent, against an average conversion rate of only 20 per cent. This means that NRI investments that are approved are actually translated into action, probably because the bulk of these are small projects that do not wither on the vine, or get lost in approval and financial closure formalities, as happens with mega-projects. This is a big plus factor for the NRIs.

There are no separate data on investments by Indians from South-East Asia. At the same time it is a common knowledge Indian community in those countries are taking an active role in promoting economic linkages between India and their adopted country. Indians in Malaysia and Singapore, for example, are involved in joint ventures with Indian entrepreneurs in southern India. Even if they do not own the companies, the Indian diaspora is playing the leading role in the policy decisions as well as persuading those companies to come to India. One notable example is the effort made by Malaysia's Samy Vellu, the influential minister in Mahatir's cabinet, who has been an important player in the emerging close relations between India and his country. Even the local Indian academics like K.S. Nathan and Mohammad Arif from Malaysia and Mukul Asher and Vanoji Rao from Singapore are doing their part through their recent publications in narrowing the gap in the negative perceptions of South-East Asian countries towards India, and sensitizing their people to the positive gains that might be achieved in improved political and economic interactions between India and ASEAN. It is no coincidence that major publications on India-ASEAN relations that have come out from South-East Asia are mostly contributed by the diaspora.

In 1996 Singapore launched the first initiative to organize what it called a 'Global Indian Entrepreneurs Conference', in a bid to network the Indian diaspora and play a catalytic role in focusing attention on India. It was ready to provide support services and some investment for PIO entrepreneurs who wanted to set up business in India. A follow up conference was hosted in 1998 in New Delhi, at the invitation of the FICCI. The stage was set for similar congregations in alternate years. Whether it provides a funnel for investments into India, it generates attention on India and a review of the investment climate and economic reforms in the country. Successive governments have taken a keen interest in these conferences. As its follow up, the Singapore Indian Chamber of Commerce and Industry, a co-sponsor for the 1996 show, set up an internet site named the Global Indian Business Network, inviting all interested parties to hook on to the expanding network. Similarly, FICCI has also launched a huge and expansive network of chambers and businessmen. To promote further the interests of business enterprises, a new regional forum called the Asia-Pacific Indian Chambers of Commerce and Industry (APICCI), comprising members from nine countries, including India, was launched in 1999 in Singapore. While launching the forum, the Singapore minister of trade and industry, George Yeo, praised the efforts of the Indian business community and said that the APICCI 'have enabled Indians to occupy strong international positions in traditional areas like the textiles, diamonds and spices, both retail and wholesale (trade)'. He further noted that such groupings could provide 'a certain amount of group insurance' to those involved. The objective of the APICCI, according to its founders, is to serve not only as a common forum for the ethnic Indian entrepreneurs of the Asia-Pacific region, the India-specific focus would also help them to facilitate the entry of capable Indian firms onto the wider regional stage and their networking thereof.

As we have pointed out earlier, in comparison with Indians in North America and Britain, the Indians in South-East Asia are not strong economic players yet. But the potentialities exist. Apart from the local Indians in South-East Asia, a new breed of expatriate Indians is slowly emerging as important players in the corporate life of South-East Asia. There is great demand in South-East Asia for Indian software engineers, chartered accountants, financial analysts and management consultants. Indian engineers who constitute about 60 per cent of the total employees in Mahatir's dream project, Multi-media Super Corridor, for example, dominate the multi-media sector in Malaysia. Singapore has employed a large number of Indians from IITs and IIMs, as well as the ones who have been trained in the United States and in Europe. Singapore Airlines have instituted a number of scholarships for bright Indians to study engineering, science and technology in Singapore Universities. After completion of the studies, the awardees are supposed to work at least for a certain number of years in Singaporean companies at a salary offered to any Singapore citizen. All over the region, one can find young Indians occupying strategic positions in corporate houses. In course of time these Indians are also going to acquire clout in the economic life of those societies, similar to the Indians in North America. At that point, it is reasonable to expect the NRIs of South-East Asia to be a force for technology sourcing and in venture capital funding, two areas in which they have done especially well in the United States. It should also be a targeted objective of Indian policy to offer inducements to this segment, because their linkages with India will lead them to develop a stake not only in the welfare of India, but also closer interactions with their adopted country.

NOTES

1. C.K. Prahalad, 'The Indian Diaspora: A Factor in Global Business?' Speech delivered at the Global Indian Entrepreneurs Conference, Singapore, 18-20 June 1996, unpublished.
2. Mukul G. Asher, 'The Indian Diaspora: Strengthening the Economic Base', unpublished Paper, June 1996.
3. Ibid.
4. Ibid.
5. *Asia Times*, 4 June 1996. Quoted in Mukul Asher.
6. In his paper mentioned above Asher lists certain measures through which the Indian diaspora can enhance their economic strength and develop a pan-Indian consciousness. He suggests that the diaspora must devise a strategy to take advantage of opportunities arising from India's drive for much greater international integration and competitiveness, and to cultivate the ability to cooperate and enter into alliances with others, including its competitors. To quote Mukul,

   Increasingly, the Indian diaspora's plans and actions would need to be predicated on the basis that the future economic prospects of the diaspora on the one hand and India on the other are increasingly inter-linked. For its part, India will need to make the appropriate changes in the overall economic policy regime and in attitudes towards the diaspora to make this possible. If Drucker (the management guru) in arguing that in the 21st century, knowledge (and brain power) and not capital, raw materials or labor will be a key resource, then the Indian diaspora and India are in a good position to take advantage of this development. However, translating this potential advantage into actual competitive advantage will not be an easy task. It will require the enabling physical infrastructure, policy environment, cultivation of what Fukuyama has called 'social capital' and necessary confidence in the ability to compete and to meet challenges.

7. *International Herald Tribune*, 11 October 1999.
8. *New York Times*, 22 July 1999.
9. Quoted in *Times of India*, 20 October 1999.

Financial Markets and Stability: Reforms in India from the BOP Crisis to the East Asian Crisis

Manmohan Agarwal and Dipankar Sengupta

INTRODUCTION

India has always been a reluctant reformer. But influence in international affairs (something that India has always strived for) depends essentially on three factors: *military might*, *economic performance* and *significance*, and *policy innovation* in handling important issues. Military might and economic size are traditional measures of national power. While policy innovation in handling important issues does not give a nation as much influence as the other two factors, nevertheless if such innovation promises to achieve higher growth and greater military power, its contribution is by no means insignificant. For example, in the 1950s and the 1960s, India wielded significant influence on economic issues on the international stage because of its path-breaking adoption of the planning process, which was intended to accelerate rates of growth and improve the living standards of its people. Even as its performance slipped behind the newly industrializing countries of East Asia in the 1960s and the 1970s, India still commanded respect among certain quarters because of its ability to manage the economy in the aftermath of the 1973 oil crisis, and because of its vigorous internal debates on important economic issues.

However, by the 1980s, India had beeome an increasingly marginalized player in the international arena. Policy makers only realized the extent of India's marginalization with the establishment of global unipolarity after the demise of the USSR. By then it had become increasingly clear that, the five-year plans notwithstanding,[1] the economy had not performed up to

* A version of this chapter was presented at the conference in January 1999, in New Delhi organized by the World Policy Institute, New York on 'Emerging Powers, India, Brazil, South Africa'.

expectations. After several five-year plans, India remained a poor country with vast sections of the population living below the poverty line and lacking basic amenities. *Obviously policy innovations that fail or that are not sufficiently successful do not contribute much to a country's influence.* Even India's reputation for managing the economy had been severely eroded by the crises of 1980-1 and 1990-1. This was because of the extremely poor state of the public finances, the very depressing financial and technical health of public sector enterprises (PSEs), and the general feeling that vested interests rather—than national interests—governed economic policy making.

Externally India's share of world trade plummeted from 2 per cent at the time of independence to 0.4 per cent by the 1980s. All this could not but lower the country's influence in international economic affairs. It is widely believed that India was completely sidelined in the later stages of the Uruguay Round of multilateral trade negotiations.[2] India's negotiating stance was not consonant with the emerging trends in international economic affairs, and the country obviously did not have the economic clout to influence the negotiations to serve its national interests. So while many countries remained sceptical of US backed proposals on intellectual property rights, investment measures and trade in services, India was unable to provide sufficient leadership to devise alternative strategies that could unite disagreeing participant countries.

It is the contention of this chapter that improved economic performance is necessary to increase India's influence in international economic affairs and to maintain its freedom of action in the sphere of international relations. But the evolution of India's society, particularly the concept of social justice that has evolved since independence makes the adoption and implementation of many reforms very difficult. It also contends that it is extremely unlikely that India will be able to undertake innovative measures to manage the increasing integration of the world commodity and financial markets and, at the same time, maintain its economic sovereignty.

The necessity of such reforms became clearly apparent when India suffered a severe balance of payments (BOP) crisis in March 1991. The purpose of this chapter is to discuss what followed: the steps taken by the successor government to tackle the crisis, the theoretical underpinnings and the implications of these policies, their immediate impact and their long-term effects. The paper also discusses the extent to which India's policy-making has been affected by the ASEAN experience of rapid economic growth, as well as the 1997 East Asian economic crisis.

The chapter is organized as follows: The first section describes India's economic performance in the period before the 1991 BOP crisis. This is followed by a discussion in section two on the reforms introduced, the initial successes, the re-emergence of negative trends, and the difficulties in building a consensus regarding the need for further reforms. Section three looks at the nature of further reforms (especially in the realm of infrastructure), the possibility of financial innovations, public finances and financial markets, and the rise and fall of Indian capital. The fourth section analyses the implications of capital account convertibility, its potential benefits and liabilities. The fifth section deals with crisis management under capital account convertibility and the lessons should be learnt from the East Asian crisis; this section also introduces the concept of Strategic Central Banking and discusses the rise of a new player the Voluntary Lender of Last Resort. The paper concludes with a discussion of the economy under a regime of completely liberalized capital markets.

I. PRELUDE TO REFORMS

THE GENESIS OF INDIA'S ECONOMIC REFORMS

Because India has always been a reluctant reformer, economic reforms in India have always been crisis-driven. The crisis that finally ushered in the reforms that buried the Nehruvian economic regime started shortly after the fall of Rajiv Gandhi's Congress government in 1989. The National Front government, led by Mr. V.P. Singh[3] was blamed for the severe BOP crisis in India in March 1991 which also coincided with the end of the cold war that eliminated India's ability to manipulate superpower rivalry and coming out with the best deal to extricate herself from her present predicament without undertaking painful measures to reform the economy. Mr. Singh was blamed for following policies that created a climate of political instability[4] and were fiscally imprudent.[5] However, more knowledgeable observers realize that such a view was extremely simplistic, if not unfair. The central government had managed its finances very imprudently throughout the 1980s; they ran continuous revenue deficits while previous governments had generally managed to generate a surplus on the revenue account.[6] In effect, the government was borrowing to meet even its consumption requirements, and instead of soft loans from multilateral and bilateral sources, it was increasingly relying on short-term loans from commercial banks and Non-Resident Indian (NRI) deposits at substantially higher rates of interest.

In 1990, following Iraq's attack on Kuwait, India's import bill rose steeply because the price of crude oil skyrocketed and simultaneously remittances dropped from the troubled region. The unstable minority government had neither the power nor the inclination to undertake harsh and unpopular adjustments. Commercial banks refused to extend short-term credit to the government and the NRIs also started to withdraw their deposits from the Indian banking system. India's foreign exchange reserves plummeted until by March 1991 they were just sufficient to finance three weeks of imports. India started to adjust only in July 1991 when a newly elected government took office.

This crisis was not as sudden as may have appear on the surface. India's economic growth accelerated in the 1980s, averaging about 5.5 per cent a year and reached 6 per cent at the end of the decade. This rate of growth was much higher than the rates achieved earlier (see Table 1). However it was accompanied by worsening fiscal and BOP deficits.[7]

Because of higher fiscal deficits, increased borrowings resulted in interest payments rising to over 20 per cent of government expenditure. The BOP deficit (at about 2.5 per cent of GDP), though low by international standards, was high when compared to the slow growth of India's exports and resulted in the debt/GDP ratio rising from under 10 per cent at the beginning of the decade to over 20 per cent by the end.

The reforms after the 1991 crisis were prompted by the conditionality attached to the IMF loan that India had received earlier, and were also needed to meet the dire situation at hand. But the crisis also provided an opportunity to those who believed that it was within India's power to excel economically and that it was India's policy framework that held back its progress. It is unclear to what extent policy makers desired the achievement of a higher rate of growth in order to raise the people's standard of living, and to what extent they wished to reverse the decline in India's international

TABLE 1: ECONOMIC PERFORMANCE 1969- 95
(FIGURES EXPRESSED IN PER CENT)[8]

	4th Plan 1969-73	*5th Plan 1974-8*	*6th Plan 1980-4*	*7th Plan 1985-9*	*Rao 1991-5*	*NF Govt 1996-8*
Real GDP Growth	3.4	5.0	5.5	5.6	5.1	6.1
Inflation, CPI	6.5	6.9	10.5	7.7	9.6	9.7
Budget Deficit/GDP	5.6	6.4	9.7	11.7	6.3	5.8
CAB/GDP	-0.7	0.5	-2.5	-2.5	-1.22	-1.3
Exports/GDP	3.7	5.4	4.9	5.0	9.5	10.7
Imports/GDP	4.1	6.4	8.1	7.3	11.4	13.9
Personal Consumption	71.9	69.8	71.7	69.5	67.7	70.7[9]
Government Consumption	8.8	8.6	9.8	11.3	10.9	12.5[9]
Fixed Investment	15.1	17.4	19.8	21.9	22.6	22.9

prestige as seen by the frequent unfavorable comparisons with the East Asian economies. The isolation which India had experienced during the Uruguay Round may have made policy makers feel more vulnerable after the collapse of the Soviet Union.

The reformers believed that the growth of the 1980s, which had occurred during a period of liberalization, vindicated their belief in the wastefulness and inefficiency of the licensing system. But earlier reforms had left the regime of the licence raj itself intact. Now the time was ripe to eliminate the heavy hand of government regulation and intervention in all aspects of the country's economy. It was also a time when politicians and bureaucrats, who had long used the rhetoric of self-sufficiency and socialism, suddenly made globalization a mantra for progress.

II. THE REFORMS

The reforms that got underway from mid-1991 were designed to bring about a dramatic change in the Indian economy. The government started to dismantle substantially the regulatory regime that had evolved since the beginning of the second Five-Year Plan, i.e. 1957. Private capital, including foreign private capital was allowed to enter almost all the industries that until then had been exclusively reserved for the public sector. The government eliminated the plethora of licenses and controls that regulated private investment and allocated imports. Henceforth, the forces of demand and supply would be relied upon to allocate investment and imports. Licensing and quantitative restrictions only remained on the import of consumer goods.

In the same vein, the exchange rate of the rupee was gradually allowed to be determined by market forces and the rupee was made totally convertible on the trade account. This marked the transition from a foreign trade managed by licenses to one managed by the exchange rate. Similarly, the state set out to reform the capital markets as well as the financial sector. The intention was to reduce state interference and increase the role of the market in borrowing and lending decisions. (We will discuss capital market reforms later.)

Except for the year 1991-2, when a stabilization policy to counter the BOP problem was undertaken and the GDP fell by 0.9 per cent, the economy performed quite well. It boomed in the years 1993-4 to 1995-6, growing even more rapidly than it had in the late 1980s. However this boom was different: export earnings in dollar terms, which had grown by only 2.6 per cent per annum in the first half of the 1980s and by 7.7 per cent during the second half, now accelerated to 22 per cent growth in 1993-4 and 15 per cent in 1994-5 and India's share of world trade almost doubled. Despite the introduction of import liberalization, the current account balance (CAB) deficit declined to 1 per cent of GDP and actually reached a low of 0.3 per cent in 1993-4. Furthermore, the liberalization of foreign capital inflows resulted in the increase of both portfolio and direct investment, so not only was the current account deficit financed but also India's foreign exchange reserves were built up and swelled to over 20 billion dollars, a far cry from the situation in 1991.

However, the reforms did not live up to expectations. In the medium term, many of the favourable trends have been reversed and the negative trends have been accentuated. The reduction in the public sector deficit was not maintained, and this could severely affect future economic performance. Initial deficit reductions were limited to the central government, and there has been some reversal in even that trend. Furthermore, the adjustment was not through the curtailment of government consumption, which was 11.2 per cent of GDP in 1995-6 and rising to 12.5 per cent in 1996-8, but through cutbacks in investment in infrastructure and social sector spending.

There have also been other setbacks. From 1996 onwards the growth rate of GDP has shrunk to 5-5.5 per cent a year mainly because of a sharp fall in the growth of manufacturing output. The level of investment by the organized sector is stuttering because of the difficulties in devising an appropriate strategy to meet the challenge of foreign competition in the form of imports or multinational production on domestic soil. The ability of firms to modernize their production facilities is at present limited by a feeble capital market, which has not fully realized its potential to draw on personal savings. This market was greatly damaged when India's government liberalized it without instituting adequate supervisory and regulatory mechanisms. The small size of the market and the stagnation of the economy limit the inflow of foreign portfolio capital.

Policies regarding foreign direct investment (FDI) have also been inadequate. The government would like such investment to be channelled to the infrastructure-building sectors, but major institutional hurdles remain before such investment can take place. Foreign investment has largely flowed to the consumer goods sector since quantitative restrictions (QRs) and tariffs continue to provide high returns for the government. The rationale for maintaining these barriers and enabling transnational corporations (TNC) to earn large returns is not clear—it does not seem justifiable on economic grounds. However, the poor performance of foreign companies in India should raise the morale of their Indian competitors. Their pricing and marketing strategies have not been successful and many of them are experiencing losses. As the growth of exports has declined, the trade and current account deficits were expected to have increased to above 2 per cent of GDP, towards the levels that prevailed in the pre-crisis period, had it not been for the slow down in the economy, which depressed imports. Here also the signals emanating from the government have been confusing.

Tariffs on imports were raised in the 1998 budget by about 10 per cent, and the exchange rate has been managed to limit devaluation, either to influence market sentiments or to curb its impact on inflation. The exchange rate policy, together with the slow down in world trade have resulted in the slowing down of export growth. Actually there was a substantial increase in the volume of exports, but since it was achieved at the cost of a sharp drop in export prices, the increase in the value of exports has not been significant.

The question that policy makers must answer is whether the economy's slow down is due to the international economic environment, or domestic political uncertainty, or lack of further reform.[10] If further reforms are the answer to India's economic woes, then the government must face a difficult challenge—how to make them acceptable to the people. Although there was very little opposition to the 1991 reforms, the issue of additional reforms is very controversial. In particular there is concern about the adverse effect of reforms of public sector enterprises (PSEs) and the ability to maintain adequate investment in the national infrastructure. Additionally, there are questions about the future of the mostly government-owned banking system, and about the roles of foreign capital and capital account convertibility. The government has not made a significant effort to build a consensus on a future policy framework. As the crisis has receded, many would like the status quo to be maintained.

It is difficult to build a consensus for future reforms in India because of its prevailing notion of social justice and equity. One can distinguish between procedural justice and justice based on actual outcomes, and in India the prevalent majority seems to support the concept of justice based on actual outcomes, that is, most Indians appear to believe that a policy is just only if its outcome is equally beneficial to all groups in the society. It is our belief that various groups should get a fair share in the outcome, but the question whether or not all groups wanting a fair share are disadvantaged is open to debate. It is important to note however, that the debate is conducted in terms of having equal outcomes. This belief is in direct conflict with the prevailing view in advanced capitalist economies, which rationalizes a reliance on market forces. According to this view, the reliance on the market mechanism is justified by its beneficial effect on economic performance, while questions about distribution are often dealt with on the basis of procedural justice, not on the basis of the equity of the outcome.[11] It is not easy to foresee how the political forces in India will reconcile the different notions of justice. But they must successfully resolve this issue if India is to reap the benefits of productivity and efficiency gains that the market is expected to bring about.[12] It is perhaps ironic that the reliance on the market mechanism is justified by its beneficial effect on economic performance but questions about distribution are often dealt with on the basis of procedural justice and the notion of judging on the basis of results is rejected.

We now discuss the nature of these reforms and the reasons why they are regarded as controversial.

III. THE DIFFICULT STEPS AHEAD OR THE ROAD NOT TAKEN

INFRASTRUCTURE AND THE POWER SECTOR

India's energy sector illustrates the typical problems faced by its public sector, particularly the infrastructure sector. One major challenge is how to finance the large investments required to increase power supply to meet the demands of industry. Since independence this sector has been the preserve of the state governments, except for a few privately owned power plants in some states. Power distribution remains firmly in the hands of the state governments, since private plants sell their power to the state electricity boards (SEBs) in the various states, which then sell it to the final consumer. The tariffs charged by the SEBs provided subsidies to important constituencies of the various political parties. For example, as is well known, agriculturists have often been exempted from paying for electricity.[13] Cross-subsidization by other consumers is never enough, so most SEBs are in debt and they have little or no funds to maintain the existing power plants, let alone money to finance new investments. Most states are experiencing power deficits because of poor maintenance of power plants and inadequately installed capacity. Decision makers in these states seem to prefer to provide inadequate power very cheaply rather than to make sufficient power available at prices that truly cover the costs of production and distribution.

The power shortage has been a major bottleneck to rapid economic growth. The Congress government, unable or unwilling to reform the SEBs, invited foreign companies to generate power to sell to the SEBs, and guaranteed the rate of return in order to circumvent the problem of the inability of the SEBs to pay for the power. That this was indeed a step to postpone a pressing problem was proved when the Dabhol Power Corporation, set up by the Enron Corporation, issued notices declaring their intention to terminate their agreement with the Maharashtra government. Ironically, this development took place when the same political formation which had invited Enron to invest in the energy sector in Maharashtra was in power. Irony is compounded by the fact that foreign investors are needed because Indian players lack money for such investments, but are chary of coming in unless there are reforms, i.e. unless the SEBs price and distribute power without political interference, so that they earn a reasonable return on their capital. But should these reforms be carried out, the SEBs would themselves be in a position to finance much of the additional generating capacity that is required. Indeed, an improved financial position would lead to an increased supply of power since existing equipment would be better maintained.

In fact, Rakshit[14] advances a good case for deficit finance for investment in the power sector. Rakshit holds that since most of the plants/factories involved in the manufacture of power plants are state owned (e.g. Bharat Heavy Electrical Corporation (BHEL), the public sector steel plants etc.), it would not be inflationary to create money to pay these factories for power generating equipment. This is because the funds given to them can be divided into three exhaustive parts: profits, wages paid to the workers, and payment for raw materials. Profits would come back to the state, wages are paid anyway, and payments for raw materials go mainly to other public sector firms whose profits also come back to the state, and whose workers would have to be paid anyway, etc. The inflationary effect will be limited to the demands on the non-public sector of the economy. Taxes need to be raised only for this component of the cost. Thus, Rakshit makes a case for a careful and judicious mix of deficit finance and commercial borrowings, and/or taxes. Heretical as such a scheme may sound, it is an innovation geared to do away with an infrastructure bottleneck and pave the way for faster rates of growth.

However, this does not mean that foreign investment in the energy sector is to be discouraged. Indeed, if our policy makers wish to ensure that the power shortage does not continue to constrain the Indian economy under its desired 5-6 per cent rate of growth, then they must recognize that BHEL/ other PSEs cannot produce the massive scale of investment required in this sector. Rakshit's proposal should be seen as a supplementary device rather than as an alternative to foreign investment. However, it is a supplementary device with great potential to generate national savings and investment by putting idle resources/capacity to work. We will examine in a later section whether this proposal is compatible with the policy of financial liberalization.

In any case, foreign investment in the power sector has not exactly poured in.[15] This is not surprising given that the tariffs/returns offered to foreign investors by the SEBs are not perceived to be enough or sustainable since the basic pricing problems of this sector still remain. Until the SEBs are allowed to charge appropriate prices they cannot offer power suppliers realistic tariff rates for power generated, nor can they set up their own power plants.

Successful implementation of power sector reforms would mitigate a serious infrastructure bottleneck and investments in this sector could jump-start the entire economy.[16] Large volumes of investment in the power sector would greatly boost the engineering and construction industries.

Reform of Government Finances

Conventional wisdom holds that the financial crisis of 1991 had its roots in the 1980s, when the government borrowed to meet even its consumption requirements. Prior to that, all was well, as the government ran a surplus on the revenue account,[17] even though there was an overall fiscal deficit. However, merely observing the presence or absence of a surplus on the revenue account is an arbitrary way of measuring the sustainability of a deficit, since a revenue surplus does not indicate if and how the accumulation of public debt and interest payments on such debt will be paid off. Anand and Wijnbergen provide a simple criterion for classifying sustainable/unsustainable budget deficits. They believe that a budget deficit is sustainable when the non-interest deficit of a budget, plus the interest payments and foreign debt, do not exceed what can be financed through debt issue at target-output ratios, plus the revenue from steady state seigniorage, and an inflation tax at the target inflation rate.[18]

Agarwal[19] (1997) has shown that even under the assumption of a 5 per cent growth rate of GDP and an 8 per cent inflation rate, India has rarely been able to meet this criterion of sustainability (see Table 2). Between 1969 and 1994, there were only two years in which the criterion was met, in 1972-3 and 1973-4.

Thus, when considered together, the budget deficits of the 1970s were unsustainable, notwithstanding the surpluses generated on the revenue

TABLE 2: FINANCING OF INDIA'S FISCAL DEFICITS

Year	*Actual Deficit*	*Sustainable Deficit*	*Seigniorage*	*Inflation Tax*
Average 1969-74	0.030	0.022	0.006	0.006
Average 1975-8	0.063	0.030	0.007	0.016
Average 1979-84	0.097	0.038	0.007	0.020
Average 1985-9	0.117	0.047	0.008	0.026
Average 1990-4	0.113	0.049	0.008	0.027

account. When we say that those deficits were unsustainable, we mean that the government investments funded in the 1970s did not sufficiently increase productivity in the economy to compensate for the costs of such investments by way of increased taxes due to rising incomes. Of course, it is true that the gap between the actual deficit and the sustainable deficit widened over the 1980s.

FINANCIAL SECTOR REFORM

The major questions being considered in the reform discussion have been: to what extent should the *financial sector* be deregulated and especially whether the *capital account* should be made *convertible*.

The attainment of a liberalized financial sector or a convertible capital account are obviously not ends in themselves, but are means to an end. The liberalized financial sector is the logical conclusion of a movement towards market allocation of investment funds. Additionally, extra resources, which hitherto had remained untapped, could now be exploited via the capital market. Capital account convertibility, on the other hand, is aimed mainly at increasing/supplementing the resources available for investment.[20] The growing movement towards capital account convertibility was stemmed by events in East Asia. We examine below the state of the Indian capital market and the potential effects of adopting capital account convertibility.

THE INDIAN CAPITAL MARKET

The Indian capital market, though over a century old, has played only a marginal role in financing industrial growth in the country. Long-term investments were financed mainly by special public sector financial institutions.

The situation changed in the 1980s when the middle class increased their demand for stock and other capital instruments. Their appetite had been whetted by the substantial capital gains they experienced on the shares floated by the TNCs to meet the requirement that they reduce their share of their hitherto wholly owned companies to 40 per cent or below. Additionally, the increase in the prices of gold and land meant that small savings could not be used to buy these traditional assets; it was easier to use such savings to purchase shares. Furthermore, the rate of inflation had increased and the middle class wanted instruments that would provide positive returns in an inflationary environment, and this was no longer true of fixed deposits at banks, the earlier preferred destination for financial savings.

Many companies wished to raise public capital in order to free themselves from the constraints imposed by the reliance on financial institutions. The government was also keen that large companies reduce their dependence on financial institutions and rely more on the capital market, since it was no longer able to fund these financial institutions through budgetary transfers.

As a consequence of the above developments there was a rapid growth of the capital market. By the early 1990s, 20 per cent of the financial savings by households was being channelled through stock markets. The middle class was well compensated for its shift to the capital market. The rate of appreciation averaged 17 per cent for the period 1980-90. This figure underestimates the capital appreciation in some of the more popular scrips.

An important change in the operation of the capital market was introduced after the 1991 crisis. The role of the Controller of Capital Issues (CCI) in vetting issues of new or existing companies and in fixing the price for issues of existing companies was eliminated[21] and companies were free to set their own issue price. Investors were in no position to evaluate the price. The price of the stock in the period before the issue was not a reliable guide since companies inflated this price through various practices in order to mislead investors. The financial press provided no analysis and their reports read like publicity handouts by the companies.

A consequence of this inadequate information and regulatory system was that several fraudulent schemes hit the stock markets. Small investors experienced huge losses when many companies that had floated shares simply disappeared. In the ensuing panic the stock prices of most other companies plummeted to levels below the issue price. The government's laxity in holding accountable the people involved in the scams, and the explicit statement that high-level officials needed to be protected (ostensibly to maintain the credibility of the system) shook the confidence of the small investor. The continued lack of any regulatory and supervisory mechanism has prevented a recovery of the capital market. It has been almost moribund and indeed in 1999 there were no IPOs and the share of household financial savings channelled through the stock market was almost nil.

The foreign financial institutions (FFIs) allowed in after the reforms have brought some capital into the country. These amounts, though small relative to the CAB deficit or the requirements of the economy, are large compared to the amounts normally transacted on the stock market, and so have contributed to increased volatility in the market. Additionally, most mutual funds floated by the FFIs are selling at a substantial discount, raising serious doubts about their capabilities. The small size of the market and the lack of new issues limit the investments of the FFIs in the Indian stock market.

Moves towards creating an information and regulatory framework appropriate to the reformed system have been tentative so far; it is very difficult to create such a framework without a clear vision of the financial system being aimed for. Financial systems fall into two general types: One is the Anglo-American system based on 'arms-length transactions'; the other is the corporatist model where there is an ongoing relationship between the suppliers of capital (i.e. banks) and the consumers of capital (i.e. the companies).

It is difficult to assess the advantages and drawbacks of the two systems, but one thing is very clear: the 'arms-length' system will not work without a panoply of institutions that perform specialized functions.[22] Such institutions have evolved only gradually in the USA. Until the 1960s, the financial system there was very akin to that of Japan and Germany. It is unrealistic to expect such an infrastructure to spring up instantaneously in India, and without it reforms based on market institutions are a recipe for disaster, as the Indian experience has shown.

The potential of the Indian capital market as a source of funds was severely damaged by the lack of an adequate regulatory framework necessary for any capital market to function properly. Moreover, the reluctance of the state to penalize even those who are caught under these lax rules signals that the influential will not be held accountable for fraud. It is therefore no surprise that the capital market has not lived up to the promise it showed in the 1980s. Without significant reforms the capital market is not likely to attract domestic savings or foreign financial capital, and it is likely to generate considerable instability. These reforms are necessary whether or not the capital account is made convertible. In the following section we discuss the question of capital account convertibility.

IV. POLICY MAKING IN A REGIME WITH CAPITAL ACCOUNT CONVERTIBILITY

Over the years, capital flows to developing countries have taken many forms, changing from mainly bond finance in the ninetheenth century and the first half of the twentieth century, to mainly loans and grants from bilateral and multilateral agencies after the Second World War, to loans from commercial banks after the oil price increase of 1973-4, and finally to portfolio and FDI in the 1980s.

Financial crises[23] have occurred in the developing countries during most of these periods, irrespective of the form of capital inflow. Crises were minimal in the 1950s and 1960s, and were usually met by the rescheduling of official loans. Other financial/debt crises have also ultimately been resolved through debt restructuring, though the process has taken much longer.[24] (For instance some of the debt negotiations started during the Great Depression of the 1930s were not concluded until 20 years later.)

The Mexican and East Asian experiences clearly show that credit transactions between private agents can be as misguided as loans to governments, and can also lead to crises.[25] Therefore, Indian policy makers must decide what can be done to maximize the benefits from access to a large pool of international savings while minimizing the costs associated with the possible breakdown of such flows.

In India there is not much dispute or controversy about the desirability of FDI, especially in sectors such as power or infrastructure where the gestation periods are typically long.[26] However, FDI does not necessarily require capital account convertibility. Why is capital account convertibility then still held desirable by a section of economists and policy makers?

The argument in favour of capital account convertibility in the Indian context has never been explicitly stated, but the gist of it seems to be as follows. Given that India is a capital scarce country with high rates of interest, capital account convertibility would enable the business community to tap cheaper sources of capital. If the government follows prudent fiscal and monetary policies that are credible to investors, they will expect growth and will invest. The very fact that they invest will boost growth, thus fulfilling their previously held expectations. This virtuous cycle of self-fulfilling beliefs will ensure that capital inflows, although nominally short-term in nature, will be continually rolled over, since no rational investor would withdraw money from a booming economy. Thus, the distinction between long term capital and short-term capital flows would become irrelevant.

Technically, capital account convertibility is not expected to greatly change the usual patterns of macroeconomic management in India, except in one respect.[27] The large differential that exists between Indian and international interest rates, as well as between the deposit and lending rates of banks, will survive with a floating exchange rate system under free capital mobility only if the rupee is expected to depreciate. A depreciation could be forced. If there is no expectation of devaluation, then capital inflow will lead to an increase in money supply, which might raise inflation and lead to an increasingly overvalued exchange rate. The overvaluation might only be corrected by a devaluation in a crisis situation. Until then, an increasing trade deficit resulting from the overvaluation might be comfortably financed by the capital inflows.[28]

Thus, it might be impossible to maintain such a large interest differential. However, policy makers are hesitant to abandon it since lower differentials would require that they rectify the large non-performing assets in the financial system and reduce the large public finance deficit.[29]

One concern about short-term portfolio capital is that it cannot be safely relied upon as an important source of investment. The share market usually plays a relatively minor role in financing industrial investment.[30] But some argue that if the capital account were made convertible, Indian businessmen would be able to borrow the cheap short-term capital that comes in the form of short-term flows.

Consider a hypothetical case in which Indian businessmen borrow cheap short-term capital denominated in dollars from abroad, to finance productive investments. Since investment is generally long term, it can lock capital into a venture. If such investments are to be of any consequence, they will, more often than not, be financed by mostly short-term loans, since these constitute the bulk of capital inflows.

Financing long-term schemes with short-term funds requires the rollover of short-term debt whenever it matures. As long as the going is good, i.e. as long as the economy grows and lenders across the globe expect it to grow, investors who have taken short-term loans from global capital markets are able to roll over their debt.

A problem would arise only if the performance of the economy falters or is expected to falter. Mere cyclical downturns, which do not represent any fundamental problem with the economy, could nevertheless stir up expectations of doom among investors. Such expectations may turn out to be self-fulfilling and a financial and currency crisis would occur.[31] The crisis would commence with lenders calling in their loans when they mature. Those loans denominated in dollars have to be repaid in the same currency.

As borrowers buy dollars to pay off their loans, the exchange rate of the rupee would fall, causing other lenders of dollar loans to call in their loans on maturity. This would set off a run on the rupee, and all those who had taken short-term loans denominated in dollars would necessarily have to buy dollars to pay off their creditors. This would lead to increased borrowing domestically in order to buy dollars. The subsequent increase in the rate of interest would squeeze domestic demand, reduce the profitability of domestic companies, depress stock markets, and encourage a further run on the currency. Thus, the vicious cycle of self-fulfilling beliefs is complete. Even a hike in interest rates, which *ceteris paribus* increases the attractiveness of holding rupees, may be ineffective in stemming the devaluation.

Indeed, rising interest rates may themselves signal that the economy is in deep trouble and thus may cause investors to flee.[32] One may ask, with some justification, whether seasoned international investors would really be unable to distinguish a cyclical downturn from a downturn arising out of unsound fundamentals. However, as Keynes[33] pointed out over six decades ago, an individual investor's belief about what others (that is the rest of the market) think may be more important than his own belief about the economic situation. Indeed, the former assumes greater importance because the 'others' are obviously much more numerous, and hence much more significant, than the individual investor.[34] In a climate of uncertainty, it is quite possible for investors who know that the economy is sound, to withdraw money because they fear that their knowledge and sentiments are not shared by others.

The dire consequences of such self-fulfilling investor panic suggest that it might be possible to assert that some kinds of capital flows are more desirable than others. While there is no unanimity of views, a considerable body of literature exists which implies that portfolio investment does not complement a nation's pool of investible resources, and tends to reduce savings. On the other hand, FDI leads to increased domestic savings and has a crowding-in effect (that is, it leads to more domestic investment). Also, while FDI flows may also be volatile, they rarely, if ever, become negative, whereas portfolio investment flows can and do become negative, creating problems for macro management.

V. CAPITAL ACCOUNT CONVERTIBILITY AND THE EAST ASIAN CRISIS

While the East Asian experience with export-led growth and foreign direct investment has been very good and is worthy of emulation, the same cannot be said of its experience with capital account convertibility. Indeed, we argue here that an export-led growth strategy combined with capital account convertibility increases the chances of a currency crisis.

With hindsight and a better knowledge of the sequence of events, a model of a crisis may even be constructed.[35] As an export-led economy with capital account convertibility (for example, Thailand) grows rapidly, its demand for investment rises. The short-term foreign capital which flows in is absorbed by the domestic capital market which uses it to finance long-term investments. As long as the economy grows this process repeats itself over and over again. However, if the demand for exports slackens due to recession in the major trading partners, fresh equity is not issued while short-term capital keeps on flowing in. This capital is then invested in the secondary market and the real estate leading to an artificial financial boom at a time when GDP growth is tapering off. This would attract even more international investors before the realization about the true nature of the boom dawns. When this bubble bursts, as it must at some time, international investors will try to liquidate their positions in this particular market and repatriate their investments. This puts the currency under pressure and if the magnitude of the outflow is large enough leading to fears of a large depreciation, others may join in, resulting in the fulfilment of these fears. The situation becomes worse if domestic banks have been supplementing their reserves through short-term borrowings from foreign investors. If these borrowings are recalled, the bank may be forced to liquidate at a heavy discount perfectly sound projects to meet the demand of wary investors. Second, if some of these borrowings are denominated in dollars, then a crashing currency would mean that the bank would need to raise far more money in terms of domestic currency to pay its international creditors than it received from them when it invited the dollar-denominated loans. Indeed, if the bank has borrowed from these sources very heavily, there might be a run on the bank.

Indeed, this is roughly what happened with the Thai baht. The run on the baht triggered off runs on currencies across East Asia. Economic contagion[36] was not the initial trigger. It was merely the transmission mechanism through which it spread across East Asia. While the lack of arms-length business relations between banks and firms and the consequent moral hazard problems that this entailed may not have been the best form of business organization for the long-term growth of the economy, the explanation or responsibility of the crisis cannot be laid entirely at its door, especially given the speed at which the region recovered. We find it very difficult not to subscribe to the view that the 1997 East Asian crisis was the result of a self-fulfilling panic which penalized these economies far more than was called for by their structural shortcomings. A temporary slow down in exports (largely beyond the control of Thailand, the epicentre of the crisis) led to a secondary market bubble which burst leading to a run on the Thai baht. Contagion ensured that it spread across East Asia, disrupting economies across the region. The economy that suffered least was Malaysian economy which suspended convertibility. It follows that while India has much to learn from the experiences of these countries regarding export promotion and measures on attracting FDI, the same cannot be said about the policies of financial liberalization.

Crisis Management with Capital Account Convertibility

When an economy with capital account convertibility is hit by a currency crisis, the central banks, especially those of the developing countries, are reduced to being helpless observers. Indeed, any action they take usually compounds the problems rather than serving to restore confidence in their currencies.

If the government decides to let its currency find its 'own level', this level may be an intolerably low one which stokes inflation (by raising import prices) and drains public finances, as the costs (in domestic currency) of servicing foreign debt increase. If the central bank hikes interest rates to defend its currency, fresh investment may become unattractive. This leads to a recession and a depression in the domestic stock market and causes foreign investors (who are able to realize that the economy is in trouble) to flee rather than to stay.

If the central bank chooses to defend the currency by running down its foreign exchange reserves, it will in all probability lose its reserves without managing to prevent depreciation (as happened in South-East Asia).

There is a fundamental difference between a banking crisis brought about by a run on the domestic currency and a usual domestic banking run; in the latter case, the central bank has the ability to fulfil its duty as a 'lender of last resort'. In the case of a usual bank run, when there is no capital account convertibility, the central bank as a 'lender of last resort' can use its discretion to lend money (by merely issuing notes) to 'sound' banks, whose problems are mostly due to self-fulfilling predictions/ prophecies of panics. By preventing the collapse of the financial system, the central bank ensures that the flow of credit to business is not choked.[37] The impact on the exchange rate of the domestic currency is minimal.

However, in a banking collapse brought about by a run on the currency (as described above), the central bank cannot act as a lender of last resort because international investors have to be repaid in foreign currency. While the central bank has the right to issue domestic currency, it does not have the ability to print foreign currency. Therefore, when there is a run on domestic banks, since short-term lenders no longer roll over dollar-denominated debt, it is futile for the central bank to pump money into their cash reserves, as it does not increase the supply of dollars. Instead, as banks try to buy dollars with this fresh infusion of cash, the value of the domestic currency plunges, further shaking the confidence of international investors in the domestic currency. The soaring value of the dollar causes the price of imports to rise sharply and may even set off hyperinflation. Indeed, if the local population loses faith in the currency, a 'flight from cash' may be witnessed and the country may become a barter economy. This scenario might appear undesirable, but the alternative is perhaps worse. If the central bank chooses to do nothing, its banking system will collapse and a subsequent collapse of credit and investment will occur, which will lead to a severe contraction of GDP.

The problem of exchange rate management is further complicated when there are several objectives with various trade-offs. An example of this is provided by the behaviour of the Japanese yen in the 1980s, though the problems of the LDCs differ from those of certain developed countries.

The Strategic Central Banker[38]

The United States experienced huge and growing trade deficits vis-à-vis Japan and Germany from 1980 onwards. In accordance with economic theory the Deutsche Mark did rise in response to these deficits, but the yen did not appreciate as quickly as expected. Even when the yen rose against the dollar, Japanese exports to the United States continued to grow steadily, and the trade deficit with Japan unexpectedly did not fall.

The failure of the dollar to depreciate during the 1980s can only be partly explained by the Federal Reserve's tight monetary policy (to control domestic inflation) as higher interest rates attracted capital from the rest of the world to finance the huge trade deficits. However, the dollar refused to fall to a level compatible with the US trade deficit even after the US Federal Reserve relaxed its monetary policy. This was partly because the Bank of Japan (BOJ) shored up the value of the dollar. Even more dynamic was the role played by the USA when it decided to come to Mexico's rescue in 1994. Although the international institutions were also brought in to effect this rescue, there is little doubt that the US Fed itself could have undertaken the responsibility. The question is why did the BOJ and the US undertake measures for the benefit of another country?

One possible explanation of the BOJ's action is that it wished to protect the competitiveness of exports to the USA, and to prevent erosions in the value of Japanese investments in the United States, since it was feared that such erosions would create havoc in the financial markets in Japan. Thus, a goal other than macroeconomic stability was added to the objective function of the central bank. This additional goal was to encourage and protect the acquisition of overseas assets by domestic agents. Similarly, the US Fed defended the peso because American investors had a considerable stake in the Mexican economy. Additionally, after the signing of NAFTA, Mexico also became a large market for American goods. Hence, it was in US's interests that Mexico's peso stay afloat.

The multiple objectives pursued by the Japanese Central Bank as well as by the US Fed can be summarized by the term *Strategic Central Banking* (SCB). SCB not only encompasses the traditional duties/roles of a central bank to maintain macroeconomic price stability, but it also includes a dynamic method of exchange rate management to promote exports and the acquisition of overseas investments. In doing so these central banks may become voluntary lenders of last resort, bailing out currencies of certain panic-hit economies if their stakes in these economies are high enough.

It is clear that the attainment of the goals of the *Strategic Central Bankers* imply trade-offs. The central bank/state (given the Phillips' Curve) may have to choose between employment and inflation. By devaluing the currency, it chooses export growth over the acquisition of foreign assets, which will become more expensive. If the economy is fairly open, then devaluation also leads to inflation. The timing of policies is also very important. For example, devaluation may imply a trade-off between exports and the acquisition of foreign assets in the short term. If however the exporter has a monopoly in the export market, then devaluation is no longer useful to boost exports. Thus, by our definition, *Strategic Central Banking* can be practiced by only a few players in the international economy—those large economies whose currency is a de facto currency of the world, or those which have been running up large trade surpluses and which have the reserves to effectively control their exchange rates. Size alone will not suffice.

India is too small to be able to indulge in *Strategic Central Banking*. But the central bank already faces certain policy dilemmas. For example, there is the question of whether it should devalue the rupee to compete more effectively with the East Asian countries, or whether it should maintain the value of the rupee to retain investor confidence and control the domestic rate of inflation. For the moment the Reserve Bank of India (RBI) seems to have chosen the second option. Again, India's inability to indulge in SCB notwithstanding, it may have to take into account the strategic economic interests of others. Devaluing the currency at this stage may be considered injurious to the successful adjustment of the economies of the East Asian countries and may be frowned upon by important financial powers, such as the United States and Japan, especially if such powers have a substantial stake in the economic stability of these economies. For example, the Western financial press was very concerned that the Chinese Yuan might be devalued. One does not know whether any advice was given to the Chinese not to devalue.

Financial Markets and Stability: Capital Account Convertibility and Innovation

Economies with capital account convertibility always face the risk of capital flight, which, through its effects on the exchange rate also has an influence on inflation and the level of domestic economic activity. Facing the crisis requires the help of important economies that practice *Strategic Central Banking*. Whether such help would be forthcoming depends on the extent to which the interests of the SCBs are affected by the depreciation of the rupee.

Therefore, the question arises: does there exist a powerful economy whose SCB would intervene if India faced difficulties? This response depends on several factors:

(1) Whether India is a large export market for any SCB economy.
(2) Whether the exports of the SCB economy to India compete with Indian goods.
(3) Whether the SCB has investments in India, and the nature of these investments.
(4) Whether the business community in that country of the SCB wish to acquire assets in India in the future and the nature of these assets.
(5) The size of the market for rupees.

If India is a large market for the goods of a powerful economy, and if a rupee devaluation threatens this market, then that country's SCB may help to defend the rupee. On the other hand, if these exports do not compete with Indian goods, and the demand for them is price and income inelastic, then the devaluation will not greatly affect their competitiveness, and the SCB would be inclined to allow the rupee to devalue. If investments in India are in facilities for exports elsewhere, a depreciation may not call for the SCB's intervention. But profits in dollar terms, from investments for the domestic market, would be hit by a fall in the value of the rupee and the SCB may intervene. The SCB's future investment in the Indian economy would become cheaper after a fall in the value of the rupee and so if potential investments are larger than the existing investments, then the SCB may not intervene.

Lastly, the size of the market for rupees is also of fundamental importance. Even if there is good reason to intervene and defend the rupee, this may not be done if it would require a large amount of the SCB's foreign exchange reserves. This is likely to be the case if the market for the rupee is large. On the other hand, in a narrow market relatively small amounts can have appreciable effects in reining in adverse sentiments during a run on the currency. The market for the rupee (at least on the sellers' side) will be larger if India goes in for capital account convertibility.[39]

The analysis is necessarily somewhat rough since, unfortunately, it is difficult to judge whether or not, and to what extent, the above criteria for the five categories apply to any country. However, it is our conclusion that no SCB is likely to bail out India should a crisis strike. This is because there is no economy that has invested heavily enough in India to have a stake in the stability of the rupee. A fall in the value of the rupee, insofar as it makes potential acquisitions cheaper, is not wholly unwelcome. Second, India disagrees with the USA, the European Union and Japan on some very important political and economic issues, such as nuclear non-proliferation, trade, and environment-related issues. The question of extending assistance might be tied to resolution of these issues. Suitable actions on such issues might be made preconditions for providing assistance. Alternatively important economic powers might conjecture that assistance should not be provided as an India, weakened economically after a currency crisis, might be more willing to make concessions. We believe that India might have to pay a high price that might be both economic and political for being rescued.[40]

Financial Liberalization and the Poor: An Asymmetry of Costs and Benefits

How are the poor, most of whom live in the rural areas, affected by financial liberalization?

We have indicated that there are two components to financial liberalization. One is the reform of the domestic capital markets, and the other is the introduction of capital account convertibility. It is our view that capital market reform, coupled with the introduction of new credit institutions such as the Grameen Bank (in Bangladesh), promises to greatly benefit rural India.

For years vast sections of the rural poor have been deprived of credit because of their inability to provide the collateral required by existing institutions, because of bureaucratic red tape, and because of the monopolization of existing credit by richer farmers who often defaulted on their loans. A capital market in which institutions that specialize in micro-credit can borrow and lend to the rural sector has the potential to emerge as a great emancipatory force for poor farmers. Not only will it increase output, but it will also free the small borrowers from the clutches of the indigenous moneylenders who generally charge usurious rates of interests.

It should be borne in mind that although these micro-credit institutions are profit-driven institutions (not charitable ones) that charge appropriate rates of interests, their existence enlarges the pool of potential lenders and increases the probability of profitable borrowing. General capital market reforms that make the raising of funds for investment easier only benefit them indirectly. Crises in the domestic financial markets such as a run on domestic banks can be tackled by loosening the money supply, a step which does not really harm the poor.

Capital account convertibility does not promise to be as universally beneficial as capital market reform. There is, however, an asymmetry between the benefits and the costs of capital account convertibility where the poor are concerned. Simply put, while the poor would not gain much from this measure, the steps taken in the aftermath of any resulting crisis would have a disastrous effect on them. Capital account convertibility would not greatly benefit the rural poor because short-term capital, by its very nature, would not go to small holders in agriculture or small-scale companies. Given the seasonality of agriculture and its dependence on unpredictable weather conditions, it is of the utmost importance that lenders should be willing to wait out temporarily adverse conditions. Foreign short-term capital is notorious for its flightiness when faced with even temporary negative fluctuations.

Additionally, in the event of a financial crisis, the poor are severely affected in the aftermath. As in all such crises, incomes contract because of restrictive credit policies. Anti-inflation policies, designed to combat the inflation that invariably follows, call for the slashing of government expenditure, which usually implies a reduction in social sector expenditure and investment. The short-term and long-term effects of such a reduction are borne mainly by the poor. They thus are victims of a policy from which they do not benefit, but whose costs they are called upon to bear when it backfires.

It is true that there are some short-term investments/loans which may benefit the poor. Certainly, short-term debt may be used for loans to exporters, and this may raise the incomes of the poor by boosting labour-intensive exports. But it is doubtful that this contribution will be significant. The majority of the capital flows are in the real estate market, or the secondary market in the stock exchange, where they have extremely limited impact on the standard of living of the poor.

The Stability of the Rupee

How stable will the rupee be if it is made convertible on the capital account? Could the existence of capital account convertibility negatively affect economic policy making?

Let us first answer the second question. Financial markets do not accept any move away from orthodox/conservative policy prescriptions. For example, conservative economists are likely to call Rakshit's plan to use deficit finance to fund projects in the power sector 'voodoo economics', and they would probably accuse the government of pursuing irresponsible fiscal policies. Such a negative reaction could dent confidence in the rupee.[41] Because the TNCs which compete with domestic power suppliers for such projects,[42] also have subsidiaries that specialize in foreign exchange transactions, it is in their interest to join the naysayers. Even SCBs of countries which specialize in making power equipment now have an incentive to discourage financial innovations of this type by moulding market sentiment accordingly.[43]

Other government policies might invite similar disapproval. For example, to improve productivity in agriculture India may invest in labour-intensive mini-irrigation projects rather than in massive projects that call for the building of large dams. Although such a decision may be in total conformity with neoclassical economics, it may well be branded 'Maoist' and retrogressive by interests that lose out because of it. Thus a decision that is perfectly justifiable on economic grounds may be impossible to implement because of fears about the signals that it sends to the capital market.[44] Thus, paradoxically, the globalization of finance may prevent the transition economies from carrying out reforms that are necessary for them to take advantage of the globalization of trade and commerce. The need for conformity where financial markets are concerned does not always gel with the financial innovations peculiar to a particular economy.

Thus, capital account convertibility may inhibit public finance innovations not only because of vested interests operating in capital markets, but also because the fears about perfectly legitimate schemes/plans may turn out to be self-fulfilling.

Turning our attention now to the first question: what would happen to the stability of the rupee if public finance innovations were given up?

The outbreak of irrational panics aside, the health of the rupee depends equally upon the fundamentals of the economy, the state of the government finances, and the expectations of investors. If the public deficit is incompatible with the maintenance of a critical level of inflation, capital flight may be provoked. If interest rates are hiked, the self-fulfilling fears may none the less render such a policy ineffectual and toothless. Even if the increases did work in the short run, they would ultimately harm the economy, since higher interest rates reduce the levels of investment and increase the deficit by increasing interest payments and reducing revenue receipts. This scenario would be made even worse if it is perceived that the government lacks the political will necessary to put its finances right, even if just in the short term. The inadequacy of the rudimentary regulatory mechanism of the financial system would add to investor panic. All these factors would combine to provide the ultimate grounds for capital flight.

In a situation where there is no capital account convertibility, this extreme situation would not occur, since inflation forcibly extracts savings from the people and into the hands of the state.[45] Painful as this experience might be, it certainly appears to be more attractive than a prolonged capital flight.

However, it must be remembered that foreign financial investors and large Indian investors already enjoy capital account convertibility. Thus, the ingredients for a crisis exist. One has not yet occurred only because India's short-term liabilities are small compared to its reserves, making it likely that any speculative attack will be beaten back.

Given the fact that currency crises today demand far more by way of reserves to be stemmed and have to be tackled in far less time than before, it is not likely that the IMF, the institutional international lender of last resort, can do much. As seen in the East Asian crisis, its advances to the panic-hit countries were too little and came very late. This is not surprising given the rapid growth of financial transactions[46] thanks to the telecommunications revolution. The IMF does not have the resources to operate in such a climate and nor does it have the organizational structure to take decisions as quickly as desired.

It is our conclusion that in the current circumstances the costs of capital account convertibility for India may well exceed the likely benefits. This is because, with such a financial policy, there is a high likelihood of a crisis being generated, the *Strategic Central Bank* of no economic power would have an incentive to support the rupee during a run on the currency.[47] A SCB would have the incentive to do so only after having acquired considerable investments in India.

Quasi-convertibility

Over the last few years the Government of India has decided to relax some of the restrictive provisions that govern capital movements. For example, up to US $100 million is now automatically approved for overseas private direct investment by Indian corporations. This is a highly welcome step as this extends a degree of assistance to Indian corporations as they invest in companies abroad or establish subsidiaries in order to become global players and take advantage of global markets. The question is whether this particular step will be one of the first steps leading inevitably towards quasi-convertibility.

At the outset, we would like to point out that this step, although welcome, is also arbitrary. It is clear that different companies will need to act with different speeds and with differing magnitudes of capital requirements as they globalize. To set an arbitrary figure is not the best way to go about helping Indian corporations to do so. A more logical step would have been to make this figure a function of variables such as the applying company's nature of business, turnover, profit, net worth, etc. Thus, giants like Infosys or Wipro, whose capital requirements are higher and for whom the time available to complete deals is shorter than the requirements of a cotton textile mill, are not inhibited by the arbitrary figure of $100 million.

To return to the main question, that is whether this step constitutes a move towards quasi-convertibility, the answer in our opinion is: not necessarily. What is being proposed is not that foreign investors be allowed to bring in portfolio capital into the Indian capital market and withdraw it at will. Indeed, this step is not about economic agents in India being allowed to use cheap foreign capital. Instead, Indian companies are being given the freedom to invest abroad. Against the $100 million that they get from the

Reserve Bank, are their assets already in India as well as the acquisitions abroad whose value on grounds of synergy with the parent company may well be above the price paid for it. Furthermore, a rush of applications for $100 million loans just when a currency crisis strikes is likely to lead to a temporary withdrawal of this facility. Second, as a desperate measure during an emergency, the state may even ask companies that have already invested abroad to liquidate their holdings and repatriate the proceeds. It cannot do so when there is full capital account convertibility.

CONCLUSION

In the aftermath of the stabilization programme, the performance of the Indian economy improved. GDP and exports grew, and the fiscal deficit was reduced. Economic growth during the period 1995-2000 has been the same as it was in the five years before the crisis—a not too discreditable 5.5-6 per cent and has not generated as many macro-imbalances as before. But there has been something of a relapse in the same period.

There is a consensus on the *need* for further reforms, but no agreement on the *nature* of these reforms. Governments have failed to develop a consensus on future economic policy. In particular, it has been difficult to convince many of the need for market-oriented reforms since the Indian polity stresses an outcome of economic equity and social justice for different groups.

Governments have sought to circumvent the need for further reforms by raising the level of investment, and to achieve this they have invited both FDI as well as portfolio investment to provide the resources for the modernization of Indian industry and the development of the nation's infrastructure. But the lack of reforms in the infrastructure sector and the capital market are themselves inhibiting the inflow of capital.

We have argued in this chapter that the contribution of portfolio capital to industrial development is likely to be small, and the benefits are likely to be outweighed by the costs of any cessation in the flight of such capital. In particular, we see no incentive for any other country to act as a white knight should the Indian economy run into problems.

The lesson that India should draw from the ASEAN countries is how to remove barriers on production and investment and how to attract FDI. It should learn from these economies how important investment in infrastructure to attract investment and lay the foundations of an investor-friendly and efficient economy. However, when it comes to capital account convertibility, it is obvious that the lessons to be learnt from the East Asian crisis are different. The crisis has shown how even economies that are fundamentally sound can be driven into recession because of a panic. Here emulation on the part of India is certainly to be avoided.

In conclusion, we believe that it is necessary to accelerate the pace of reforms in India's infrastructure sector, public sector, and financial markets. These reforms have to be crafted to ensure that they do not aggravate the inequities in Indian society; in particular, the poor have to be protected from any adverse consequences of rampant globalization. Arguments about portfolio capital and capital account convertibility are not as important as this main issue.

NOTES

1. Others would argue that we were in bad shape precisely because of the planning process.
2. See B.L. Das, 'India's Trade Negotiations: Past Experiences and Future Challenges', *International Studies* 35 (4) (October-December 1998), pp. 397-408.
3. That India had still to find its moorings in the Post-USSR age was symbolized by P.V. Narasimha Rao's gaffe when he warned about the need to carry out reforms with utmost care, pointing out to the coup attempt against Gorbachev in May 1991. The coup failed hours later and it turned out, not surprisingly, that the successor regime headed by Boris Yeltsin had not taken kindly to Rao's statements.
4. He accepted the recommendation of the Mandal Commission, which called for the reservation of a per centage of government jobs for the Other Backward Classes.
5. His government's decision to write off loans to farmers was criticized as fiscally irresponsible and imprudent. Also, his speech upon taking office, saying that India's coffers were empty, did little to boost the confidence of overseas creditors in India's ability to repay its loans.
6. Indian budgets have two parts: the revenue account and the capital account. The revenue account deals with the consumption expenditure of the government, and on the receipts side it denotes the resources raised by way of taxes. The capital account deals with the investment/capital expenditures of the government, and on the receipts side it shows the resources raised by the government by way of loans, bonds and other forms of borrowings. Prior to the 1980s, the government borrowed only to finance capital formation, which enhances the productive capacity of the economy.
7. The government stemmed the adverse effects on exports and investment by raising government expenditure in a regime of fixed exchange rates and no capital account mobility through exchange rate depreciation and using other export incentives to encourage exports and loans at lower rates of interest from public sector financial institutions.
8. The figures shown here are taken from the various issues of *RBI Report on Currency and Finance* and may not be consistent with other figures issued by the various governments. This is because statistical discrepancies may be as high as 7 per cent of GDP.

9. Calculated from the International Financial Statistics Yearbook, 2000, IMF, Washington.
10. Some simulations suggest that, with the current policy framework, India is capable of maintaining the 5.5-6 per cent growth rate achieved in the 1980s. But more rapid growth will require policy changes.
11. This difference surfaces very often and very early in seminars when NGOs and economists are present. Whether a situation should be evaluated by its results is discussed extensively by Sen under the name of 'consequentalism'; see A.K. Sen, *On Ethics and Economics* (Oxford: Oxford University Press, 1987), pp. 75-8.
12. This difference in approach is discussed in S. Tendulkar, 'Foundational Propositions Underlying the Indian Economic Reforms', in *Indian Economy in Transition*, ed. Manmohan Agarwal, Alokesh Barua, Sandwip Kumar Das and Manoj Pant (New Delhi: Har-Anand 1998); see also M. Agarwal, 'Economic Reform, Acquisitive Instinct, and Individual Will', *International Studies* 55 (4) (1998), pp. 409-24.
13. The costs of such subsidies in 1998-9 are estimated at over Rs. 230 billion, whereas the total plan allocation for education was less than Rs. 50 billion.
14. Mihir Rakshit, 'Uses and Abuses of Instruments for Resource Mobilisation: The Indian Experience', in *The Indian Economy: Recent Development and Future Prospects*, ed. R.E.B Lucas and G. Papanek, New Delhi: Oxford University Press (1988), pp. 319-42.
15. Where MNCs have come in and actually started producing power, they have run into problems. Apart from Maharashtra, Orissa also has faced problems with its suppliers.
16. Simulations with a number of macroeconometric models suggests that public investment raises significantly the level of economic activity. But they also support the theoretical position that effects of such investments on the BOP may be negative and would need to be closely monitored.
17. The budget deficit, which averaged about 6 per cent until the 1980s, jumped to 10 per cent in the early 1980s and to over 12 per cent at the time of the crisis.
18. Ritu Anand and Sweder van Wijnbergen, 'Inflation and Financing of Government Expenditure: An introductory analysis with an application to Turkey', *World Bank Economic Review* 3 (1) (1987), pp. 17-38.
19. Manmohan Agarwal, 'India', in *Going Global: Transition from Plan to Market Economy in the World Economy*, ed. Padma Desai (Cambridge Massachusetts: MIT Press, 1997), pp. 473-96.
20. However, there are others who claim that capital account convertibility brings about better corporate monitoring.
21. The pricing formula used was very conservative and almost guaranteed a substantial capital gain.
22. For a discussion of these issues, see T. Hellman and K. Murdock, 'Financial Sector Development Policy: The Importance of Reputational Capital, and Governance', *Development Strategy and Management of the Market Economy*, ed. I.P. Szekely and R. Sabot (Oxford: Clarendon Press, 1997).
23. For a discussion of these crises and the manner of adjustment one may see among others, B. Eichengreen and P.H. Lindert, eds., *The International Debt Crisis in Historical Perspective* (Cambridge, Massachusets: MIT Press, 1989); H. Handelman and W. Baer, eds., *Paying the Costs of Austerity in Latin America* (Boulder, Colorado: Westview Press, 1989).
24. When investors invest in sovereign debt, they run the risk (as in any other financial loan) of the borrower defaulting. When a large number of projects in an economy fail,

the borrowing country may be forced to default. One of the problems in International Relations is to devise a mechanism, whereby genuine defaulters can be distinguished from strategic defaulters (defaults as cases of bad faith).

25. There is an extensive literature on capital flows and instability, see G. Calvo, *Varieties of Capital Market Crises*, Mimeo, IMF, Washington (1994). On the Mexican crisis, see J.A. Sachs, A. Tornell and A. Velasco, 'The Collapse of the Mexican Peso: What Have We Learnt?', National Bureau of Economic Research, Working Paper, no. 5742 (1995). On the East Asian crisis, see J. Sachs and S. Radelet, 'The East Asian Financial Crisis: Diagnosis, Remedies, Prospects', *Brookings Papers on Economic Activity*, no. 1 (1998); R. Wade, *Governing the Market: Economic Theory and the Role of Government in East Asian Industrialization* (Princeton, NJ: Princeton University Press (1990). Many of the issues about the currency crises are discussed in M. Agarwal, 'Capital Account Convertibility: Fact and Frenzy,' *Indian Economy in Transition* (1998). For a less formal but informative history of currency crises see C.P. Kindleberger and J.P. Laffargue, *Financial Crises: Theory, History and Policy* (Cambridge: Cambridge University, 1982).
26. Opposition to FDI generally comes from businessmen who have long enjoyed the fruits of protection, and are unable to compete in the new environment.
27. See Agarwal, *Economic Reform.*
28. There is a large body of literature that discusses situations like these; see P. Krugman, 'A Model of BOP crisis', *Journal of Money, Credit and Banking* 4 (August 1979), pp. 311-25; P.R. Agenor, J.S. Bhandari and R.P. Flood, 'Speculative Attacks and BOP Crises', *IMF Staff Papers* 39 (2) (1992), pp. 359-94; Calvo, *Varieties . . .*, Capital inflows encouraged by a pre-announced devaluation, which was less than the interest rate differential, fuelled inflation and resulted in increasing overvaluation; this is considered the cause of the Southern Cone crises of the late 1970s and early 1980s .
29. It has been recognized that large differentials between borrowing and lending rates is one way of recapitalizing banks faced with large non-performing assets; and this was done in the US, for instance, in the wake of bad loans to Latin America, real estate deals, etc.
30. New share issues account for less than 5 per cent of the external finance raised by US companies in the period 1970-85 (F.S. Mishkin and S.G. Eakin, *Financial Markets and Institutions*, New York: Harper Collins, 1995). Most of the borrowing is from banks because of the well-known problems of asymmetric information and principal-agent compatibility of interests.
31. See Sachs and Radelet, *East Asian . . .*, for an analysis of such situations.
32. That such fears are not idle is borne out by the large literature in currency crises e.g. Sachs and Radelet, *East Asian. . . .* It is also borne out by the South-East Asian currency crisis! After all, the large loans at high interest rates imply that the balance sheet of companies has deteriorated.
33. John Maynard Keynes, *The General Theory of Interest, Employment and Money* (London: Macmillan, 1936).
34. Unless it happens to be a *Strategic Central Banker*. See next section.
35. In this section we borrow heavily from Rajdeep Sengupta 'Capital Inflows and the Crisis in East Asia: A Macroeconomic Analysis', unpublished M.Phil thesis, Centre for Economic Studies and Planning, JNU, New Delhi (1999).
36. The term ***contagion*** despite its pejorative connotations refers to the phenomenon that certain markets in different countries may move in the same direction because of links between these different markets.

37. In the wake of the stock market collapse on October 1987, the US Federal Reserve assured important market players of almost unlimited credit to ensure that they intervened in the market and prevented further declines on subsequent days. This prevented a major stock market debacle, which could have caused a recession.
38. This player has been defined and discussed in detail in M. Agarwal, and Dipankar Sengupta, 'Tackling International Financial Crises: Voluntary Lenders of the Last Resort', *International Studies* 38, 2 (2001), pp. 97-112.
39. Actions of a *SCB*, a lender of last resort can lead to dramatically different results. In the case of the East Asian crisis, it was argued that there should be no interventions to salvage weak financial institutions and the law of the market should be allowed to prevail. Many financial institutions failed. The resulting financial stringency and financial pessimism more difficult. In the case of the LT hedge fund, the Fed stepped in immediately in the name of systemic risks and the problem was surmounted with hardly a blip in the financial markets.
40. In this connection it is important to remember that the 1991 programme with the Fund was supposed to be part of an extended programme that was to be negotiated later. But such a programme was not negotiated. One is left to wonder whether even the merely economic preconditions for a such a programme were unpalatable to the Indian government.
41. In January 1998, Indonesia proposed a budget, which was severely criticized by the IMF, and the US government as contravening earlier agreements. It was pointed out that the increase in expenditure was on account of the devaluation of the Indonesian rupiah and did not fully compensate for it. The IMF accepted this an even higher level of government expenditure, but by then the damage had been done in the currency market.
42. The importance of the psychological impact on foreign investors was used to explain the choice of the finance minister in the Vajpayee government in 1996.
43. It has been argued by some that the very cost-effective methods devised by C-DOT for rural telecommunications were stopped in part by pressure from foreign equipment suppliers.
44. Many observers have been struck by the overtly negative comments by the western press about the Korean chaebol. Yet no merger among western corporations elicits a similar negative reaction. Also one may note the many negative stories about China's economic performance after its criticisms of NATOs actions in Kosovo.
45. In situations of poor tax administration, an inflation tax may be the least inefficient way for the government to raise resources.
46. In 1947, the maximum speculation against the pound was $100 million which rose to a record flow of $1500 million in favour of the DM in May 1969. This was topped by $1000 million flowing into Germany in half an hour in May 1971; see C. Kindleberger, *Panics, Manias and Crashes* (Basingstoke, Macmillan 1978). By the late 1990s foreign exchange transactions were $1.5 trillion a day; see R. Gilpin, *The Challenge of Global Capitalism* (Princeton: Princeton University Press, 2000).
47. On the contrary, it may have the incentive to provoke such a flight, especially if there are serious differences on political issues.

Lessons for India from the Asian Crisis: A South-East Asian Perspective

Sakulrat Montreevat

Many economic troubles that the world has suffered are now the sort of thing we had learned to prevent. In 1997-8, the world experienced the effects of crises in Asia that started with the Thai baht and spread to a number of regional currencies. The Asian crises were the third region-wide currency crisis of the 1990s, following Europe in 1992-3 and Latin America in 1994-5. The Asian crises involved currencies, finance and economies.[1] Krugman describes the crises as:

> I hereby proposed another name: The Great Recession. I call it a recession rather than a depression because, catastrophic as the last two years have been for some countries, at a global level the damage has so far been well short of Depression levels (cross your fingers). But it deserves the honorific 'great', because for the afflicted countries it has indeed been the worst (economic) thing they have experienced in half a century. And the allusion to the Great Depression seems to me entirely appropriate: as Mark Twain might have said, recent events may not have repeated those of the 1930s, but they do rhyme.[2]

While policy makers have learned their lesson, the Asian crises have also challenged economists. Many economic studies, both descriptive and empirical, have debated causes, policy approaches, and prevention. This paper reviews the studies from economic points of view. Lessons from this study may benefit India.

This paper describes causes of the Asian crises, exploring empirical evidence from various studies. Crisis management is dealt with thereafter. Policy responses to the crises are reviewed. Recovery paths and legacies of the crises are then discussed. Lessons from the Asia crises are discussed and implications for India are derived.

THE CAUSES OF THE ASIAN CRISES

There have been many studies on the causes of the Asian crises. The conclusions drawn were various, based on different indicators and methodologies.

A recent study by K.S. Jomo presents the causes of the crises based on macroeconomic indicators in four most crisis-affected economies—Thailand, Indonesia, South Korea and Malaysia. Apparently, the savings and investment rates were high and rising in the three South-East Asian economies. Foreign savings supplemented high domestic savings in all four economies, especially in Thailand and Malaysia. Unemployment was low while fiscal balances generally remained positive before 1997-8. Also, the incremental capital output ratio (ICOR) rose in all the three South-East Asian economies during the 1990s before 1997, with the increase greatest in Thailand and least in Indonesia. The rising ICOR implies declining returns on new investments before the crisis. Export-led growth had been followed by a construction and property boom, fuelled by financial systems favouring such 'short-termist' investments—involving loans with collateral preferred by bankers—over more productive, but also seemingly more risky investments in manufacturing and agriculture. The exaggerated expansion of investment in such 'non-tradeables' exacerbated their current account deficits. In addition, after mid-1995, the South-East Asian currency pegs to the US dollar—which had enhanced the region's competitiveness as the dollar declined for a decade after the 1985 Plaza Accord—became a growing liability as the yen began to depreciate once again. The overvalued currencies became attractive targets for speculative attacks, resulting in futile but costly defences of the Thai baht and Malaysian ringgit and the rapid regional spread of panic aptly termed 'contagion'. The resulting precipitous asset price collapses—as the share and property market bubbles burst—undermined the East Asian four's heavily exposed banking systems, debilitating financial system liquidity and causing economic recession. Although widespread in East Asia, for various reasons, the property-finance nexus was particularly strong in Thailand, which made it all the more vulnerable to the inevitable bubble burst.[3]

Jomo also points out that the national financial systems in the region did not adapt well to international financial liberalization. The bank-based financial systems of most crisis-hit East Asian countries were especially vulnerable to the sudden drop in the availability of short-term loans as international confidence in the region dropped dramatically during 1997. Noble and Ravenhill[4] examined how liberalization of capital movements, vastly increased capital flow, poor prudential supervision of banking systems and unproductive investment, all within a context of fixed exchange rates, combined to increase the vulnerability of East Asian economies in the first half of the 1990s. Their statement is presented in Table 1. Neither inflexible exchange rate alone (the case of China) nor inadequate prudential regulation alone (the case of Japan) caused the problem. Also, China and Taiwan did not experience a severe financial crisis in 1997-8 because of restrictions on capital movements. Japan, China and Taiwan had accumulated substantial foreign exchange reserves and had relatively insignificant levels of foreign debt compared to reserves. They were thus far less vulnerable to a speculative panic than other economies in the region. Among the crisis-hit economies, Malaysia was in a better situation in terms of short-term foreign debt in relation to foreign exchange reserves. Based on this, it is doubtful whether the crisis was worse in Indonesia, Korea and Thailand than in Malaysia.

Burnside and others[5] built a dynamic general equilibrium model to articulate a view of the Asian currency crisis. Using the model calibrated to Korea and Thailand data, their study finds that the Asian currency crisis was caused by large prospective government deficits associated with implicit bailout guarantees to failing banking systems. It is summarized that regardless of country's fiscal position, a speculative attack is inevitable once the present value of future government deficits rises.

Regarding initial triggers leading to the vulnerable economies, Noble and Ravenhill inferred that much of the enormous literature that the Asian crises generated falls into one of two broad camps, '*fundamentalists*' and '*panic-stricken*'. To the *fundamentalists*, the problems of the crisis economies arose because the governments had not liberalized their financial system enough. The system of relational banking and close ties between the state and private business had to be dissolved to remove the worst of the moral hazard problems. Also, the admission of foreign financial institutions would provide a new element of competition for local institutions and foster the adoption of higher standards of financial rectitude. Meanwhile, to the *panic-stricken*, the crisis arose because of premature liberalization of capital market and the activities of speculators. The policy implications were international surveillance of the activities of hedge funds, and measures to penalize short-term international capital flows.

In another view of the crisis trigger[6] based on chronological record, the Thai baht contagion may have triggered the 1997 financial crisis elsewhere. Table 2 shows that the crisis appears to have affected the immediate neighbours in Asia first, then spread to the stock markets, and then to the world at large. In addition, the contraction in regional trade brought declines

TABLE 1: KEY ECONOMIC VARIABLES OF EAST ASIAN ECONOMIES

	Indonesia	Korea	Thailand	Philippines	Malaysia	Japan	China	Taiwan
Exchange rate	Crawling peg	Managed float	Peg	Managed float	Managed float	Freely floating	Peg	Managed float
Significant accumulation of short-term foreign debt in relation to foreign exchange reserves	Yes	Yes	Yes	No	No	No	No	No
Significant real exchange rate appreciation, 1996	Partial	No	Yes	Yes	Yes	No	No	No
Capital account liberalization	Yes	Partial	Yes	Yes	Yes	Yes	No	Partial
Inadequate prudential regulation	Yes	Yes	Yes	Partial	Partial	Yes	Yes	Partial
Current account deficit,1996	Moderate	Moderate	Large	Moderate	Moderate	No	No	No

SOURCE: Nobel and Ravenhill (2000).

TABLE 2: CHRONOLOGY OF EVENTS SURROUNDING THE ASIAN CRISIS, MARCH 1997-JULY 1999

Date	*Country*	*Description of Events*
1997		
3 March	Thailand	First official announcement of problems in two unnamed finance companies, and a recapitalization programme.
March-June	Thailand	Sixty-six finance companies secretly receive substantial liquidity support from the Bank of Thailand. Significant capital outflow.
April	Malaysia	Bank Negara Malaysia imposes limits on bank lending to the property sector and for the purchase of stocks.
29 June	Thailand	Operations of 16 finance companies suspended and a guarantee of depositors' and creditors' funds in remaining finance companies announced.
2 July	Thailand	Baht is floated and depreciates by 10% of its pre-float value, and 17% in a week.
8-14 July	Malaysia	Bank Negara Malaysia intervenes aggressively to defend the ringgit: efforts to support the ringgit are abandoned; ringgit is allowed to float.
11 July	Indonesia	Widening of the rupiah's band.
	Philippines	Peso is allowed more flexibility.
13 July	Korea	Several Korean banks are placed on negative credit outlook by rating agencies.
20 July	Philippines	IMF grants US $1000 million as emergency grant after peso falls outside a widened band to defend the basket peg.
24 July	Malaysia	Malaysia ringgit comes under speculative attack.
5 August	Thailand	Measures adopted to strengthen financial sector. Operations of 42 finance companies suspended.
14 August	Indonesia	Authorities abolish band for rupiah, which plunges immediately.
20 August	Thailand	Three-year Stand-by Arrangement with IMF approved.
25 August	Korea	Government guarantees banks' external liabilities; withdrawal of credit lines continues.
8 October	Malaysia	Malaysia spend US $20 billion to prop the share market.
14 October	Thailand	Financial sector restructuring strategy announced; Financial Sector Restructuring Agency and asset management company established; blanket guarantee strengthened.
24 October	Thailand	Emergency decrees to facilitate financial sector restructuring.
31 October	Indonesia	Bank resolution package announced; 16 commercial banks closed; limited deposit insurance for depositors in other banks; other bank closures to follow.

(Contd.)

TABLE 2 (Contd.)

Date	Country	Description of Events
3 November	Hong Kong	Hong Kong share market declined by nearly 25% in value.
5 November	Indonesia	Three-year Stand-by Arrangement with IMF approved.
Mid-November	Thailand	Change in government. Significant strengthening of economic reform programme.
19 November	Korea	Exchange rate band widened. Won falls sharply.
24 November	Japan	Japan's third financial house to apply for closure: the seventh largest Yamaichi Securities goes under.
November	Korea	Korea Asset Management Corporation's (KAMCO) non-performing asset fund is established.
3 December	Japan	Tokyo City Bank, a regional bank, closes.
4 December	Korea	IMF approves three-year Stand-by Arrangement; rollover of short-term debt continues to decline.
8 December	Thailand	Fifty-six suspended finance companies are permanently closed.
Mid-December	Indonesia	Deposit runs on banks, accounting for half of banking system assets.
18 December	Korea	New government is elected; commitment to programme is strengthened.
24 December	Korea	Foreign private bank creditors agree to maintain exposure temporarily.
25 December	Malaysia	Malaysia imposes tough reforms including expenditure cuts.
29 December	Korea	Legislation passed strengthening independence for Bank of Korea and creating Financial Supervision Commission.
31 December	Thailand	Bank of Thailand intervention in a commercial bank; shareholders' stakes eliminated.
December	Korea	Fourteen merchant banks are suspended and two large commercial banks taken over by the government.
1998		
1 January	Malaysia	Measures announced to strengthen prudential regulations.
12 January	Korea	Korean won plunges further with fresh problems of Hanna.
		IMF and lender nations move to finance US$10 billion loan to Korea.
15 January	Indonesia	Second IMF-supported programme announced. Indonesian Bank Restructuring Agency (IBRA) established and blanket guarantee announced.
17 January	Hong Kong	Peregrine of Hong Kong files for liquidation from share market loss.
20 January	Malaysia	Bank Negara Malaysia announces blanket guarantee for all depositors.

(Contd.)

TABLE 2 (Contd.)

Date	*Country*	*Description of Events*
23 January	Thailand	Bank of Thailand intervenes in two commercial banks; shareholders eliminated.
26 January	Indonesia	Indonesian Bank Restructuring Agency (IBRA) established and blanket guarantee announced.
28 January	Korea	Agreement with external private creditors on re-scheduling of short-term debt.
January	Korea	Ten of 14 suspended merchant banks closed; 20 remaining merchant banks are required to submit rehabilitation plans.
15 February	Korea	New president and government take office.
February	Indonesia	President Suharto re-elected. Doubts about future of financial sector program grow stronger amid political uncertainty. Rupiah depreciates further and currency board is debated.
11 March	Thailand	One commercial bank purchased by foreign strategic investor.
25 March	Malaysia	Programme to consolidate finance companies and to recapitalize commercial banks is announced.
31 March	Thailand	New loan classification and loss provisioning rules introduced.
March	Philippines	Three-year Stand-by Arrangement agreed with IMF.
4 April	Indonesia	IBRA closes seven banks and takes over seven others.
End-April	Korea	Four of 20 merchant banks' rehabilitation plans rejected; banks are closed.
18 May	Thailand	Bank of Thailand intervention in seven financial companies; shareholders eliminated.
Mid-May	Indonesia	Widespread riots. Rupiah depreciates, deposit runs intensify, and Bank Indonesia must provide liquidity.
21 May	Indonesia	Indonesian president fires the central bank governor. Indonesia's President Suharto resigns after a wave of bloody riots.
29 May	Indonesia	A major private bank taken over by IBRA.
5 June	Indonesia	International lender and Indonesia companies agree on corporate debt restructuring.
29 June	Korea	For the first time, government closes five commercial banks (small ones). Two merchant banks are closed and two merged with commercial banks.
30 June	Korea	New loan classification and loss provisioning rules introduced.
June	Malaysia	Danaharta, an asset management company, is established.
Mid-July	Indonesia	Authorities allow market-determined interest rates on Bank Indonesia bills.

(Contd.)

TABLE 2 (Contd.)

Date	*Country*	*Description of Events*
14 August	Thailand	Comprehensive financial sector restructuring plan announced, including facilities for public support and bank recapitalization. Intervention in two banks and five financial companies; shareholders' stakes eliminated.
11-27 August	World	Stock market plunge around the world in expectation of interest rate rises in the USA. Hong Kong mounts an expensive support to prop up the stock market.
30 August	Thailand	Majority ownership in one medium-sized commercial bank by foreign strategic investor.
August	Malaysia	Danamodel, bank restructuring and recapitalization agency, is established.
23 September	Indonesia	Indonesia's bilateral external debt to official creditors refinanced.
27 September	Japan	A major leasing company in Japan files for bankruptcy.
30 September	Indonesia	Bank Mandiri created through merger of four largest state-owned banks. Plans announced for joint government-private sector recapitalization of private banks.
September	Malaysia	Capital controls introduced, exchanged rate pegged (RM 3.8/ US $1), disclosure requirement relaxed, and measures to stimulate bank lending adopted.
2 October	USA	The Long Term Capital Fund is reported to have lost US $5 billion.
6 October	Indonesia	Amended Banking Law passed, which included strengthening of IBRA.
17 October	USA	The Federal Reserve mounts a rescue by putting together a consortium to rescue the Long Term Capital Fund.
October-November	USA	The Fed announces interest rate cuts, and the share market rebounds. This averts world panic from spreading. Two more rate cuts follow by 20 November 1998. Russian ruble tumbles 12%.
December	Asia	Most currencies that had overshot (baht, rupiah, peso, ringgit and won) recovered about half-way from their worst declines. Rupiah gained the most from its low of some Rp 17,000 to Rp 7,600/ US $.
1999		
16 January	Brazil	Speculative attack on Brazilian currency: 8%, then a 18% devaluation.

(Contd.)

TABLE 2 (Contd.)

Date	*Country*	*Description of Events*
		Free-floated the currency. Capital outflow of US $40-80 billion.
January	Europe	The euro starts phase one to replace 11 EU currencies by 2002.
	China	About 240 mutual funds suffered loss: decision to close the second largest fund and notice given of further reduction of a total of 40 of them.
		It was later revealed in a Guangdong court that the total loss from GITIC would amount to about US $50 billion.
15 February	Malaysia	Capital controls replaced with declining exit levies.
13 March	Indonesia	Government closes 38 banks and IBRA takes over seven others. Eligibility of nine banks for joint recapitalization with government announced.
March	Japan	Japan announces far-reaching reforms, which pulls the stock market from its low of around 13,000 to somewhere close to 16,000.
21 April	Indonesia	Closure of one joint-venture bank.
April	Indonesia	Government announces a plan to recapitlaize the three other state banks (all insolvent).
May	London	George Soros announces that the currency crisis is over. No reactions in the markets. Reserves of several countries improve, one of which is Korea.
9 June	USA	The long-term bond yield goes up to 6 per cent triggering dollar to depreciate, and the stock markets to begin losing value.
30 June	Indonesia	Eight private banks recapitalized jointly through public and private funds.
June	World	Interbank and discount rates and bond yields go up, signaling an expectation of interest rises in the future, Stock Market declining.
	Europe	The euro, the third world currency, loses out, reaching parity with dollar. This prompts speculation that the British pound will not find its way into the euro since the expected euro's strength not revealed.
5 July	Indonesia	Government announces plan for resolution of IBRA banks.
31 July	Indonesia	Legal merger of component banks of Bank Mandiri.
July	Thailand	One small private bank intervened and put up for sale; one major bank announces establishment of an asset management company.

SOURCES: Lingren (1999); and Ariff and Khalid (2000).

in the exchange rates of several other countries—i.e. the Singapore dollar, the Australian dollar, and the Yen. By the end of 1998 the Asian financial crisis began to assume a world dimension. The crisis was made worse by political destabilization and mistakes in the implementation of the IMF rescue programme. These factors led to the crisis being dragged out to the end of 1998 and into 1999. Cointegration test results show that the contagion has not just a Thai origin, but a common origin from other currencies in the region all moving together to cause the overshooting. Unidirectional and reverse causation tests show that the financial crisis had a multi-country origin. It is mentioned that the greater integration of the countries in the region through a significantly greater degree of financial and trade flows is the reason for the severity of the crisis effects in all these countries. In other words, the contagion appeared first in Thailand, but had several sources. The common idea that the problems of Thailand and of Indonesia were the main factor in the financial crisis can be rejected.

A recent empirical study by Forbes[7] confirms that trade effects were highly significant in the international transmission for 48 crisis economies during 16 crises between 1994 and 1999. The study explains that trade can transmit crises via three channels: competitiveness effect, income effect, and bargain effect.[8] The empirical result finds that the competitiveness and income effects both remain highly significant and economically important. Countries which compete with exports from a crisis country and which export to the crisis country had significantly lower stock market returns during the crises. The study also finds that trade effects have a much larger impact than other macroeconomic variables of a country in explaining its vulnerability to a crisis.

Many empirical studies have attempted to answer whether the Asian crises were due to deterioration in their macroeconomic fundamentals or due to financial contagion. Woo, Carleton and Rosario[9] employed two methods to find out the answer for the five Asian crisis stricken countries—Indonesia, Malaysia, the Philippines, South Korea and Thailand. Based on the competitor weighted real exchange rate (CWRER) index for each country over 1986-97, general appreciation of the CWRER was not accompanied by a general increase in the current account deficits before the crises in the case of Indonesia, the Philippines and Malaysia. Only South Korea and Thailand satisfied the condition. The results, then, were ambiguous about loss in trade competitiveness being the overriding reason for the crisis. Based on a fundamentals-based logit model by pooling annual data of 57 countries over 1970-96, the empirical result shows that macroeconomic fundamentals did not predict the 1997 Asian financial crises. Woo and others interpreted this result as evidence that financial contagion was the main cause of the Asian crisis. They also declared that their logit model did not include all the relevant fundamentals, and that this omission may have led to an under-prediction of the crisis. However, they concluded that the well-known currency crisis models of other researches had also been unable to predict the Asian crises.

In conclusion, as far as the theoretical and empirical literatures reviewed, it was financial contagion, rather than the weakness in fundamentals, that was the main cause of the 1997 Asian crises. There is no perfect model that would be able to represent the crises. Undoubtedly, policy responses at the wake of the crises were inappropriate.

CRISIS MANAGEMENT

In 1996, short-term foreign debt plus current account deficit as proportions of international reserves revealed to be more than 100 per cent for Thailand (153 per cent), Indonesia (138 per cent), and South Korea (127 per cent), relative to 55 per cent for Malaysia.[10] Thereby, the first three countries inevitably required the IMF emergency credit in 1997. Exceptionally, large official financing packages were approved and provided to Thailand, Indonesia, and South Korea, respectively. The funding was provided by the IMF and other multilateral financial institutions, the World Bank and Asian Development Bank (ADB), and commitments of substantial bilateral support.

The IMF said that the Asian crisis differs from previous crises in key respects, and it may indicate faultlines in an increasingly integrated global economic and financial system. The root of the Asian crisis was at financial sector fragility, stemming in part from weaknesses in governance in the corporate, financial, and government sectors, which made these economies increasingly vulnerable to changes in market sentiment, a deteriorating external situation and contagion.[11] Given the nature of the crisis, the policy response, in the context of the IMF-supported programmes, was framed into three main elements: official financing packages; structural reforms; and macroeconomic policies.

Financing: The financing packages assembled to support the Asian crisis countries were impressive: US $36 billion for Indonesia, US $58 billion for Korea, and US $17 billion for Thailand (Table 3). The IMF support was made available in tranches over the life of the programmes in order to ensure that the authorities have a continuing incentive to adhere to the adjustment policies agreed under the programme.

TABLE 3: IMF: OFFICIAL FINANCING

Original Package[1]	*In billions of SDRs*	*In billions of US Dollars*	*In per cent of Annual GDP*	*In per cent of IMF Quota*[2]
Indonesia[3]				
IMF	7,338	10.1	5	490
World Bank and ADB		8.0	4	
Bilateral Sources[4]		18.0	9	
Total package		36.1	17	
Memorandum items:				
Short-term external debt[5]		33.2		
Net international reserves[6]		24.5		
South Korea				
IMF	15,500	21.1	5	1,938
World Bank and ADB		14.2	3	
Bilateral Sources[7]		23.1	5	
Total package		58.4	13	
Memorandum items:				
Short-term external debt[8]		100.0		
Net international reserves[9]		6.2		
Thailand				
IMF	2,900	4.0	3	505
World Bank and ADB		2.7	2	
Bilateral Sources[10]		10.5	7	
Total package		17.2	12	
Memorandum items:				
Short-term external debt[11]		36.9		
Net international reserves[12]		1.6		

NOTES: [1] The figures refer to the financing packages announced at the time when the stand-by arrangements were approved: 20 August 1997 in Thailand; 5 November 1997 in Indonesia; 4 December 1997 in Korea.

[2] Duration of original arrangements was 36 months for Indonesia and Korea, 34 months for Thailand.

[3] Original financing package, not including augmentations since July 1998

[4] Financing from Japan, including US $1.6 billion disbursed under the original package, and US $1 billion disbursed under the Miyazawa Initiative.

[5] End June 1997.

[6] End September 1997.

[7] Second line of defense

[8] Estimate for end September 1997, including debt contracted by residents nonresident branches and affiliates of domestic financial institutions, and offshore banking debt contracted by domestic banks.

[9] Usable reserves as of 2 December 1997, excluding Bank of Korea deposits at overseas branches of resident banks.

[10] Bilateral official financing in the form of non-renewable 6-month swaps, disbursed in conjunction with Fund disbursements.

[11] End June 1997.

[12] Gross reserves as of August 14, 1997, adjusted for outstanding obligations from swaps and forward contracts amounting to US $26.4 billion.

SOURCES: Boorman et al. (2000); Lane et al. (1999).

Structural Reforms: The structural reforms worked out in cooperation with the World Bank and the ADB was mainly focused on the financial and corporate sectors. To limit the risks of bank runs and uncontrolled liquidity expansion, unviable institutions were closed and potentially viable ones strengthened. To put the system on a sound footing, measures to strengthen financial supervision and regulation were imposed (Table 4). Besides, measures were addressed to facilitate corporate restructuring and strengthen governance, disclosure and accounting standards. In addition, the structural reforms also covered many other areas such as trade liberalization, competition policy and privatization, which aimed at enhancing the resilience and growth potential of the crisis economies (Table 5). In the light of concerns over the effects of the crisis on the poor and vulnerable, the reforms included measures to strengthen and broaden existing social safety nets.

Macroeconomic Policies: Given massive market pressures to float the currencies, the main reasons for not trying to re-establish currency pegs were that the authorities had neither the reserves nor the commitment to use monetary policy unstintingly to defend them. However, monetary policy in the programmes faced a difficult trade-off between the desire to avoid a depreciation-inflation spiral and the desire to limit the adverse effects of monetary tightening on the real economy. Meanwhile, to make room for the estimated carrying costs of bank restructuring without increasing the overall fiscal deficit as well as to the needed current account adjustment, the initial programmes prescribed fiscal surplus. Later, in the light of the collapse of private domestic demand under way, fiscal policy went into a reverse, accommodating a substantial widening of deficits to support economic activity (Table 6).

The large official financing packages, together with the restructuring and macroeconomic policies, were intended to restore confidence and limit private capital outflows. However, the programmes were not initially successful in restoring confidence, and private capital continued to exit. The currencies continued to depreciate after the programmes had been adopted. Moreover, the economies sank into deep recession, contrary to initial IMF projections of only a mild slow down. Now many criticisms of the programmes have come out.

TABLE 4: IMF: MEASURES TO ADDRESS THE FINANCIAL SECTOR TURMOIL

Measure	*Indonesia*	*South Korea*	*Thailand*	*Malaysia*	*Philippines*
Emergency measures					
Liquidity support	Yes	Yes	Yes	Yes	Yes
Introduction of a blanket guarantee	Yes	Yes	Yes	Yes	No
Institutional measures					
Establishment of an overarching restructuring authority	Yes	Yes	No	Yes[1]	No
Establishment of a separate bank restructuring authority	Yes	No	No	Yes	No
Establishment of a centralized asset management corporation	Yes	Yes[2]	No[3]	Yes	No
Adoption of a special corporate debt restructuring framework	Yes	Yes	Yes	Yes	No
Operational autonomy of restructuring agencies	Limited	Yes	n.a.	Yes	n.a.
Restructuring measures					
Intervention in financial institutions that were weak or insolvent	Yes	Yes	Yes	Yes	Yes
Mergers of weak institutions	Yes[4]	Yes	Yes[4]	Yes	Yes
Closure of insolvent institutions	Yes	Yes	Yes	No	Yes
Use of public funds to purchase nonperforming assets	Yes	Yes	No	Yes	No
Use of public funds to recapitalize institutions, including:	Yes	Yes	Yes	Yes	No
State intervention in banks	Yes	Yes	Yes	Yes	No
Elimination or dilution of current shareholder stakes of insolvent banks	Yes	Yes	Yes	Yes	Yes
New direct foreign investment	Yes	Yes	Yes	Limited[5]	Yes
Other measures					
Measures to encourage corporate restructuring	Yes	Yes	Yes	Yes	Yes
Steps to improve prudential supervision and regulation	Yes	Yes	Yes	Yes	Yes

NOTES: [1] Steering committee chaired by the central bank.

[2] The powers and resources of a preexisting asset management company were substantially increased.

[3] The Financial Sector Restructuring Agency (FRA) was established to liquidate 56 closed finance companies, and the asset management company to deal with residual FRA assets.

[4] Between government-owned intervened institutions.

[5] Foreign banks are allowed to purchase up to a 30% stake.

SOURCE: Lindgren (1999).

TABLE 5: IMF: STRUCTURAL REFORM PROGRAMMES FOR INDONESIA, SOUTH KOREA, AND THAILAND

Reform	*Indonesia*	*South Korea*	*Thailand*
Domestic trade	Eliminate monopolies in foods, plywood, and clove distribution.		
Foreign trade	Reduce tariff on broad range of items, including agricultural products, chemicals, and metal products. Phase out all non-tariff barriers. Eliminate or reduce export taxes and quantitative restrictions on palm oil, leather, cork, minerals, logs, timber, and other exports.	Phase out Import diversification Programme. Align import certification procedures with international practice. Permit foreigner to engage insecurities dealing, insurance, leasing, and other property-related businesses.	
Fiscal issues	Eliminate subsidies and raise prices on domestic fuel, electricity, rice, soybeans and soymeal, sugar wheat flour, corn, and fishmeal. Discontinue tax, trade, and credit privileges for national car and aircraft projects.	Review and rationalize subsidy programmes	
Privatization	Privatization of state enterprises over the medium term.	Privatize five state-owned enterprises immediately, another six by 2002	Privatize and restructure energy, telecommunications, water and railways.

NOTE: Financial and corporate restructuring and reform programmes are not included.
SOURCE: World Bank (1999).

TABLE 6: CENTRAL GOVERNMENT FISCAL BALANCES

(in percentage of GDP)

	1987-91	1992-6	1996	1997	1998			
					Initial Package	First Revision	Second Revision	Third Revision
Indonesia	-1.0	0.9	1.2	-0.2	1.0	-1.0	-3.0	-8.5
South Korea	0.0	0.2	0.5	0.3	0.0-0.3	0.0-0.3	-0.8	-1,8
Thailand	2.1	2.4	2.4	-0.9	1.0	1.0	-1.6	-2.4
Malaysia	-3.9	0.7	1.1	2.6	2.5	0.5	-3.5	
Philippines	-2.6	-0.1	0.3	-0.9	0.0	-1.0	-3.0	

NOTE: Data above for Indonesia refer to fiscal year starting that year (1997 refers to FY 1997/98 April to March), and that for Thailand ending in that year (1997) refers to FY 1996/97 October to September).

SOURCE: World Bank (1999).

Given the financial fragility, Lane expounded that the crisis became difficult to stop because of the vicious circle[12] and many unfavourable events—i.e. political events, disturbing information (especially on weak international reserves), the premature closings of insolvent banks, and doubts about how much of the announced financing packages were actually available. Krugman[13] concurred with Jeffry Sachs, an IMF critic, that 'this was less a matter of economic fundamental than it was a case of self-fulfilling prophecy, of market panic that, by causing a collapse of the real economy, ends up validating itself'. As part of a recovery strategy, increasing public spending and cutting interest rates as well as imposing capital control were recommended. Jomo criticised IMF prescriptions, saying that the deflationary macroeconomic policies and abrupt closure of financial institutions had undermined investor confidence. Such contractionary measures transformed

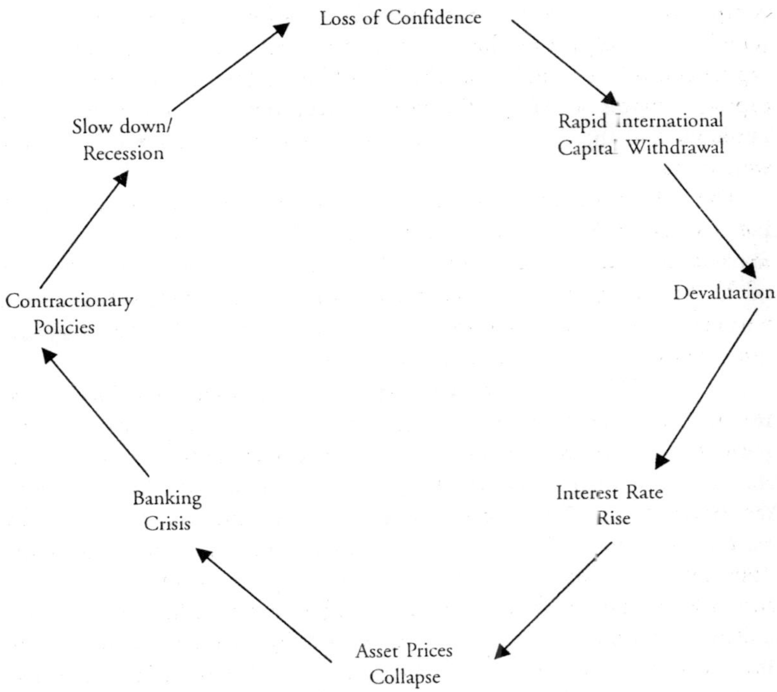

SOURCE: Jomo (1998).

CHART 1: IMF PRESCRIPTION/EAST ASIAN DILEMMA

what had started as a currency crisis and become a full-blown financial crisis, into a crisis of the real economy in 1998. He also concluded that the apparent failures of the IMF certainly did not inspire much confidence. And, though the Philippines had long been under IMF programmes and supervision, it was not spared the contagion. Reflationary measures and avoiding bank runs and consequent social instability were recommended for policy responses.

Reviewing previous work, Boorman and others[14] concluded that monetary and fiscal policies should not have been tightened at the outset in order to support economic activity. To the extent that structural reforms were needed, the reforms should have been undertaken more gradually and only as the economy recovered from the effects of the crisis. They also criticized policies adopted by Malaysia with capital controls and smaller increases in interest rates: these policies were less different than they seem from those of other countries in the region.[15] Moreover, as Malaysia's capital controls were introduced in September 1998—after market conditions had stabilized and capital outflows abated, it is hard to test the usefulness of capital controls in handling a crisis. In addition, Thailand's experience on capital controls in May 1997 was unsuccessful in staunching capital outflows, and the Baht had to be floated two months after the controls were imposed.

The IMF programme was criticised that it covered a very wide range of policies, especially for Indonesia, but ignored the core issues of financial markets and exchange rate regimes.[16] Many analysts have criticised the role of the IMF as a global crisis lender and manager. Nevertheless, besides the national and global responses, there is a question whether regional institutions had attempted in the crisis solving.

Lin and Rajan[17] summarized that there have been some substantive regional initiatives proposed in response to the crisis in South-East Asia, preventive as well as curative in nature. These include the Miyazawa and the joint US-Japan initiatives, the ASEAN Economic Surveillance process, the ASEAN Action Plan on Social Safety Nets, and the Manila Framework for Enhanced Asian Regional Cooperation to Promote Financial Stability. Apparently, apart from the multilateral assistance from the IMF, World Bank, and ADB, substantive cooperation in the region has been limited to ad hoc unilateral and bilateral initiatives, particularly by Japan. Since four of the five crisis-hit economies in East Asia are in South-East Asia, ASEAN has come under particularly sharp criticism for its perceived inaction and its delay in dealing with the crisis. One reason is that, the crisis had come at a time where political transition was taking into Indonesia as ASEAN's de facto leader. Meanwhile, APEC is still a rather loose, young and geographically elusive organization. Hence, the roles of ASEAN and APEC in dealing with the crisis were limited. Moreover, discussion on regional financial cooperation has not been able to produce any tangible result. This is primarily due to the lack of a consensus about a regional framework to respond to the crisis.[18]

DYNAMIC OF RECOVERY AND LEGACIES OF THE CRISES

WHY DID ASIA APPARENTLY 'BOTTOM OUT' IN LATE 1998?

The recession in the five crisis-hit countries in East Asia (EA5)—Indonesia, South Korea, Malaysia, the Philippines and Thailand—began to recover in late 1998 for three reasons. Changes in macroeconomic policies (relaxed monetary and fiscal policies), as exchange rates stabilized, allowed interest rates to fall and consumption to recover. Assertive structural adjustments helped restore credit flows and boosted consumer and investor confidence. And, the regional recovery, supported by strong growth in the United States and Europe, bolstered external demand. The rapid recovery in 1999 was fuelled by continuing monetary and fiscal stimulus, as well as favourable global economic environment, supported by a recovery in prices of electronics—Asia is now the world's largest supplier of such equipment.[19]

At end-2000, a report by World Bank[20] presents that within the EA5, macroeconomic policies remain stable, with slow progress in structural reforms. Inflation has stabilized at low rates. As a result, interest rates remained below pre-crisis levels. Currency values 15-20 per cent lower than their pre-crisis level in real terms, provided a healthy boost to exports. Current account surplus has netted out against the capital account to produce a continuing rise in reserves. Foreign direct investment (FDI) has dominated capital inflows (except for Indonesia), supplemented with positive portfolio investment. Short-term private foreign debt has shrunk. Short-term debt to reserve ratio has dramatically declined. A foundation of lower risk is implied.

Growth of the EA5 was reported in a continuing recovery mode since early 1999. The growth pattern however varies by countries (Table 7). Korea is experiencing the strongest recovery although problems in corporate restructuring and negative growth in construction sector remains. Malaysia is also in a fast growing mode with positive growth in all sectors but FDI, an important driver in the past, still languishes. Thai recovery was weighted down by the slow recovery of construction and the persistent and heavy losses in the financial sector. Unlike Korea and Malaysia, the Thai financial sector has mainly depended on self-recapitalization. The Philippines' recovery has been stabilized due to a decline in public construction since late-1999. Similarly, investment in Indonesia is still lagging. Indonesia's recovery has consolidated further in the first half of 2000. But financial restructuring continues to be painfully slow. In conclusion, the EA5 seems to be on a V-shaped recovery, instead of a U-shaped recovery as the initial IMF prediction—the growth would be stagnant for at least three to four years after the sharp drops in 1998. Nevertheless, the recovery is still far from complete.

WHAT ARE THE LEGACIES OF THE CRISIS?

NPLs: NPLs remain a burden on bank profitability, especially in Indonesia and Thailand (Table 8). As a result, credit extension has been limited. Large firms have had access to alternative sources of capital such as bond and equity markets. Small and medium enterprises (SMEs) have been in the bottleneck of credit release, especially in Korea and Thailand, bank-based economies. Notably, corporate debt restructuring represents the flip side of banks' NPLs.

Poverty: The crisis has substantially increased levels of poverty in all the EA5. The World Bank reports that the deep recession had pushed millions of East Asians below the poverty line—measured by consumption expenditure, and interrupted a decade-long trend of steady reductions in the number of people living below the poverty line. Under the recent recovery path, the poverty incidence has declined from the rate of 37 per cent in 1999 to 31.8 per cent in 2000—the levels however are still well above the 25.7 per cent before the crisis outbreak. In most countries, social safety nets are either lacking or rudimentary, and government face enormous challenges in fighting against poverty.[21]

Public Debts: Public debt has been driven by financial bailouts and deficit spending to boost the economies from mid-1998. It has risen to 35-50 per cent of GDP in Korea, Malaysia and Thailand, and to 90-100 per cent of GDP in Indonesia and the Philippines. Debt services has risen and squeezed non-interest public spending. Substantial improvement in expenditure management, especially on interest and amortization payments, is required to avoid crowding out of social and public expenditures.[22]

TABLE 7: RECOVERY PATH OF EAST ASIA-5

	Indonesia	*South Korea*	*Malaysia*	*Philippines*	*Thailand*
GDP					
Bottom Out	1998Q4	1998Q3	1998Q4	1998Q4	1998Q2
Recovery Path	Consolidated	Strong	Strong	Continued	Continued
Main Engine:					
- Demand Side[1]	Priv. C, X	X	Priv. C, X	X	X
- Supply Side	Manufacturing	Manufacturing	Manufacturing	Manufacturing	Manufacturing
Drawn-Down:					
- Demand Side	Investment			Investment	
- Supply Side	Agriculture Financial Construction	Construction		Construction	Financial Construction
Economic Development in 2000					
Currency	Weaken	Stable	Still Peg	Weaken	Weaken
Stock Market	New Slump	Poorly Performed	Spurt and Decline	Continue to Decline	Substantial Losses
Property Market	Remains Weak	Mixed Prospects	Consolidated	Remains Weak	Remains Sluggish
Financial Restructuring	Slow Progress	More Market-Oriented	Slow Progress	Enacted New Bank Law To Boost Securities Code	Slow Progress
Corporate Restructuring	Slow Progress	Slow Progress	Slow Progress		Slow Progress

NOTE: [1] Priv. C = Private Consumption, X = Exports

SOURCES: ADB (2000) and World Bank, 'Regional Overview', November 2000.

TABLE 8: NPLS OF CRISIS-AFFECTED COUNTRIES

(in percentage of total loans)

	1997	*1998*	*1999*		*2000*		
	Dec.	*Dec.*	*Jun.*	*Dec.*	*Jun.*	*Sept.*	*Dec.*
Indonesia[1]	...	...	...	64.0	63.5	64.7	58.8 (Nov.)
excl. IBRA	7.2	48.6	39.0	32.9	30.0	26.9	23.9 (Nov.)
South Korea[2]	8.0	16.1	16.4	15.8	18.9	17.9	...
excl. KAMCO/KDIC	5.9	10.4	11.3	10.9	13.6	12.3	...
Malaysia[3]	6.0	22.6	23.4	23.6	23.2	...	...
excl. Danaharta	...	18.9	18.1	16.7	16.2	16.1	15.3
Philippines[4]	4.7	10.4	13.1	12.5	14.6	15.3	15.1
Thailand[5]	...	45.0	47.4	41.5	34.8	30.6	26.5
excl. AMCs	...	45.0	47.4	38.9	32.0	22.6	17.7

NOTES: [1]The first line uses the 'stringent' definition of an NPL; the second line excludes transfers to IBRA.

[2]NPL figures use the BLC.

[3]Figures include commercial banks, finance companies, merchant banks, and Danaharta.

[4]Figures are for commercial banks.

[5]First line includes commercial banks, finance companies, and the estimated amount of NPLs transferred to wholly-owned private AMCs.

SOURCE: World Bank (2001).

LESSONS FROM THE CRISIS

Hindsight: Contagion is the main cause of the Asian crises. Weakness in the financial sector after the liberalization turned the currency crisis into a financial crisis. Tightening macroeconomic policies in early 1998 was an inappropriate response to financial contagion. The sudden drop in economic growth was a serious outcome. Reversal of the economic policies with the supports of external demand caused a bottom out in late 1998, a rapid recovery in 1999, and a continuing recovery in 2000.

Timing: Currencies of the EA5 collapsed within two months after the baht trigger in July 1997. Weakness of financial institutions since liberalization has induced financial vulnerability for a decade—both pre-crisis and post-crisis. Relaxed macroeconomic policies took at least 6-12 months to get the economies on a recovery. The recovery however has not completed even after two years. That said, the crisis started quickly but has taken a longer time to cure. Political problems should also be factored in for the delay in solving the crisis.

Risk: Weakness in the financial sector has been a risk factor before and after the crisis. The IMF structural reforms have been implemented slowly. Without new loans, the chicken-egg problem between financial institutions and corporate firms persists.

Prevention: The IMF structural reforms are preventive measures—to strengthen bank and corporate sectors—but they may not be appropriate when economies turn turtle and high interest rates are posed. Implicitly, the prevention will be beneficial to long-term growth.

Vulnerability: Crisis-hit countries are vulnerable to external shocks as long as the risk factors remain. Financial and corporate restructuring should be speeded up.

Ample Reserves: As long as self-help by regional cooperation is limited, the IMF is still the last-resource lender. The past became a lesson for tomorrow. Policy makers of all nations and regional and international organizations should be cautious and prudential in considering all internal and external factors to estimate outcomes before policy implementation.

IMPLICATIONS FOR INDIA

The Indian economy experienced a balance-of-payments crisis in 1990-1. It was the first time in its history that India was faced with the prospect of defaulting on its international payments. Contractionary fiscal and monetary policies were adopted in response to the crisis. Also, other economic and structural reforms have been installed. The reforms however have slowed in progress in late 1990s, partly due to political uncertainty and partly due to contagion of the 1997 Asian crisis.[23]

With the onset of the Asian crisis, foreign institutional investor withdrew funds from Indian markets during August 1997 to August 1998, while Indian companies lost access to overseas equity and debt markets. Exports to the Asian region largely declined in 1998-9, which more than offset strong export growth to the United States. As a result, the Asian crisis and its aftermath put the Indian exchange rate under downward pressure on a number of occasions. This intensified in November 1997, causing the Reserve Bank of India to intervene in both the spot and forward markets and to tighten monetary policy. Activity in the industrial and service sectors slowed in response to the fallout effects of Asian crisis.[24] The Indian economy did not, however, collapse in a serious way. The growth rate, which suddenly dropped to 4.5 per cent in 1997-8 from 7.5 per cent in the previous year, rose to 6.8 and 5.9 per cent in 1998-9 and 1999-2000, respectively. Foreign exchange reserves in terms of US dollars and months of imports showed an increasing trend in the second half of the 1990s. This can be attributed to a lower degree of openness of the Indian economies relative to that of the crisis-hit economies (Table 9).

Since the 1990s, India has sped up integration into the world economy. Deregulation has been significant. Trade barriers have declined significantly. Export and import shares in GDP have become larger. Foreign investment has increased gradually but persistently. The opening up of the capital account has spurred capital inflows, leading to greater capital formation in the economy and an increase in foreign exchange reserves. This has reduced the risk of another balance-of-payment crisis. External commercial borrowings provide an additional source of funds to Indian companies, allowing them to augment domestically available resources and to take advantage of lower international interest rates.[25]

Financial development has also improved, especially on the depth of financial intermediation, private sector participation in banking and the activity of stock markets.[26] Apparently, the financial sector is still dominated by state banks, which hold more than three-quarters of banking-sector assets. It is criticized that state banks lent money without sufficient credit checks.[27] (Deutsche Bank Research 2001). Explicitly, NPLs as a percentage of outstanding loans of state banks have been larger than that of domestic private banks and of foreign banks.[28] On privatization, the Indian government announced a plan to reduce its minimum share in state banks from 51 to 33 per cent in order to make fresh capital inflows possible. So far, the government is yet to take a concrete step. However, the financial system will probably not lead to a crisis as it is sheltered from international capital flows by the limits on currency convertibility and the high share of government paper in the banking sector. Implicitly, the large shares of state companies in both industrial and financial sectors, about a quarter of GDP, are an indicator of a government budget risk.[29]

The lesson learnt from the 1997 Asian crises is that as long as weaknesses in the financial sector remain, a country is vulnerable to external shocks. When a crisis occurs and the economy collapses, high NPLs, increased poverty level and larger public debt become legacies. India has been facing fiscal imbalances and the poverty problem. Public deficit remains at an unacceptable 9-10 per cent of GDP over the second half of the 1990s.[30] The burden of public debt could eventually undermine confidence and erode India's comfortable-looking foreign-exchange cushion.[31] Strengthening the financial sector then should speed up and is necessary to put in place

TABLE 9: OPENNESS OF ECONOMIES: INDIA AND CRISIS-AFFECTED ASIAN ECONOMIES

	Trade/GDP (%)		*Loan in Foreign Currency from Overseas Commercial Banks (% of Short-term Loan)*		*FDI Inflows (Millions of US $)*			*Bonds and Equity Issued on Internatidonal Markets (Billions of US $)*					
								Bonds			*Equity*		
	1997	*1999*	*1998*	*1999*	*1997*	*1998*	*1999*	*1997*	*1998*	*1999*	*1997*	*1998*	*1999*
India	18.7	19.2	40.1	37.4	3,577	2,635	2,168	6.0	5.7	4.7	1.0	0.1	0.9
Indonesia	44.7	51.1	52.7	49.6	...	...	...	6.5	5.7	3.5	1.1	0.0	1.2
Malaysia	150.9	183.6	44.5	42.3	6,513	2,700	3,532	12.7	12.2	14.3	0.4	0.2	0.0
Korea	58.8	64.9	45.3	53.6	3,088	5,215	10,340	49.4	50.6	46.7	0.6	0.5	6.9
Philippines	66.7	87.2	53.7	49.6	...	...	...	8.2	9.1	12.6	0.3	0.5	0.2
Thailand	77.3	85.6	58.2	54.8	3,732	7,449	6,078	11.7	11.8	12.8	0.0	2.3	1.7

SOURCE: CEIC Database; United Nations (2001).

TABLE 10: SIZE OF FINANCIAL MARKET: INDIA AND CRISIS-AFFECTED ASIAN ECONOMIES

	Size of the Financial Sector Average 1998-9		
	Deposit Money Banks/GDP (1)	*Stock Market Capitalization/GDP (2)*	*(1)+(2)*
India	0.26	0.33	0.59
Indonesia	0.36	0.35	0.71
Malaysia	0.99	1.65	2.64
Korea	0.76	0.56	1.32
Philippines	0.45	0.59	1.04
Thailand	1.11	0.39	1.50

SOURCE: United Nations (2001).

the second generation of reforms to limit crisis risk. It should be implemented while the country continues to gain an economic growth from the first generation of reforms, which has faded.

India has to push harder in financial sector reforms. Table 10 shows the significance of India's financial sector: it holds more than 50 per cent share of GDP. Direction of capital account convertibility has been put in place for India to go. As learnt, a collapse in the financial sector will cause a liquidity shortage and recession, which will take a long time to overcome. As preventive measures, bank reforms are obviously important. These should include new strategies of privatization and prudential regulations and supervisions—requiring transparent accounting, capital requirements at least up to the international norm. India should rethink deposit insurance and legal institutional designs. Further development of securities markets is needed to diminish a possibility of bank crisis. Bail-out guarantees to a failing banking system associated with prospective larger public deficits should be avoided. Costs of a crisis have been so massive in the crisis-hit economies. India should avoid similar disasters in the future.

CONCLUDING REMARKS

The 1997 Asian crises are not only financial experiences but also involve long-term growth as well as large and lasting social costs of the economies and region. The form of crises is hard to predict and challenges both economists and policy makers. Many economic models have been developed to capture the speculative attacks, weakness in economic fundamentals, banking sector fragility, contagion channels, and appropriate policy responses. Prudential indicators and preventive measures expected are generated from the models. Despite these attempts, it is difficult to represent the crises by a model with all influential factors. Debate then continues. With a longer time period, the indicators and preventive measures should be evaluated and could be firmed. Also, appropriate exchange rate regime under international financial liberalization is recommended for further studies and debates.

As a lesson, the Asian crisis is an expensive experience for the crisis-hit economies from which others can learn too. India considered East Asian countries as models for economic reforms, prior to their deep recession in 1997-8. Before the second generation of reforms are implemented, the lessons from the 1997 crisis should be realized and taken into consideration in order to prevent another crisis.

NOTES

1. Definitions of financial crisis in literatures vary with specific manifestations of the crisis being studied. The terms financial crisis and banking crisis are used interchangeably, an acceptable usage for countries where the banking system dominates financial intermediation (Sundararajan and Balino 1991).
2. Paul Krugman, *The Return of Depression Economics*, New York: W.W. Norton & Company, 1999, p. xi.
3. K.S. Jomo, *Malaysian Eclipse: Economic Crisis and Recovery*, London: Zed Books, 2001.
4. Gregory Nobel and John Ravenhill, *The Asian Financial Crisis and the Architecture of Global Finance*, Cambridge: Cambridge University Press, 2000.
5. Craig Burnside, Martin Eichenbaum and Sergio Robelo, 'Prospective Deficits and the Asian Currency Crisis', World Bank Policies Research Paper, August 1999. (http://www.worldbank.org).
6. Mohamed Ariff and Ahmed M. Khalid, *Liberalization Growth and the Asian Financial Crisis: Lessons for Developing and Transitional Economics in Asia,* Cheltenham: Edward Elgar, 2000.
7. Kristin J. Forbes, 'How Important is Trade in the International Spread of Crises?' 9 December 2000. (http://web.mit.edu/kjforbes/www/)
8. A competitiveness effect occurs when one country devalues its currency, increasing the relative competitiveness of its exports and hurting the competitiveness of exports from other countries. An income effect occurs when a crisis affects income and growth with the crisis country, thereby affecting purchases of imports from abroad. A bargain effect occurs when a country devalues its currency, reducing the relative price of its exports and thereby reducing prices in countries that import these goods (Forbes 2000).
9. Wing Thye Woo, Patrick D. Carleton, and Brain P. Rosario, 'The Unorthodox Origins of the Asian Currency Crisis: Evidence from Logit Estimation', *ASEAN Economic Bulletin*, vol. 17, no. 2 (August 2000), pp. 120-34.

10. Jomo, *Malaysian Eclipse*, op. cit.
11. T. Lane, Atish Ghosh, Javier Hamann, Steven Phillips, Mariane Schulze-Ghattas, and Tsidi Tsikata, 'IMF-Supported Programs in Indonesia, Korea, and Thailand: A Prelimiary Assessment', IMF Occasional Paper 178, 1999, p. 1.
12. Currency depreciation plunged more institutions into insolvency, further undermined creditors' prospects of repayment, and accelerated the exit of capital. T. Lane, 'The Asian Financial Crisis: What Have We Learned?', *Finance & Development*, vol. 36, no. 3 (1999), pp. 44-7.
13. Paul Krugman, 'Capital Control Freaks: How Malaysia Got a Way with Economic Heresy', *Slate*, 27 September 1999. (http.//wed.mit.edu/krugman/www/)
14. Jack Boorman, Timothy Lane, Marianne Schulze-Ghattas, Ales Bulir, Atish R. Ghosh, Jvir Hamann, Alexandros Mourmouras and Steven Phillips, 'Managing Financial Crises: The Experience in East Asia', IMF Working Paper WP/00/107, June 2000. (http://www.imf.org).
15. The initial reaction of Bank Negara Malaysia was to ward off the attacks by raising interest rates, followed by tightening monetary conditions instead. After a signal of a severe recession in mid-1998, fiscal budget turned to be a deficit of 1.5 per cent of GDP in 1998 from a surplus of 2.5 per cent of GDP in 1997. In addition, the Malaysian authorities embarked on wide-ranging reforms in the regulatory and supervisory framework for the financial sector. (Boorman et al., 2000, pp. 11-13).
16. Radelet, Steven and Jeffery D. Sachs, 'The East Asian Fianncial Crisis: Diagnosis, Remedies, Prospects'. Brrokings Papers on Economic Activity, no. 1 (1998), pp. 1-74; and Morris Goldstein, 'IMF Structural Programs', December 2000. (http://www.nber.org/books/woodstock00/structural12-15-00.pdf)
17. Chang Li Lin Lin and Ramkishen S. Rajan, 'Regional Response to the Southeast Asian Financial Crisis: A Case of Self-Help or No Help?' *Australian Journal of International Affairs*, vol. 53 (3) (1999), pp. 261-81.
18. Yunjong Wang, 'The Asian Financial Crisis and Its Aftermath: Do We need a Regional Financial Arrangement?, *ASEAN Economic Bulletin*, vol. 17 (2) (August 2000), pp. 205-17.
19. Asian Development Bank, *Asian Recovery Report 2000*, October 2000. (http://aric.adb.org/external/arr2000/arr_oct.htm); International Monetary Fund, 'World Economic Outlook: A Survey by the staff of the International Monetary Fund', Advance Copy, September 2000; (http://www.imf.org); World Bank, *East Asia: Recovery and Beyond*, Washington, D.C.: The World Bank, 2000.
20. World Bank, 'Regional Overview', November 2000. (http:wbln0018.worldbank.org/eap/eap.nsf/Attachments/Thailand+Quarterby+brief/$file/Thailand+QB+final.pdf)
21. Asian Development Bank, 'Asia Recovery Report 2000', October 2000. (http://aric.adb.org/external/arr2000/arr_oct.htm)
22. World Bank, 'East Asia: Recovery and Beyond', Washington, D.C.: The World Bank, 2000; World Bank, 'Regional Overview', November 2000.
23. Lawrence R. Klein, and T. Palanivel, 'Economic Reforms and Growth Prospects in India', August 2000 (http://economics.anu.edu.au/asarc/klein.pdf)
24. International Monetary Fund, 'India: Recent Economic Developments', IMF Staff Country Report, no. 00/155, November 2000.
25. Asian Development Bank, *Asian Development Outlook 2001*, New York, Oxford University Press, 2001.

26. Lawrence R. Klein and T. Palanivel, 'Economic Reforms and Growth Prospects in India', August 2000 (http://economics.anu.edu.au/asarc/klein.pdf)
27. Deutsche Bank Research, 'India', *Economic & Financial Outlook—Asia*, 3 April 2001, pp. 15-17.
28. International Monetary Fund, 'India: Recent Economic Developments', IMF Staff Country Report, no. 00/155, November 2000.
29. Deutsche Bank Research, 'India', *Economic & Financial Outlook—Asia*, 3 April 2001, pp. 15-17.
30. International Monetary Fund, 'India: Recent Economic Developments', IMF Staff Country Report, no. 00/155, November 2000.
31. *The Economist*, 2 June 2001.

REFERENCES

Jomo, K.S., *Tigers in Trouble*, London: Zed Books, 1998.

Lane, Timothy, 'The Asian Financial Crisis· What Have We Learned?' *Finance & Development*, vol. 36, no. 3 (September 1999): 44-7. (http://www.imf.org/external/pubs/fi/fandd/1999/09/lane.htm).

Lindgren, Carl-Johan, Tomas J.T. Balino, Charles Enoh, Anne-Marie Gulde, Marc Quintyn and Leslie Teo, 'Financial Sector Crisis and Restructuring: Lessons from Asia', IMF Occasional Paper 188, 1999. (http://www.imf.org)

Sundararajan, V. and Tomas J.T. Balino, *Banking Crises: Cases and Issues*, Washington, D.C.: IMF, 1991.

———, 'Unlocking India's Potential', *The Economist*, 2 June 2001.

United Nations. *Economic and Social Survey of Asia and the Pacific 2001*, New York: United Nations, 2001.

World Bank, *Global Economic Prospects and the Developing Countries: 1998/99 Beyond Financial Crisis*, Washington, D.C.: The World Bank, 1999.

———, 'East Asia Update', March 2001. (http://wbln0018.worldbank.org/eap/eap.nsf/Attachments/Special+Focus:+EA+Financial+&+Corporate+Restructuring/$File/Fin&Corp.pdf)

Fiscal Reforms in ASEAN: Lessons for India

Mahesh C. Purohit

The Association of South-East Asian Nations (ASEAN) is one of the most dynamic groups of nations in the world economy.[1] Like the European Union, ASEAN has attained a special significance in the global economy in recent years. With a combined area of 43,13,820 sq. km. it has a market of around 500 million people[2] with a combined gross domestic product of US $800 billion. It has achieved high real GDP growth (7.2 per cent), stability and significant degree of poverty alleviation over the past few years (Table 1). The members of ASEAN have enjoyed substantial trade and investment flows by adopting liberalization policies. It is estimated that ASEAN has more than doubled its share in world output and income since 1975 to reach almost 6 per cent. This confers on ASEAN an economic weight about halfway between those of Germany and Japan.

Over the years, the share of ASEAN in world trade has increased 3½ times to about 8 per cent, equivalent to the share of Japan. Moreover, the share of total foreign investment received by developing countries is estimated to be approximately 25 per cent during the 1990s, compared with just a trickle in the early 1970s. Per capita GDP in purchasing power parity terms has increased from less than US $1,000 to almost US $10,000 in a very short period. This is an enormous achievement. At the same time, the dynamism of the economy of the region has been an important factor in sustaining the growth of the world economy.

ASEAN has achieved sustainable and 'high-quality growth' rates that foster human development, promote equity, safeguard environment, and allow an enhancement of the cultural values of those countries. The members of ASEAN have a reputation for adopting prudent and responsive fiscal policies since 1970 to the onset of the sudden and severe economic crisis beginning July 1997.[3] While the members of ASEAN have almost recovered from the sudden and severe crisis, it has led to a more realistic and informed appraisal of the fiscal practices and institutions in these countries.

TABLE 1: SELECTED ASEAN INDICATORS (1996)

Countries	*Land Area (sq. km)*	*Population ('000)*	*Pop. Growth (%)*	*Labour Force ('000)*	*GDP (US $ billions)*	*Real GDP Growth (%)*	*GDP/Cap. (US $)*	*Exports (US $ million)*	*Imports (US $ million)*	*Current Acc (% of GDP)*
Brunei	5,765	305	3.1	138	5.3	3.5	17,377.0	2,608.9	2,505.2	-1.9
Indonesia	19,19,317	2,00,000	1.6	78,300	222.5	7.8	1,112.5	49,814.7	42,928.5	-3.4
Laos	2,36,800	4,800	2.4	2,030	2.1	7.0	437.5	313.1	678.1	-16.5
Malaysia	3,29,758	21,170	2.3	8,200	99.2	8.6	4,686.1	76,703.0	72,691.2	-4.9
Myanmar	6,76,577	45,570	1.84	26,860	121.0	5.8	2,655.0	885.6	1,829.2	-0.28
Philippines	3,00,000	71,900	2.3	29,733	83.8	5.7	1,165.4	20,543.0	31,885.0	-4.5
Singapore[1]	648	3,612	4.2	1,802	94.1	7.0	26,041.0	1,25,006.7	1,31,326.4	15.0
Thailand	5,14,000	60,000	1.1	32,800	186.7	6.6	3,111.7	55,770.6	72,386.9	-7.9
Vietnam	3,30,955	75,350	2.07	34,700	23.5	9.37	311.7	6,800.0	10,200.0	-12.2
Total	43,13,820	4,82,707	1.78	2,14,563	838.2	7.2	1,736.5	3,38,446	3,66,430.5	-5.7

NOTE: [1] Data on exports (FOB) and imports (CIF) are from Customs Trade Data.

SOURCE: Countries' submission for AMO 1997.

This paper provides an account of fiscal reforms attempted in the ASEAN and attempts to draw lessons for India. The scheme of presentation is as follows: Part I presents analysis of fiscal reforms attempted in ASEAN in the last three decades. Part II provides an analysis of the reforms in this area so far attempted in India. Finally, Part III presents lessons from the experiences of ASEAN and recommends the tasks ahead for India for achieving high and self-sustainable growth.

I. FISCAL REFORMS IN ASEAN

In ASEAN fiscal reforms played a role in bringing about macroeconomic stability. The main objectives of fiscal reforms in these countries were to carry forward the structural reforms of the real sector already under way and to attain efficiency in resource allocation and their use, as also to mobilize resources to deal with the problems of rising fiscal deficits. In consonance with this, tax reforms were carried out to help the process of globalization, attract foreign investment and provide greater integration of the world economy in tax systems.

Overall fiscal trends indicate that in the 1960s and 1970s most ASEAN countries followed conservative macroeconomic policies. The growth of public expenditure was high and fiscal deficits huge. Also, as in most countries following socialist patterns, considerable amounts of money were diverted to the public sector, which did not yield expected revenues. Therefore, efforts were made to reduce public expenditure drastically. Emphasis was on reducing unwarranted subsidies and on reforming public sector undertakings. At the same time, efforts were made to increase productive expenditure and lay emphasis on infrastructure and human resource development. It was realized that the best policy was to maintain fiscal balance. This was attempted though massive additional resource mobilization through taxation.

Thailand experienced structural changes in the overall economy through reforms in the fiscal sector. The structure of production shifted from agriculture to industry. The modern sectors had overcome the traditional sectors. Moreover, there was less and less of barrier between Thailand and the rest of the world. The value of imports and exports to GDP was growing by more than 65 per cent.[4] On the tax front, Thailand attempted reforms at a time when its growth rate was high and the fiscal situation comfortable. The overall reforms aimed at: (a) improving the competitiveness and investment climate of the economy, encouraging efficiency of the productive capacity through neutral tax treatment and elimination of distortions and interference by the government, and (b) improving tax compliance through a broad-based, equitable and transparent system, promoting structural changes through neutrality and equitable tax treatment, and reducing import tariff.[5] With these objectives in view, Thailand introduced a comprehensive VAT by replacing the existing system of sales and other taxes.[6] Also, it restructured the excise duties to provide the role of a selective tax and reformed the customs tariff. On the income tax front, Thailand rationalized the rates of personal income tax and introduced a uniform corporate tax.

Indonesia undertook a comprehensive tax reform, the process of which was initiated in early 1981. The resulting programme was enacted by Parliament in December 1983. However, due to a sharp increase in revenue from the petroleum sector, the reforms were postponed. Reforms in income tax were carried out in January 1984, in commodity taxes in April 1985 by introducing VAT and luxury taxes, and in land and building tax and stamp duty in January 1986. Thus, the major elements of tax reforms in Indonesia consisted of introduction of VAT, restructuring of direct taxes and improving tax administration.[7] After reforms, domestic sources accounted for the majority of tax revenue. The percentage of tax to GDP has risen noticeably. This, coupled with debt payment and reduction in revenue expenditure, has resulted in lower domestic budgetary impact, curbing the growth of aggregate demand and dampening inflation.[8] All in all, these reforms broadly brought the new system of Indonesia in conformity with the international thinking on the subject. These reforms were based on a well thought-out blueprint[9] prepared by international agencies.[10] The reforms aimed at a tax system that would increase its buoyancy and raise the ratio of non-oil tax revenue to GDP, thereby reducing dependence on the income tax revenue from the petroleum sector. It aimed at providing efficiency in transfer of resources to the public sector, and in reducing tax induced distortions in allocation of resources.

The Philippines attempted fiscal reforms mainly to target at lowering fiscal deficits. The reforms were at the background of growth of GDP around 5.9 per cent during 1960 to 1970 with high inflation during the 1970s. Since growth in this period was largely driven by public investment financed by foreign borrowings, inflation went up considerably. Hence the Philippines resorted to a structural adjustment programme whose emphasis was on tax reform, privatization, public enterprise rationalization, and fiscal and financial liberalization.[11] On the expenditure front, most of the reforms instituted were dominated by cuts, especially related to maintenance and investment. By 1986, the deficit as well as inflation was under control. On the tax front, major reforms were carried out in tariffs. The peak tariff was brought down from 100 in 1981 to 50 per cent in 1985. Quantitative restrictions were also lifted. All export taxes with the exception of that on logs were abolished. The 1986 measures represented the first attempt at a comprehensive tax reform. The major components of the package were: (i) a shift from the scheduler to a global approach in income tax, (ii) rationalization of increase in withholding tax rate, (iii) unification of dual corporate tax rate to a single rate of 35 per cent, and (iv) introduction of VAT in place of sales/turnover and a host of other taxes. In addition, reforms were attempted in administration.

Vietnam being a centrally controlled economy, in transition to a market economy, reforms in this country have been on different lines. While attempting reforms it has maintained its macroeconomic stability with the control of inflation in 1994-5.[12] In the late 1980s and the beginning of the 1990s Vietnam had a large fiscal deficit that could not be financed by domestic revenues. Accordingly, it adopted several policies to restrain its expenditure and curb inflation. From 1989, it abolished all direct subsidies to state-owned enterprises and shifted investment in commercial state enterprises outside the government budget. On the tax front, some important changes have been introduced both in the structure and administration of taxes. While there were fourteen different kinds of taxes before 1989, these were rationalized and reduced to nine, which resulted in increased buoyancy of the tax system.

The following common points emerge. First, the marginal rates of income tax (both personal and corporate tax) have been reduced, the number of individual income tax brackets has been curtailed and the base of the tax has been broadened. Second, except for Brunei, all the members of ASEAN have gone in for a system of VAT. Third, there is a better appreciation of the fact that the structure of the tax should be in accordance with the capacity of the administration. Most countries have, therefore, given increasing attention to improving tax administration. Finally, both for direct and indirect taxes, there has been a strong feeling that incentives do not play any role in attracting investment or affecting any activity significantly. These were termed as 'harmful tax competition' and curtailed in most of the countries.

All the members of ASEAN witnessed a record economic growth during the last three decades. Most of the countries grew at an average annual rate of more than 5.5 per cent between 1965 and 1990. Singapore, for example, transformed itself from a struggling mini-state to one of the richest, most dynamic economies in the world. However, some of the member countries such as Myanmar and Vietnam are among the world's poorest nations.[13]

Consequent upon the reforms, many of the countries had large fiscal surpluses. Singapore, for example, has been running large fiscal surpluses for many years. Thailand has also been in budgetary surplus for some time. Most members of ASEAN, including the Philippines and Vietnam, have moved in the same direction. High rate of domestic savings and foreign direct investment has been mainly responsible for this. The efforts of these countries have ensured that their current account deficits are driven by export-oriented investment, rather than consumption; and also by the private sector, rather than government spending. These deficits are financed to a large extent by long-term capital inflows. Emphasis on infrastructure investment and anti-poverty programmes has helped increase productivity growth, and social spending, thereby reducing poverty and ensuring political sustainability of the reform process.

Although the members of ASEAN have been performing well, they were not prepared to face outcomes of the process of globalization such as large capital inflows, taxing cyber transactions, and large outflows of skilled labour in the area of information technology. In some countries, strong domestic demand has raised external current account deficits and put pressure on private sector credit and domestic prices. These strains have also been felt, in varying degrees, in labour markets, especially for skilled labour and in real estate markets. More recently, many countries have faced the consequences of slow down in exports from the region. This was the result of collapse of the financial market in Mexico and later in Brazil. However, its effect percolated through to the members of ASEAN, which resulted in collapse of exchange rate, decline of international trade, fall in confidence, and consequential outflow of foreign investment. The reforms in fiscal sectors attempted since then have aimed at avoiding recurrence of such crisis in future.

Since 1999 the ASEAN economies have been recovering from the financial and currency crisis of 1997-8 and their growth has continued to widen and deepen in 2000. After its V-shaped economic recovery in 1999, ASEAN consolidated its gains with sustained growth in the first half of 2000. The region's gross domestic product was expected to grow by some 4.9 per cent for the whole year. Stronger growth is expected due to continued expansion of exports, a revival in consumer spending, and a turnaround in investment. As private-led demand plays a greater role in supporting economic recovery, governmental pump-priming would be beginning to taper off.

Owing to a number of steps taken to reduce macroeconomic imbalances, inflation rates in member countries of ASEAN have begun to moderate especially where overheating has been a concern. However, current account adjustment continues to be on the reform agenda of all the countries to check the slow down in exports and to strengthen domestic financial sectors.

In financial and macroeconomic cooperation, the members of ASEAN have created a stable, prosperous and competitive region by maintaining macroeconomic and financial stability. ASEAN has promoted closer consultations and liberalization of the financial services and closer cooperation in money and capital market, tax, insurance and customs matters. Over the short term, the plan is meant to spur the region's economies to recover; and to protect the region's poor from the effects of the crisis. In the long run, the members of ASEAN plan to preserve the environment and to lay foundations for solid and equitable development. It is, however, important that a few additional elements are added to the strategy to safeguard external and financial stability over the medium term. These include reducing reliance on foreign savings, helping to ensure that private capital inflows take the form of long-term investment, strengthening prudential norms for the domestic banking and ensuring an appropriate role for the state.

REFORMS IN FISCAL SECTOR IN POST-LIBERALIZED ERA IN INDIA

As compared to most members of ASEAN, India has followed the path of planned economic development since Independence. The five-year plans were geared to provide an important role to the public sector. Keeping this in view, the fiscal sector aimed at accelerating growth with social justice based on a socialistic pattern of society.

The Nehru-Mahalanobis model behind the Indian plans was based on the plateau of market failure. Externalities, public goods, monopolies and monopsonies were considered the main factors causing such a failure. Government intervention was considered truly justified on this basis.

With a view to removing the imperfection of the market and have coordination within and between different sectors, government intervention and for that purpose elaborate five-year plans were considered important. Within the democratic set-up of the federal structure, the five-year plans focused on physical consistency of the investment targets within input-output frameworks for a given time horizon. This called for a larger involvement of the public sector. Hence, an enlarged role for the government was envisaged to control and influence the allocation and distribution of resources.

In this framework fiscal policy was intended to raise larger resources from the richer sections of the society to direct massive investment in the public sector, especially in infrastructure development and areas having large externalities.[14] With these tasks assigned to fiscal policy, there have been significant gains made during the planned economic development. The notable achievements were among others the expansion in food production through the green revolution enough to attain self-sufficiency, also to evolve a broad base for industrial growth and to improve various socio-economic indicators.

The achievement in the growth rate of the economy was, however, below target. The results on many of the fronts were not up to the expectation. On the other hand members of ASEAN in similar situations attained a very high rate of growth during the same period, leaving India behind in many aspects. Lack of growth of the Indian economy created problems in balance of payments and financial stability was on the brink of collapse just before the adoption of the structural adjustment programme.

Since 1991, the structural adjustment programme coupled with fiscal reforms has been in the forefront. These reforms aimed at correcting the imbalance and achieving a higher rate of growth in the economy. Under the new regime, fiscal policy gave a thrust to investment in the absence of trade barriers and quantitative restrictions. Also, fiscal policy got an added impetus in directing the flow of investment in the context of delicensing of industries.

One of the important aspects of reform in the early phases was to restore the macro balance of the economy. The emphasis was on reducing the fiscal deficit of the government. In 1986-7, it was running at over 8 per cent of GDP. The effort was to bring this down to around 6 per cent. Due to conscious efforts of the central government the fiscal deficit was gradually brought down to 5.9 per cent in the year 1991-2. It further declined to 5.2 per cent in 1996-7 (Table 2). Thereafter, the deficit again increased. The deficit of the centre is likely to be around 5.1 per cent in 2000-1(RE) and 4.7 per cent in 2001-2 (BE). The total deficit of the centre and the states put together is likely to be more than 10 per cent in 1999-2000.

The consequences of high fiscal deficit depend on the way it is financed. As is well known, it could either be financed by monetization or by borrowings in the domestic financial market. Excessive monetization leads to uncontrolled expansion of money supply and an increase in domestic inflationary pressure. Alternatively, deficit could be financed from the domestic financial markets. This causes the real interest rate to be very high. The government has been borrowing at around 11 per cent when inflation averaged around 5 per cent. That is, the government is borrowing

TABLE 2: CENTRE AND STATES: AGGREGATE BUDGETARY BALANCE

(% of GDP Old Series)

Year	Fiscal Deficit			Revenue Deficit			Primary Deficit		
	Centre	*States*	*Combined*	*Centre*	*States*	*Combined*	*Centre*	*States*	*Combined*
1990-1	8.33	3.28	9.64	3.47	0.84	4.31	4.32	1.69	5.00
1991-2	5.89	2.93	7.17	2.64	0.81	3.45	1.58	1.19	2.19
1992-3	5.69	2.92	7.38	2.63	0.72	3.36	1.29	1.06	2.23
1993-4	7.43	2.49	8.68	4.04	0.47	4.51	2.90	0.56	3.39
1994-5	5.99	2.86	7.36	3.22	0.73	3.95	1.42	0.84	1.93
1995-6	5.38	2.75	6.81	2.66	0.77	3.43	0.91	0.86	1.61
1996-7	5.23	2.97	6.82	2.56	1.43	3.98	0.57	0.97	1.35
1997-8	6.21	3.10	7.74	3.24	1.29	4.53	1.63	1.00	1.40
1998-9	6.80	4.47	9.50	4.08	2.72	6.80	2.13	2.34	3.23
1999-2000 (RE)	5.96	4.98	10.40	4.03	3.13	7.16	0.96	2.55	2.13
1993-4	*7.01*	*2.35*	*8.19*	*3.81*	*0.45*	*4.25*	*2.74*	*0.52*	*3.20*
1994-5	*5.71*	*2.73*	*7.02*	*3.07*	*0.70*	*3.77*	*1.35*	*0.80*	*1.84*
1995-6	*5.10*	*2.60*	*6.44*	*2.52*	*0.73*	*3.25*	*0.86*	*0.81*	*1.52*
1996-7	*4.90*	*2.79*	*6.40*	*2.40*	*1.34*	*3.73*	*0.53*	*0.91*	*1.26*
1997-8	*5.87*	*2.93*	*7.32*	*3.06*	*1.22*	*4.28*	*1.54*	*0.94*	*1.33*
1998-9	*6.43*	*4.23*	*8.99*	*3.85*	*2.57*	*6.43*	*2.01*	*2.22*	*3.06*
1999-2000 (RE)	*5.64*	*4.71*	*9.84*	*3.81*	*2.96*	*6.77*	*0.90*	*2.41*	*2.02*

NOTE: Figures in *italics* indicate as per cent of GDP (New Series). Old Series for 1997-8 to 1999-2000 have been derived from the New Series by using a conversion factor 1.0577. For 1999-2000, FD and PD of the Centre exclude the States' and UTs' share of small savings.

SOURCE: Government of India, Report of the Eleventh Finance Commission, New Delhi, 2000, p. 7.

at the real interest rate of around 6 per cent.[15] In view of this, banks have no incentive to lend to creditworthy private investors causing crowding out of private investment.

Planned development in its earlier phases has witnessed a phenomenal growth in the size of public sector that has grown both in terms of proportion of investment and in terms of ratio of GDP. Initially, public sector undertakings were established to provide public as well as merit goods and also to create surpluses for the general budget. Later on, several of the PSUs started incurring losses. This was true of both the central and state PSUs, though the situation has been more critical at the state level. This has created an added burden on the already enlarging expenditure of the government. Also, the practice of the government taking over loss making private enterprises to prevent their closure for the sake of employment has caused an increase in expenditure. A situation has arrived when even revenue expenditure of the government is met by borrowings. Hence, as considered by the members of ASEAN, a school of thought is gaining momentum that the public sector is inherently inefficient. Accordingly, it is argued that the public sector should be contracted with increasing dependence on market mechanism and French-type indicative planning.[16] Based on the new thinking, the government has started privatizing these PSUs and liberalizing the private sector. Commission for Disinvestment is already working in this direction, but progress has been slow and so far the PSUs are a drain on resources and result in an increase in debt and interest.

On an average, during the last fifteen years, the revenue receipts increased by 15 per cent and the revenue expenditure, both plan and non-plan, by 19 per cent. The faster growth of government expenditure as compared to revenue has been a major concern for fiscal policy.

Interest payment is an important component of non-plan expenditure, causing great concern. It is an outcome of resorting to an increasing amount of borrowings in the recent past. The indebtedness of the centre as well as of states has increased considerably since 1984-5. In the last few years, it has been growing by Rs. 4,000 crore a year. Consequently, the combined domestic debt of the government (centre plus state) as proportion of GDP, has increased from 38.75 per cent in 1960-1 to 59.66 per cent in 1990-1. Thereafter it decreased to 56.62 per cent in 1994-5. The growth of debt coupled with inadequate returns from the use of borrowed funds increased the burden of interest payment. As a result, whereas in 1980-1 it was approximately 2 per cent of GDP for the centre, state and union territories, it increased to approximately 6.33 per cent of GDP in 1994-5. Consequently, the total interest expenditure (26 per cent) is greater than the internal borrowings (25 per cent), creating an eternal vicious circle causing internal debt-trap forcing the government to mobilize fresh loans from the market to pay the interest obligations.

In the early phases of planned development it was argued that a limited amount of deficit financing was useful to give a boost to the economy. However, in the later phases, there has been no check on the increase in deficit that was often determined as a residual. Consequently, the combined domestic debt of all governments has been growing at a rate of about 16 per cent during the later part of the 1990s. However, it exceeded the nominal GDP growth since 1997-8, posing problems for fiscal policy. This has also caused a steady increase in the combined debt (of centre and states) to GDP ratio that is now around 65 per cent. The level of debt is now so high that India has to borrow even to service the debt.

The tax GDP ratio has been stagnating over the years. In fact, the ratio in the first two years of reform has declined by two percentage points, i.e. from 16.4 to 14.2 per cent. This was due to the fact that the prevailing tax structure was complex, causing adverse effects on efficiency and neutrality. In addition, it gave rise to a parallel economy, that expanded every year. This called for various reforms both in taxes in income and property and on taxes on commodities and services.

Reforms in taxation of personal income were first initiated in the Budget for 1992-3 and were carried further in the later years. Rationalization has been attempted in the rates, as well as the base of the tax. The rate structure was simplified, the marginal tax rate reduced and tax base widened. The surcharge on the tax payable by the assessees was withdrawn in 1994-5. While it was temporarily reintroduced in 1999-2000 and raised further next year, it has been withdrawn in the Budget of 2001-2 except for a 2 per cent surcharge for earthquake relief.

Simultaneously, several exemptions related to the computation of taxable income were rationalized to avoid any erosion of tax base. A ceiling of 20 per cent of tax rebates on eligible savings of up to Rs. 60,000 per annum was instituted. While the general eligibility remains the same for all, this has been increased to 30 per cent for persons having income up to Rs. 1 lakh in the Budget of 2001-2.

A beginning was made to broaden the tax base by introducing a system of presumptive taxation for small traders. A voluntary scheme of presumptive taxation was devised for small dealers to bring all such dealers into the tax net. A flat annual tax of Rs. 1,400 was fixed for such dealers with an annual turnover of less than Rs. 5 lakh.[17] In addition, an 'estimated income method' was introduced in the Budget for 1994-5 for taxpayers engaged in civil construction (including construction or repair of buildings, dams, bridges, or other road or canal structures) or the supply of labour for construction or any other works contract. Its coverage was extended to all assessees having gross receipts not exceeding Rs. 4 lakh.[18] The scheme was also applicable to truck operators owning up to ten trucks and engaged in the business of plying, leasing or hiring trucks.[19] To curb tax evasion, it was made mandatory to submit tax returns (irrespective of income) if one had fulfilled one of the criteria enumerated by the government.[20]

Along with rationalization, efforts were made to curb the parallel economy and to bring tax evaders under tax umbrella. Accordingly, a scheme of immunity was announced in Budget for 1994-5 to provide such people an opportunity to deposit unaccounted money with the National Housing Bank with the proviso that 40 per cent of this would be deposited in a special fund for financing slum clearance. A more liberal provision was announced in the Budget for 1997-8 known as the voluntary disclosure of income scheme. At the same time it provided relief to small taxpayers. The general exemption limit for all taxpayers and the standard deduction for the salaried taxpayers were raised.

Structural reforms have been attempted in regard to capital gains tax, gift tax and wealth tax. Long-term capital gains tax has been revised to a 20 per cent flat rate system with an adjustment concerning inflation for individuals, domestic company and foreign company. Gift tax has been confined to large amounts by raising the exemption limit to Rs. 30,000. In view of its insignificance both in raising revenue and in curbing evasion, gift tax has been abolished in 1998. Wealth tax has also been rationalized. Wealth exceeding Rs. 15 lakh is taxed at a flat rate of 1 per cent. One residential house and productive (financial) assets such as bonds and shares have been exempted. Provisions for the taxation of other wealth have also been rationalized. In an attempt to encourage development, urban land held by a person as stock-in-trade, is now exempt for a period of five years (as against three years until 1994-5).

Changes in corporation tax have been effected both in content and rate structure through the budgets for 1994-5 and 1997-8. Prior to this, a distinction was made between closely and widely held[21] domestic companies. This has now been withdrawn and equal treatment is extended to all companies. The changes have brought the corporation tax very close to the structures prevailing in other countries of ASEAN.

The tax rate on income of companies incorporated abroad and earning in India has been reduced from 65 per cent to 48 per cent in 1997-8. A five-year tax holiday for investment in infrastructure was introduced in 1995-6 and subsequently in 1996-7; these concessions were extended to the power sector as well to boost investment in this sector. In addition, surcharge on corporation tax earlier levied at the rate of 15 per cent in 1995-6 and 7.5 per cent in 1996-7 on domestic companies having income in excess of Rs. 75,000 has been dropped in the year 1997-8. An important change in the structure of corporation tax relates to introduction of a Minimum Alternate Tax (MAT). This tax was first levied through the Budget 1996-7 on all those companies that have gradually become zero-tax companies due to various incentives for investment and concession. All such companies are now subject to MAT if their total income was less than 30 per cent of their book profits. The MAT was levied at the rate of 43 per cent of book profits, which is deemed to be the total income. Thus, the effective rate of MAT is 12.9 per cent. However, the tax is not levied if the company is engaged in: (i) the business of generation and distribution of power, (ii) development and maintenance of infrastructure facilities, and (iii) the unit is 100 per cent Export Oriented Unit (EOU) or established in Export-Oriented Zones (EOZ). With further amendments in Budget 1997-8, the income earned from exports was exempted from MAT and a credit system was introduced to enable a company to carry forward its tax liability for five years.[22] In this way, almost all zero-tax companies pay corporation tax at not less than 10.5 per cent on their book profits.

As part of structural reforms aimed at opening up the frontiers of the economy, a major reform in customs duties has been to lower its peak rates. The maximum rate was brought down from 330 per cent to 85 per cent in 1993-4 and gradually to 40 per cent in the 1996-7 and to 30 per cent in 1997-8. Also, a large number of end-use exemptions (causing disputes, litigation and misuse) have been withdrawn and the number of rates reduced. However, the Budget for 1998-9 introduced a Special Additional Duty (SAD) to correct the distortions caused by irrational domestic trade tax. Accordingly, on all imports across the board, SAD at the rate of 4 per cent was levied to have level playing field for the domestic industries. This compensated for the domestic trade taxes borne by domestic industries and not levied on imports. The SAD was, however, removed in the budget for 2000-1.

At the federal level, Union Excise Duties (UEDs) are levied on goods produced or manufactured.[23] Initially, under UEDs there were various rates and a plethora of exemptions. However, reforms over the years have converted UEDs into a system of CenVAT with a single rate of 16 per cent on almost all goods. In addition, there is a Special Excise Duty (SED) of 16 per cent on specified products. Most of the items under SED are final products but some of the items also fall in the category of intermediate goods. The CenVAT allows instant credit for the taxes paid on inputs in the form of excise duty[24] as also of countervailing duty (CVD)[25] paid on inputs and capital goods[26] received in a factory for the manufacture of any dutiable final product (except matches).

At the state level, many taxes are levied on commodities and services. These include sales tax, state excise, motor vehicle tax and passenger and goods tax. Sales tax is the most important tax yielding almost two-thirds of the states' own tax revenue. All the states levy sales tax at the first-point of sale within the state under the state's sales tax laws.[27] Inter-state transactions are covered by the Central Sales Tax (CST) Act, 1956.

The reforms so far attempted have made a good beginning. An evaluation of these reforms, however, points to the following aspects, which are still required to be attended to:

(a) *High fiscal deficit*: The fiscal deficit of the centre and states put together is very high which could cause damage to the economy. It requires corrective action urgently. The efforts in the Budget 2001-2 have already taken a step further. Implementation of the Fiscal Responsibility Act[28] would further help taking care of this aspect.

(b) *Expenditure control*: Despite efforts by the centre, it has not been possible to control non-plan expenditure. The situation is worse at the state level. It is very important that stern measures are adopted to curtail non-plan expenditure. Various measures could be adopted: no increase in government employment, suspension of transfers, economy in inventories, curtailing activities based on zero-based budgeting, and reducing subsidies. The Expenditure Reforms Commission has started giving its reports and the government must take immediate action on its recommendations. A beginning has been made in the Budget proposals for 2001-2.

(c) *Reducing interest payments*: While recognizing the fact that interest payment has been a very substantial part of government expenditure, in the Budget of 2001-2 the administered interest rate has been reduced to lower the interest burden of the government. In general, it is important that we review all the schemes, plan and non-plan, and examine the inefficacy. The Budget for 2001-2 has made some efforts in this direction.

(d) *Subsidies and user charges*: Rationalization of subsidies is a critical area. Some hard decisions have to be taken to look into the overall impact of subsidies on food, fertilizer, kerosene, railway fares, education, etc. Also, user charges should have an upward revision to make these realistic.

(e) *Adverse effects on savings and investment*: While rationalizing personal income tax, the government has withdrawn two specific concessions relating to postponed expenditure.[29] This has resulted in a decline in savings. The trends in gross domestic savings indicate that it increased from 12.7 per cent of GDP in 1960-1 to 24 per cent in 1989-90. As a percentage of GDP it was at its maximum (27.4 per cent) in 1990-1. Since then it has declined (22.7 per cent in 1993-4 and 25.3 per cent in 1995-6). The ASEAN experience in this regard is certainly enlightening.

(f) *Failure of presumptive taxation*: The scheme for bringing small dealers into the tax net through the mechanism of presumptive taxation, which commenced with the Budget for 1992-3 and extended further through the 'estimated income method' contained in the Budget for 1994-5, has failed to meet expectations. The yield from presumptive taxation was only Rs. 110 million in 1992-3, and Rs. 275 million in 1993-4. This is due to paucity of the necessary administrative machinery supported by market surveys required to bring the targeted taxpayers into the tax net. In this context the experience of the *forfeit* system, as used in France, provides some lessons.[30]

(g) *Increase in number of taxes*: In addition to the reforms enumerated above, the centre has attempted to raise resources through a 'service tax' by taking advantage of the residuary entry in the union list. To begin with, a service tax at the rate of 5 per cent was imposed in the Budget for 1994-5 on three services: stockbrokers, telephones and non-life insurance. Since then many more services have been brought under the tax net, bringing the total to 40. Since an extensive use of this base results in cascading of tax and also complicates the tax system, it is important to bring this under the net of VAT.

(h) *Simplification of procedures*: With regard to procedural reforms, the government has, so far, touched only the tip of the iceberg. In fact both under the UEDs and the sales tax there are various time-consuming and involved procedures both in regard to declarative requirements and accounting obligations.[31] The reforms must emphasize the simplification of these aspects.

III. LESSONS FOR INDIA AND TASKS AHEAD

The experience of members of ASEAN who have achieved high-quality growth until the onset of sudden and severe economic crises provides an opportunity for a realistic and informed appraisal of fiscal practices and institutions in these countries. It also offers some important lessons for a country like India.

While India has attempted some reforms during the last decade and achieved growth in some sectors, the experience of members of ASEAN suggests that India is capable of sustaining higher rates of growth provided it addresses the issues of structural weaknesses in fiscal and financial sectors. Greater efforts are needed to facilitate the continuance of structural reforms, particularly relating to debt and corporate restructuring.

Fiscal consolidation needs to be carried out in a way that reduces the size of the public sector. This would help in sustaining performance of the governments that must maintain an environment conducive to high-quality growth. Moreover, today's increased competition for private capital inflows calls more than ever for domestic institutions that can formulate and implement effective economic and financial policies, make efficient use of domestic resources, and fulfil government functions in a way that provides excellence in governance. This includes reducing regulations and restrictions that foster rent-seeking activities; ensuring that fiscal and central bank accounts and budgetary procedures and controls are transparent; protecting property and contract rights; and guaranteeing the professionalism and independence of the judiciary. There are other important activities of the government, such as safeguarding natural resources and the environment, fighting corruption, and streamlining the civil service.

An important lesson to be drawn from the experience of the members of ASEAN relates to reducing external vulnerability by curtailing current account deficits. Since the greatest threat of instability was posed by more volatile short-term inflows, macroeconomic and structural policies should be geared to encourage foreign direct investment and other long-term investment flows. The most important policies in this regard are those encouraging domestic investment—a stable macroeconomic environment and continued structural reform, including further trade liberalization and, with it, the outward orientation of the economy. It is important to learn from the experience of ASEAN that direct quantitative controls on capital inflows rarely work for any sustained period. Moreover, such controls run counter to the thrust of external liberalization that has been a hallmark of the success of ASEAN. Also, increase in domestic rates of saving play a crucial role. Most ASEAN countries had private saving rates that were among the highest in the world. Such an approach would help address the challenge posed by capital inflows, reduce the burden on monetary policy, and tend to reduce interest rates.

While public expenditure has to be curtailed, there has to be an increase in spending in critical areas of education, health, and infrastructure. The fiscal policy must protect its poor from the effects of globalization by making adequate provisions for social safety nets. A sustainable social security system is a critical priority. The choice of an appropriate mix of public and private sector provisions of pension and health care needs and the creation of contributory schemes to finance old-age retirement benefits is extremely important. This would call for an appropriate mix of revenue and expenditure measures along with avoidance of investment incentives and unproductive outlays. Also, there is room to raise revenues through steps to improve tax administration and other measures.

An important lesson for India is the adaptation of the tax system to globalization.[32] In the Indian context, while globalization had some adverse impact on the fiscal system due to lowering of rates of custom duties and removal of quantitative restrictions (due to WTO regime), the structure of excise duty had to be rationalized and rates of duty curtailed to a reasonable level for providing a level playing field for the indigenous industries. Also, domestic trade taxes are being rationalized. While the conventional tax structure might have challenges in administering current taxes, new types of taxes might become feasible with the rise of new technologies and activities.[33] Such taxes could be levied by all these countries including India.[34]

It is important to strengthen India's Surveillance Process (ISP) for regulation and timely warnings within India and with the members of ASEAN as well as of SAARC countries to develop a strong and robust fiscal and financial system. The ISP should have two major elements: monitoring of Indian (regional as well as national) economic and financial developments and providing peer review by the finance ministers of India or SAARC or other coordinating blocks.

In macroeconomic and financial cooperation, as already attempted by the ASEAN, India must promote liberalization of financial services and closer cooperation in money and capital markets, tax, insurance and customs matters. Drawing lessons from the crisis of ASEAN, India must ensure that liberalization of capital accounts is properly sequenced to allow the freer flow of capital while cushioning the impact of sudden shifts in capital flows.

In addition, India must embark on an effort to develop its own regional bond market and put in place infrastructure that would enable a corporation or a government to raise funds in any bond market within the region. A regional support mechanism to promote further regional financial stability could also been envisaged.[35] Appropriate mechanism could also be developed to enhance the participation of the private sector in crisis management and resolution. Standards of transparency and disclosure are equally important for the public and private sectors. In particular, large market participants such as highly leveraged institutions, which have systemic significance, should be subjected to regular and timely transparency and disclosure requirements. Dissemination of necessary information helps investors make better decisions so that they do not rely solely on the information of rating agencies. Given the important role that credit rating agencies play in the international financial markets, there should be greater transparency in the rating process.

ASEAN Vision 2020 consolidates extra-ASEAN regional linkages for mutual benefit for multilateral trading system. It also envisages promotion of a modern and competitive small and medium enterprises (SME) sector. In addition, it promotes financial sector liberalization and closer cooperation in money and capital market, tax, insurance and customs matters as well as closer consultations in macroeconomic and financial policies. India must also prepare and plan to implement such a Vision 2020. In addition, in designing fiscal reforms, it is essential to not just focus on macroeconomic aspect but also on technical and allocative efficiency aspects of the tax and expenditure systems. It is equally important to have emphasis on issues of coordination and effectiveness of fiscal institutions and procedures.

NOTES

* The author is a Professor at the National Institute of Public Finance and Policy, New Delhi. He is grateful to the participants at the workshop for their useful comments and especially to Mukul Ashar and Arun Kumar for their insightful comments and suggestions during the discussion of the paper at the workshop. The author wishes to express his gratitude to Ajay Halen for his help in compilation of data and to Anurodh Sharma for providing competent secretarial assistance. The author alone, however, remains responsible for the errors, if any.

1. The ASEAN founded on 8 August 1967 through the ASEAN Declaration (also known as Bangkok Declaration of 1967). The five founding countries, Indonesia, Malaysia, Philippines, Singapore and Thailand, originally signed the Declaration. Brunei Darussalam was admitted in 1984, Vietnam in 1995, Laos and Myanmar in 1997, and Cambodia in 1999.
2. It has a combined area of 30,69,581 sq. km. and accounts for 77 per cent of the world production of natural rubber, 75 per cent palm oil, 70 per cent copra, 43 per cent tin, and 18 per cent of bananas and vegetables.
3. Asian Development Bank, *Emerging Asia: Changes and Challenges*, Manila, 1997.

4. Chawin Leenabanchong, 'Thailand Towards Fiscal Reforms', paper presented at a Symposium on Fiscal Reform and Economic Development, organised by the Institute for Economic and Social Research Faculty of Economics, University of Indonesia in cooperation with the EDAP-UNDP, 1995.
5. See Somchai Sujjappongse, 'Tax Structure, Tax Reform, and its Impact on the Thai Economy', paper presented at the International Conference on Tax Reforms, held on 7-9 December 1992, New Delhi.
6. See for details, Charnchai Musignisarkorn, 'Value Added Tax in Thailand', paper presented at the International Conference on Tax Reforms, held on 7-9 December 1992, New Delhi.
7. R.J. Chelliah, 'Financial and Fiscal Sector Reforms in Asian Countries', *Asian Development Review,* vol. 11 (2), 1993, pp. 47-71.
8. Kahlil Rowter, and Rinaldi Sinaga, 'Taxation Reforms in Indonesia: Rationale and Economic Impact', paper presented at a Symposium on Fiscal Reform and Economic Development, organised by the Institute for Economic and Social Research Faculty of Economics, University of Indonesia in cooperation with the EDAP-UNDP, 1995.
9. See Mukul Asher, *Income, Sales and Property Tax Reforms in Indonesia: A Preliminary Assessment* (mimeo), 1986.
10. Harvard Institute of International Development was chosen as the external institution for technical studies and drafting the tax reform package.
11. See for details, G. Manasan Rosario, 'Fiscal Reform and Economic Develop-ment: The Case of the Philippines', paper presented at a Symposium on Fiscal Reform and Economic Development, organised by the Institute for Economic and Social Research Faculty of Economics, University of Indonesia in cooperation with the EDAP-UNDP, 1995.
12. To Din Thai, 'Some Issues of Public Finance in Vietnam', paper presented at a Symposium on Fiscal Reform and Economic Development, organised by the Institute for Economic and Social Research Faculty of Economics, University of Indonesia in cooperation with the EDAP-UNDP, 1995.
13. See for details, Asian Development Bank, *Emerging Asia: Changes and Challenges,* 1997.
14. The First Five Year Plan pronounced that the main task of the fiscal policy was to 'raise, to the extent possible, through taxation, through loans and through surpluses earned on state enterprises a considerable portion of the savings needed. The financing of investment through public savings would help to ensure a pattern of development in consonance with accepted social criteria.' See Government of India, *The First Five Year Plan,* New Delhi, 1953, p. 39.
15. Government of India, *Economic Reforms: A Medium Term Perspective, Recommendations of Prime Minister's Economic Advisory Council,* New Delhi, 2001, p. 43.
16. S.P. Gupta, 'Planning and Liberalisation', *Economic and Political Weekly,* 23 October 1993, pp. 2349-55.
17. These dealers are not required to maintain detailed books of accounts or submit detailed returns. The scheme was further pursued in the Budget for 1994-5. It now extends to civil construction, contractors and to truck operators.
18. The taxable income in such cases is estimated at 8 per cent of their gross receipts.
19. The income from each truck is estimated at Rs. 2,500 per month for heavy goods vehicles and Rs. 2,000 per month for other vehicles.
20. Initially, there were four criteria: owning a house, or a telephone, or a car or travelling abroad. This list was expanded in Budget 1998-9 to include two more items namely

holding a credit card and membership of an expensive club. Initially, this scheme applied in the four cosmopolitan towns only. It has been extended to all towns in the Budget of 2001-2.

21. A widely held company is also calleu a company 'in which the public is substantially interested', and its shares are registered in the stock exchange.
22. That is, the tax credit is allowed to be carried forward for a period of five assessment years. When the regular tax becomes payable, the difference between the regular tax and tax computed under MAT for that year provided would be set off against the MAT credit.
23. The prevailing structure includes basic UEDs, special excise duty, additional excise duty in lieu of sales tax, additional duty of excise on textiles and textile articles, and cesses on specified commodities. The additional excise duty in lieu of sales tax is levied on tobacco, textiles and sugar. This is a tax rental arrangement between the Union and the states. Cesses on specified commodities and additional excise duty on textiles are primarily meant to raise resources for the development of concerned industries.
24. This includes all the variants of UEDs such as additional excises or cesses.
25. This is levied as per the provisions of the Customs Act wherein this is referred to as Additional Duty of Customs. However, this is popularly known as CVD.
26. For capital goods only 50 per cent of the duty paid on the goods can be availed of in a financial year; the remaining credit can be availed of in the next financial year, provided the goods are still in use.
27. See for details Mahesh C. Purohit (2001), *Sales Tax and VAT in India,* Delhi: Gayatri Publications.
28. The Bill on the subject is on the anvil in the Lok Sabha.
29. The concessions were related to Secs. 80 CCA and 80 CCB. The concession under Sec. 80 CCA, was for investments under the National Savings Scheme and those related to Sec. 80 CCB were meant for investments under mutual funds. Both these schemes were for long-term investments. The National Savings Scheme is akin to the Individual Retirement Account common in the USA.
30. Mahesh C. Purohit, *Value Added Tax: Experiences of India and Other Countries,* Delhi: Gayatri Publications, 2001.
31. See Mahesh C. Purohit, 'Central Excise Duty and MODVAT', *Tax Notes International,* 26 May 1997, pp. 1709-13.
32. See J. Şlemrod, 'Comments', *Taxation in an Integrated World,* Washington, D.C., The Brookings Institute, 1995.
33. Tanzi identifies new technologies and activities as 'fiscal termites'. V. Tanzi, 'Technological Development and the Work of Fiscal Termites', International Monetary Fund, Working Paper, 2000, pp. 22.
34. See Mukul Asher and R.S. Rajan, 'Globalization and Tax Systems', in M. Asher, D. Newman and T.P. Snyder, eds., *Public Policy in Asia: Implications for Business and Government,* Connecticut: Quorum Books, 2001.
35. ASEAN agreed to establish a regional financing arrangement called the 'Chiang Mai Initiative'. To help countries meet temporary liquidity problems, ASEAN agreed to expand the ASEAN Swap Arrangement (ASA)—originally set up by the five founding member countries of ASEAN to provide financial support to members with balance-of-payments difficulties—to enlarge it as well as to include all the ASEAN. The ASEAN central banks have agreed on the principles governing the expanded facility.

REFERENCES

Asher, Mukul (1986), *Income, Sales and Property Tax Reforms in Indonesia: A Preliminary Assessment.*

—— , 'Reforming the Tax System in Indonesia', paper presented for a *Project on Reforming Taxes in Developing Countries* (mimeo).

—— and R.S. Rajan, 'Globalization and Tax Systems', in M.G. Ashar, D. Newman, and T.P. Snyder (eds.) (2001), *Public Policy in Asia: Implications for Business and Government,* Quorum Books, Connecticut (mimeo).

Asian Development Bank (1997), *Emerging Asia: Changes and Challenges,* Philippines.

Bagchi, A. (1998), 'India's Fiscal Reform: Some Signposts', *Vikalp,* 23: January-March, 9-22.

——and Pulin B. Nayak (1994), 'A Survey of Public Finance and the Planning Process: The Indian Experience', in A. Bagchi and N. Stern (1994), *Tax Policy and Planning in Developing Countries,* Oxford University Press, New Delhi.

Chelliah, R.J. (1993), 'Financial and Fiscal Sector Reforms in Asian Countries', *Asian Development Review,* vol. 11, no. 2, pp. 47-71.

Choi, Kwang (1990), 'Tax Policy and Tax Reform in Korea', paper presented at a World Bank Conference on Tax Policy in Developing Countries, 28-30 March 1990.

Choi, Kwang et al. (1992), *Public Finance in Korea,* Seoul National University Press, Seoul.

Government of India (2001), *Economic Reforms: A Medium Term Perspective, Recommendations of Prime Minister's Economic Advisory Council,* New Delhi.

——(1991-3), *Tax Reforms Committee, Interim Report, Final Report Part I, and Final Report Part II,* Ministry of Finance, New Delhi.

——(1953), *The First Five-Year Plan,* Planning Commission, New Delhi.

Jenkins, Glenn P. and Seth E. Terkper (1992), 'Viet Nam's Tax Reforms: Policies in Transition Economies', Harvard Institute for International Development, Cambridge, October.

Kim, Dong-Kun (1992), 'Structure of VAT in Korea: Lessons for Developing Countries', paper presented at the International Conference on Tax Reforms, held on 7-9 December, New Delhi.

Manasan Rosario, G. (1995), 'Fiscal Reform and Economic Development: The Case of the Philippines', paper presented at a Symposium on Fiscal Reform and Economic Development, organized by the Institute for Economic and Social Research Faculty of Economics, University of Indonesia in cooperation with the EDAP-UNDP.

Mundle, Sudipto (1998), 'Tax Reforms in Viet Nam: A Selective Analysis', Asian Development Bank, Occasional Paper, no. 18.

Musignisarkorn, Charnchai (1992), 'Value Added Tax in Thailand', paper presented at the International Conference on Tax Reforms, held on 7-9 December, New Delhi.

Owens Jeffrey and Edward Whitehons (1996), 'Tax Reform for the 21st Century', *Bulletin for International Fiscal Documentation*, November/December, pp. 538-47.

Park, Jongkoo (1995), 'The Pattern of and Role of Public Finance in Korea', paper presented at a Symposium on Fiscal Reform and Economic Development, organized by the Institute for Economic and Social Research Faculty of Economics, University of Indonesia in cooperation with the EDAP-UNDP.

Purohit, Mahesh C. (1997), 'Value Added Tax in a Federal Structure - A Case Study of Brazil', *Economic and Political Weekly*, February-15 May, pp. 357-62.

——(2001), *Value Added Tax: Experiences of India and Other Countries*, Gayatri Publications, Delhi.

Purohit, Mahesh C. and D.N. Rao (1994), 'Fiscal Intervention for Environmental Protection: A Cross-Sectional Analysis for Fiscal Prescriptions', paper presented at the 50th Congress of the International Institute of Public Finance, Harvard University, Cambridge, USA (22-25 August).

Rakshit, Mihir (1991), 'The Macroeconomic Adjustment Programme: A Critique', *Economic and Political Weekly*, 24 August.

Rowter, Kahlil and Rinaldi Sinaga (1995), 'Taxation Reforms in Indonesia: Rationale and Economic Impact', paper presented at a Symposium on Fiscal Reform and Economic Development, organized by the Institute for Economic and Social Research Faculty of Economics, University of Indonesia in cooperation with the EDAP-UNDP.

Slemrod, J. (1995), 'Comments', in *Taxation in an Integrated World*, The Brookings Institute, Washington, D.C.

Sujjappongse, Somchai (1992), 'Tax Structure, Tax Reform, and its Impact on the Thai Economy', paper presented at the International Conference on Tax Reforms, held on 7-9 December, New Delhi.

Tanzi, V. (2000), 'Technological Development and the Work of Fiscal Termites', International Monetary Fund, Working Paper, pp. 22.

Thai, To Din (1995), 'Some Issues of Public Finance in Vietnam', paper presented at a Symposium on Fiscal Reform and Economic Development, organized by the Institute for Economic and Social Research, University of Indonesia in cooperation with the EDAP-UNDP.

Towe, Christopher M. (1991), 'The Budgetary Control and Fiscal Impact of Government Contingent Liabilities', IMF Staff Papers, 38(I): 109-34.

Privatization: India, ASEAN and the Global Economy

R.K. Mishra

This paper critically analyses privatization trends in India and ASEAN and the global economy, brings out similarities and dissimilarities in the privatization trends related thereto and portends futuristic privatisation scenario.

The privatization policy and trends of ASEAN have had far-reaching effects on the other economies of Asia. ASEAN has been considered the engine of the economic growth of Asia and therefore the success of its privatization philosophy has encouraged emulation from many other economies. An attempt is made to present here a picture of privatisation in some ASEAN economies followed by a detailed case study of privatization in Singapore and Malaysia.

ASEAN has been keeping pace with privatization experiments in the US, UK, France, Australia, Mexico, Argentina, Chile, Peru, Tanzania and Uganda, etc.

Malaysia has privatized more than 800 public enterprises in a systematic fashion. It launched its privatization drive with a master plan 1985.[1] The progress of privatization in Malaysia could be rated as slow and steady. The commercialization, corporatization and privatization of the Malaysian Telecommunications Department which was the largest single transfer of fixed and net current assets, is a case in point. Malaysia later privatized its ports, air transport, shipping lines, manufacturing and commerce, energy and social services. Malaysia provides an example of an institutional structure for privatization with clearly defined responsibilities. The high point of Malaysia's privatization programme was the protection of the special interests of the Bumiputra (indigenous community and labour).

Singapore commenced its privatization programme in 1985. Ministerial departmental enterprises and non-ministerial public corporations, boards and government companies were privatized between 1985 and 1990. 650 public enterprises of one type or another, with a total staff of more than 1,80,000 representing about 20 per cent of the economy's workforce, were privatized during this period.

Since independence in 1945, the public sector has played an important role in the Indonesian economy. Article 33 of the Indonesian Constitution, stipulates state control of such sectors of production of the economy which effect the life of the people as a result of which all strategic industries were run by public enterprises as an instrumentality of the state. By 1980, 69 per cent of the investment in the Indonesian economy came from the public sector. In 1988,[2] the state owned around 50 per cent of shares in the mining industry, 100 per cent of shares in the oil and gas production, 100 per cent shares in utilities, 50 per cent share in transport and communication and a 65 per cent share in banking and finance. In 1988, the privatization programme was launched to transfer the ownership and management of departmental agencies, public corporations and publicly owned companies. The reform programme intended to provide more independence in planning and decision-making to the leftover enterprises in the public sector. The privatization drive was carried out because of pressure from the international organizations, a lack of government funds to support continuously inefficient public enterprises, and to promote the indigenous private sector.

The Philippines was compelled to reduce the role of public enterprises following their rapid expansion between 1975 and 1984 which was detrimental to fiscal position of the economy. The privatization programme launched in 1985 emphasized the reduction of the number of government enterprises to only those which were necessary for specific economic and social purposes. The Congress reviewed the Senate Bill promulgating the Government Corporation Code of the Philippines to monitor and control the leftover public enterprises. By 1989, 41 per cent of the total enterprises were privatized and in the subsequent years, excepting a few, most operating in strategic sectors were also privatized. The Philippines set up a Trust for the re-privatization of a large number of public enterprises created by the Marcos government. This Asset Privatization Trust, evolved administrative, legal and financial arrangements. The privatization programme faced problems of industrial rehabilitation, writing-off the huge accumulated losses incurred by the public enterprises and providing a safety net to the vulnerable class.

The Republic of Korea had 5 government enterprises, 25 government invested enterprises, 54 subsidiaries of government invested enterprises and 6 other government backed enterprises as on 31 March 1984. The government enterprises were departmental in nature. Railways and the government invested enterprises held at least 50 per cent of government shares. These included among others Korea Development Bank and Korea Electric Power Corporation. The subsidiaries of government invested enterprises had indirect government investment through government invested enterprises. The government backed enterprises held less than 50 per cent government shares. The first large-scale privatization was undertaken from 1968 to 1973. In this period the government privatized 11 public enterprises, prominent among which were Korea Machinery Industry Company, Korea Express Company, Korea Airlines, Korea Commercial Bank, Korea Mining and Smelting Company and Inchon Iron and Steel Company. The second privatization programme was implemented in 1981-3, during which, as a part of general liberalization policy, government sold shares of 6 of its enterprises, such as Korea Dredging Corporation, Korea First Bank, Seoul Trust Bank and Cho-Hung Bank. In 1987, the Korean government announced an ambitious privatization programme to sell part or all of the government shares in 10 public enterprises, including its largest public enterprises, the Korea Electric Power Corporation, the Korea Telecommunication Authority, and Pohang Iron and Steel Company. In 1987, the Korea Monopoly Corporation producing and selling all tobacco and ginseng products under monopolistic authority was also sold. One of the prominent features of Korean privatization was deregulation and transfer of ownership of the commercial banks through indigenous and global sell-off arrangements. The salient characteristics of the Korean privatization programme have been the sale of large-scale monopolistic enterprises with a nationwide network and the people's share programme of selling 5 trillion won worth of government-health shares. One clear objective of the Korean People's Share programme was to have a more equitable income distribution among people, by offering shares of financially sound public enterprises to benefit low income groups and small investors.

Thailand started its privatization programme in the 1980s both as a pragmatic and a doctrinaire approach. The privatization programme was motivated by huge fiscal deficits and the necessity to attract foreign direct investment. It covered strategic and non-strategic enterprises ranging from telecom to textile mills. Thailand adopted wide-ranging techniques of privatization, with public offering, private sale and lease being prominent. A sector-wise survey of privatization transactions in Thailand showed that privatization of public sector units was undertaken for agriculture/agri-business, tourism, infrastructure/construction and public services and utilities. There were 9 cases of dominant privatization completed by 1988. The privatization of the Bangkok Metropolitan Transit Organisation, a very large public organization set the pace and trend. The government adopted a variety of techniques such as contracting out of maintenance and repair services, liberalization and legalization and franchising of unprofitable and new routes. Special safeguards were provided against retrenchment of labour. The privatization resulted in increased frequency of bus services and elimination of subsidies.

CASE STUDIES

Singapore and Malaysia are the privatization leaders not only in ASEAN but also in the whole of Asia. The privatization experiences in these two countries bring out very interesting dimensions.

SINGAPORE

In its privatization policy the government was to enlist new priority industries only where private entrepreneurs did not have the will or the money to undertake projects on their own and where it was essential for government to provide the entrepreneurship. The policy further provided for divestment in shares in companies where the government of Singapore did not have a majority of shares without preventing private sector participation through listing on the stock exchange. The government decided to list all the enlisted government companies on the stock exchange. Subsequently the government appointed a Public Sector Divestment Committee[4] in March 1985 to establish principles for the identification of public sector units for disposal—partially or entirely, structure a programme for the divestment of public sector units indicting their phasing out schedule and manner and channels of disposal, identify opportunities during the disinvestment programme for the broadening and deepening of the Singapore Stock Market and look into the privatization of statutory boards. The Committee has succeeded in privatizing all the 505 government companies including all 91 of the first tier companies and 204 second tier companies. The Committee conducted the feasibility studies for privatization by consultants skilled in law and financial management. In the course of its work the Committee came across many complex issues such as conversion of partly paid and fully paid shares in readiness for public listing of the company, obtaining the consent of major shareholders to divest share holding in petrochemical corporations and conversion of statutory boards into government companies such as the Civil Aviation Authority of Singapore, the Port of Singapore Authority, the Public Utility Board, the Telecommunication Authority of Singapore, the Commercial and Industrial Security Corporation, the Gurang Town Corporation and the Singapore Broadcasting Corporation.

The Committee tackled issues concerning the need to restructure candidates for privatization into more than one company and establish a regulatory regime for efficient functioning of the privatized companies. The Committee based its recommendations on the premise that all government companies could ultimately be privatized, with the exception of companies with foreign government participation or interest, companies which have a commercial rather than social mission, companies which were not profitable and faced an uncertain future and companies that were engaged in activities relating to national defence. The second promise was that all companies which were amenable to privatization are to be privatized totally, other than where there was a perceived need for the government to maintain some degree of internal control over their operations. But it was recognized that even in such cases there was no need to have absolute majority of shareholdings as this control could be exercised by way of a golden share. The Committee determined the value of each targeted enterprise through negotiations price-earnings ratio, market capitalization and the net tangible assets method.

The privatization of Singapore Airlines and the Singapore Telecom are successful cases of divestment. Singapore Airlines was incorporated as a government owned national airline in January 1972. The company was listed on the Singapore Stock Exchange in December 1985 but ten years earlier the management had introduced a share incentive scheme under which most employees became eligible. At the time of the listing of the company, the Bank of Singapore directed the Development Bank of Singapore to extend loans to the employees to convert their shares into fully paid scrips. The company decided to float its shares in the domestic and overseas capital markets through private placements. This float of shares turned out to be a successful technique. The company ended with around 15,000 shareholders and complete elimination of government control. Singapore Telecom was set up in October 1993 as a privatized company. The interface of the company with the capital market presents a very interesting story. Initially the government divested 10 per cent of its stake in the company. Later the company was listed on the Singapore Stock Exchange. International road shows were conducted in several capital markets the world over, which received overwhelming response at each stop. A very wide coverage was given to the sell-off of the company and considerable hype in the local and foreign media was created. The investing public formed long queues at the relevant offices to buy application forms. The three-fold division of share offers,[5] shares at a fixed price of S $1.90 per share and with 40 free 'loyalty shares' for every 100 shares held over six years for adult Singaporean with a Central Provident Fund; 200 million shares at a fixed price of S$ 2.00 per share with no 'loyalty shares' but with 40.7 million shares reserved for company employees—a maximum of 1,000 shares being available to each adult Singaporean; and 550 million shares at a 'strike price' to be determined by tender with each bid being at least S $2.00—both Singaporean and foreign individuals and institutions being eligible for 1,000 shares or in multiples of it became very popular.

The pace of change was effected by a variety of factors such a special nature and significance of government's agreement with neighbouring countries, delay in getting the shares listed, valuation, creation of an appropriate regime of incentives for buyers of shareholdings and negotiations with the Securities Industry Council of Singapore about fixing the percentage of reserved shares. The share proceeds have been used for modernizing the economy.

MALAYSIA

The Malaysian privatization programme had multiple objectives, budgetary, performance-based and ideological, listed as

1. reduction of the financial and administrative burden of government;
2. promotion of competition and improvement of enterprise efficiency;
3. stimulation of private entrepreneurship and investment;
4. reduction of the role of the State in the economy; and
5. promotion of the objectives of the New Economic Policy, largely designed to correct the economic imbalance between the Malays (Bumiputra) and other ethnic groups.

Malaysia provides an example of an institutional structure with clearly defined responsibilities. The set of institutions established to manage the divestment process are as follows:

i. The main privatization committee is responsible for planning, coordinating and evaluating the programme. It also submits agreements to cabinet for approval.
ii. The privatization secretariat provides services to this committee. It is also responsible for coordinating negotiations and organizing technical sub-committees.
iii. There are four technical sub-committees, for transportation; manufacturing and commerce; energy, telecommunications, ports and information; and social and other services.

In Malaysia privatization has officially referred to sale or divestment of state concerns through the incorporated legally as a public limited company (e.g. Syarikat Telekom Malaysia Berhard to take over the activities of the Telecom Department), public issue or sale of a minority or even a majority of shares in a state owned public company (e.g. Malaysian Airlines System), placement of shares with institutional investors (e.g. Malaysian Airlines System's 5 per cent shares to the government of Brunei), sale/lease of physical assets (e.g. lease of Lady Templer Hospital to Rampai Muda), joint public/private sector ventures [e.g. the establishment of Perbadan Otomobil Nasional (Proton)], schemes to draw private financing into construction projects (e.g. North Port Kelang toll road bypass), contracting out public services (e.g. parking services and garbage disposal) and allowing private competition where the public sector previously enjoyed a complete monopoly (e.g. a third television channel replacing Sistem Televisyen Malaysia Berhard). Malaysian privatization has been criticized on account of the existence of formal and informal collusion, possible patterns in bidding for contracts, some companies enjoying special influence and privileged information, increased cost to the public, shortfall in public investments and reduced job opportunities. On the issue of foreign ownership, the Malaysian privatization plan advocates[6] minorities divestment of no more than 25 per cent to foreign investing public. In privatized entities where foreign expertise is needed, foreign participation is crucial for export market access and promotion, international linkages and exposure are required and the supply of local capital is not sufficient. The privatization plan has established a special fund to finance related expenses such as feasibility studies, preparing candidates for privatization and disbursing compensation. The privatization plan also provides for employee stock options in the enterprises. The plan distinguishes six different categories of candidates for privatization, flagships to be privatized over several years, easily privatizable government majority owned companies (especially in manufacturing and agricultural production sectors), restructuring candidates (unprofitable companies needing financial and operational restructuring), services, listed and minority shareholding and new projects (to be privatized on build, operate and transfer basis). Malaysian privatization, as in Singapore, believes in commercialization and legal corporatization.

GLOBAL SCENE

Privatization is on the rise worldwide. Since the big expansion of state ownerships in the 1960s and 1970s, the number of public enterprises worldwide has been shrinking at an accelerating pace. More than 60,000 public enterprises, at a conservative estimate, have been privatized, most of them since 1990. We now review the significance of privatization drawn from the global scenario and then portray trends in some developed and developing economies such as the UK, France, Mexico and Chile.

Between 1990 and 2000, more than US $700 billion in assets have been privatized around the world.[7] About 40 per cent of this occurred in emerging economies. Till 1996, only 10 per cent of public enterprise assets were privatized in the developing world and 30-40 per cent of the assets in these enterprises have been privatized in the transitional economies. This shows that the developing countries possess significant scope for privatization. The fiscal deficits argument is presented as a basic defense in favour of privatization in the developing countries. In India, in July 1991 when the stabilization and structural adjustment programme was launched, the combined fiscal deficit of the central and the state governments touched a two digit mark of 10 per cent. Between 1991 and 1998, the fiscal deficit declined but it again increased to 10 per cent in 1999-2000. There is an all-round demand for privatization in all the sectors of the economy where public sector is present. Central and state governments have asserted that they cannot find funds to overcome the fiscal deficit which has created serious problems of inflation, erosion in the vale of the rupee, higher incidence of public debt and interest payments and wasteful public expenditure. The core competence argument is another consideration suggested in favour of privatization. The state in many developing countries has made forays into all possible economic activities. This has resulted in un-optimal allocation of resources, their less efficient use and far less participation of the private sector than desired. In fact, the presence of the state in all sorts of economic activities has weakened private initiative. Contemporary economic thinking believes in the dictum 'government should only govern'. Analysed in detail, this argument means that the state should limit its presence to law and order. The private sector is capable of shouldering all other responsibilities if these two are in proper shape. The latter part of the twentieth century has seen the rise of management movement which presents professionalism as a universal solution for the various economic problems. Professionalism requires vision, a keen understanding of the people, high appreciation for time management and sensitization with regard to value addition: financial and non-financial. No system under government tutelage can provide an environment conducive to the germination and growth of professionalization.

The twenty-first century has begun with expressions of faith in private financial initiative. The distribution of income and wealth has been highly inequitable, rendering governments elected by popular vote economically weak, with a few having access to a large chunk of resources. Unless these few join the main stream the government of the day cannot mobilize adequate funds to improve physical and economic infrastructure which can create conditions for the rest of the people to level up with the few. Private Financial Initiative (PFI) is now the popular call for building up infrastructures. Privatization in developing countries could be seen as not only the process of transferring public sector industries to private sector but also as a measure of strengthening the private sector itself. The weak private sector in such countries needs strengthening in terms of size, funding, technology, manpower, operating management, risk absorption and integration into internal and external markets. The takeover of public sector units by the private sector provides it the much needed opportunity to strengthen itself on these parameters. The full-fledged application of the public sector theory itself makes a way for its replacement by the private sector. According to the public sector theory, public enterprises are initially set up due to political ideology. This stage continues for a period of five or ten years but in the second stage the political ideology has to balance itself with economics. This stage continues for another five or ten years. Then comes the third stage where the latter takes over the former. In this stage matters related to policy, financial and operational autonomy assume critical importance. Only those public enterprises which possess such autonomy function well as enterprises. The others are pushed out of business by market forces. An enterprise has to have considerable agility to react to the market forces, which are unpredictable and shift with great speed. By their very nature, public enterprises are devoid of these characteristics. Hence, a private firm is better suited to understand the market and come to grips with it. Social sector development is the new credo of the growth strategy of developing countries. This requires huge funding. Privatization opens the floodgates for social sector development. The allocations to important social sectors such as education, health and housing have been miniscule. Put together these do not exceed a double digit mark for a country such as India which can look to privatization as a means to step up outlays on these important heads.

Privatization has prospered a great deal as an economic movement in the developed countries. Politically this could be seen from the fact that the world is no more bipolar. The socialist economies were transitional economies, waiting for wings to join the economically developed countries. To inject a new stimulus the developed countries adopted privatization at three levels, mega, macro and micro. All three initiatives resulted in the rollback of the state from provider, producer, welfare, police to the regulator state. In mega terms the developed countries called for globalization to facilitate unhindered movement of labour, capital, technology and goods to exploit the benefits of indivisibility of scale. The property rights theory acted as the main catalyst. In macro terms the developed countries initiated privatization by liberalizing their agricultural, industrial, fiscal, monetary, trade and public sector policies. Deregulation constituted the backbone of this liberalization. In micro terms, liberalization had dealt with changing the structure and the working of firms. A package of measures was introduced to provide freedom in decision making. The developed countries saw clear gains in understanding the role of the market and allowing enterprise to interact with it instead of keeping them in the business. Competition was visualized as the most important gain. These countries also saw in the market an efficient allocator of resources, maximizing the marginal social advantage. Business theorists saw in privatization a tremendous scope for performance improvement of firms. In their opinion, privatization leads to activating market forces, broadening the scope of the private sector, transferring majority ownership, removing entry barriers, introducing competition, setting up joint ventures and reducing the number of government nominees on boards.

The post-privatization performance of the relevant enterprises has provided further motivation for accelerated privatization. Megginson, Nash and van Randenborgh compared the pre- and post-privatization financial and operating performance of 61 firms in 18 countries, from 1961 to 1990. The authors observed that after privatization the sample firms became more profitable increased their real sales and investment sending, and improved their operating efficiency. The companies also significantly reduced their debt levels and increased dividend payments. Perhaps more surprising, they increased employment. These results were generally unchanged when the analysts partitioned the data into smaller sub-samples. The broad results of the study are given in Table 1.

THE UK EXPERIENCE

The 1979 general elections in the UK were a watershed in the realm of transition from public ownership to privatization. The Conservative Party pledged itself against further nationalization and declared its intention to denationalize the recently acquired aerospace and shipbuilding concerns, to sell-off some minor shareholdings as circumstances permitted, and to

TABLE 1: PRIVATE ELECTRICITY IN DEVELOPING COUNTRIES, BY REGION 1990-7

Region	*Projects*	*Total Investments in projects with private participation (1997 US $ millions)*
East Asia and the Pacific	165	49,741
Europe and Central Asia	112	10,436
Latin America and the Caribbean	169	45,311
Middle East and the North Africa	10	6,721
South Asia	57	16,799
Sub-Saharan Africa	21	2,040
Total	534	131,048

SOURCE: Ada Karina Izaguirre, 'Private Participation in the Electricity Sector—Recent Trends, in Private Sector', December 1988, p. 7.

deregulate bus transport. Departing from the pledged mandate, Thatcher moved in the direction of the New Right doctrine and began to talk of conviction politics, the end of consensus and economic radicalism. Thatcherism had several distinguishable elements, the most relevant of which were de-regulation, disposal of public owned agencies by public floatation and direct sale to an existing private sector company, sale of public assets, contracting out services formerly performed by public authorities, imposition of user charges, espousal of consumers' sovereignty, espousal of performance measurement inside the civil service and a drive to reduce the numbers of civil servants.[8] The UK privatization movement which started in a small way in 1979 by the disposal of mainly the government's holdings of British Petroleum and the National Enterprise Board, Surplus Water Board and the New Town Corporation, gained a great momentum by the time of the 1983 general elections by which time the government has realized that privatization was a vote winner as well as an ideological commitment. By the time of the 1987 elections, the UK government had disposed of most of the manufacturing interests of the state's own portfolio in addition to most hotels owned by the British Rail, British Gas, Royal Ordinance and various subsidiaries of then existing nationalized industries including British Rail's Sea Link Ferries, British Airways' helicopter operations, and some more subsidiaries of the National Enterprise Board. The period between 1989 and 1995 saw the privatization of British Steel and British Telecommunications, Enterprise Oil, Forestry Commission, General Practice Finance Commission, Insurance Service Group, Land Settlement, Motorway

Service Area Leases, National Enterprise Board Holdings, National Seed Development Organization, Northern Ireland Electricity, Rolls Royce and Water Companies.

Forty-one UK public enterprises were privatized through public offer of shares: British Airports Authority, British Airways, British Gas, British Petroleum Company, British Steel, British Telecommunications, Jaguar, Rolls Royce, etc. Most of these public floatations were received well by the investing public. The floatations were 24 times over subscribed in the case of Amersham, 34 times in the case of AB Ports, 32 times in the case of British Airways, 8.7 times in the case of British Telecom and 9.2 times in the case of Eastern Electricity, 15.4 times in the case of Manweb, 9.5 times in the case of Midlands Electricity, 13.7 times in the case of Northern Ireland Electricity, 17.9 times in the case of Northumberland water, 13.2 times in the case of Seeboard, 15.8 times in the case of South Wales Electricity, 12.2 times in the case of South West Electric and 11.6 times in the case of Yorkshire Electricity. Privatization introduced an innovative element by combining offers made by both the respective company and the government. Such offers were made in the case of Amersham, AB Ports, British Airports Authority, British Aerospace, British Airways, British Gas, British Petroleum, British Steel, British Telecom, Britoil, Cable and Wires, Enterprise Oil, Jaguar, National Power, etc. One of the highlights of the UK privatization was the arrangement for small investors. In most cases existing shareholders were generally given preferential treatment when applying for second and third issues. For example, on the basis of one for every five shares owned in the case of Britoil and one for every twelve in the case of British Petroleum, the eligible gas customers were guaranteed a minimum of 200 shares by British Gas. Individuals registered with the British Petroleum Share Information Office at a certain date were guaranteed an allocation of 100 shares. In a large number of cases, small investors were allowed to pay share subscriptions in two or three instalments. Maximum royalty bonus shares were allotted in many a case, to subscribers who did not sell their shares during the lock-in-period.

In the case of 41 enterprises privatized between 1979 and 1995 a minimum investment by subscribers was stipulated, which they had to make in more than one instalments. The first instalment was usually 30-40 per cent of the minimum investment. Most importantly, the UK privatization programme imposed some restrictions for the post-privatization period, including restrictions on special shares. The appointment of government directors was banned in the case of Amersham, British Airports Authority, British Aerospace, British Airways, British Gas, British Steel, Cable and

Wireless, Enterprise Oil, Jaguar, National Power, Northern Ireland Electricity, Power Gen, Regional Electricity, Rolls Royce, Scottish Hydro, Scottish Power and Water Companies. Only British Airways, British Petroleum, British Telecom and Britoil were permitted to have government directors. The condition to appoint a British citizen as Chief Executive in the privatized firm was also abolished, except in the case of British Aerospace, British Telecom and Rolls Royce. The restriction on disposal of assets was removed in the case of all enterprises excepting Amersham, Jaguar and Rolls Royce. However, the restriction on the issue of new voting shares was imposed on many privatized companies except British Airports Authority, British Aerospace, British Airways, British Petroleum and Cable and Wireless. The 15 per cent foreign ownership restriction was imposed on British Aerospace and British Airways and Rolls Royce. Special voting rights/provisions were made in the case of British Airports Authority, British Gas, Britoil, Enterprise Oil, National Power, Northern Ireland Electricity, Power Gen, Regional Electricity, Rolls Royce, Scottish Hydro and Water Companies. The privatization proceeds increased from 587 million pounds in 1979-80/1980-1 to 4300 million pounds in 1994-5 (estimated). The privatization costs varied from a minimum of 1.4 per cent of proceeds in the case of Regional Electricity to 5.4 per cent in the case of British Petroleum. These costs comprised underwriting, other fees/commissions and advertising. Interestingly, they showed a tendency to decline in the 1990s. The underwriting charges constituted UK primary underwriting commission and UK sub-underwriting commission of which the former dominated the latter. Albeit the regulation was an ignored factor in the initial cases of privatization, the UK government imparted greater attention to it the 1980s. The setting up of the OFTEL (Office of the Telecom Regulatory Authority) provided an important push to the institution of regulation. The OFTEL ensured the healthy protection of the interests of the telecom customers. Its price cap ensured a price gain to the customers. The UK privatization experiment clearly points out that privatization can ensure sustainable economic, social and political development through reforms.

MEXICO

Mexico's privatization commenced in 1983. Initially, small public enterprises were privatized to improve the health of public finances and productivity. This effort has continued with added intensity with the completion of large and some more complex privatization transactions. During the 1990s the government offloaded all sugar mils, hotels, airlines, telecom, banking and steel units. Of the 1,150 public enterprises under state control in 1982, Mexico has privatized about 900, with sales totalling to US $15 billion (about 5 per cent of the GDP). Mexico proposes to privatize another 87 enterprises in the near future. The sale of public enterprises has resulted in the transfer of 2,50,000 employees to the private sector. The macroeconomic factors shaping the process include macroeconomic conditions, shareholder control and creation of a competitive environment. The privatization of public enterprises in Mexico has had three elements: a legal framework, a simple non-discriminatory procedure and a set of principles applying both laws and procedures concerning specific cases for privatization. The legal framework is contained in the Mexican Constitution which sets the limits of public sector participation and of the programme of privatization as a whole. The private sector has been barred entry into strategic sector such as minting, printing money, generating nuclear power and electricity, telegraph services, radio and satellite communications, oil and hydro carbons, petrochemicals, radioactive minerals and railways. The Constitution specifies the modality of privatization through public auction completed through bids in sealed envelopes to be made public to ensure that the state gets the best price opportunity. The sale of a public enterprise goes through a twelve-step process comprising presentation of a proposal, deciding how to divest, authorizing the sale process, appointing a sales agent, developing guidelines, announcing the sales, determining a reference price, evaluating the offers, closing the sale, signing the sales contract, completing the divestiture and preparing the 'white book' (with all the relevant papers for forwarding to the Ministry of Finance). The valuation process adopted in Mexico comprises steps such as estimating book value, benchmarking internationally and identifying justifiable multiples of book value, projecting cash flows, working out optimal value, maximizing the value through restructuring and choosing the right time to privatize.

Chilean Experience

Privatization in Chile commenced in 1973 and its scale since then has been on of the largest in the developing world, covering sectors from banks and automobiles to fisheries and agro-industries. By 1973, the government of Chile owned and managed 600 enterprises, accounting for almost one-half of the GDP. About half of these enterprises were inherited whereas the remaining half were created afresh. The policy of liberalization was initiated in 1973 to reduce the fiscal deficits from 25 per cent of GDP to 10 per cent. The government decided to privatize public enterprises also to cure the malaise of inflation. The first phase[9] of privatization in Chile took place in 1974-5, involving the outright transfer or return to previous owners of about 240 enterprises nationalized in the preceding years. The second phase, implemented during 1975-83, involved privatization of created enterprises. The third phase, 1985-6, involved the re-privatization of enterprises divested during phases one and two. The fourth and current phase involves the divestiture of the last 40 large industrial enterprises which had performed well and in some cases better than the private sector. To improve the efficiency of the economy the government of Chile created a separate mechanism to oversee divestiture. The preparation of privatization in Chile includes steps such as selection of units, unravelling the character of the public enterprise, identifying legal constraints, and finding the importance of the enterprise, in the specific industry. Competitive bidding was the preferred technique of privatization. The instruments and mechanisms employed in the four phases of privatization turned out to be de-nationalization, debt-led sale of shares, equity-led sale of shares and spreading ownership through popular capitalism. During the third phase labour capitalism through the sale of shares and employee buyouts, also found its way. The Bank of Chile was privatized through popular capitalism. The sale of National Computing and Informatics Company was executed through labour capitalism. The National Electricity Company was privatized through break-up. The Chilean experience points out the prerequisites of a sweeping programme comprising setting up an adequate institutional framework to oversee privatizations, establishing special incentives for small investors, passing legislation specifically aimed at guiding the participation of large domestic and foreign investors and pension funds and applying the lessons from previous attempt at privatization to avoid the same pitfalls. The Chilean privatization also suggests that it may be preferable to carry out any large-scale privatization programme over an extended time-frame and avoid ownership concentration through a conscious policy of widespread share ownership involving if necessary special discounts, incentives, quotas, etc.

French Experience

Chronic losses, low productivity, rigid trade unionism and constant down trend in public finances forced the French government to embrace privatization in 1986-8. The first wave[10] was ushered in as a reaction to the programme of nationalization introduced under the Public Law of February

1982. Although, 47 companies passed into public ownership as part of this programme, a Right wing government with an explicit commitment to privatization as much as possible of the state's extensive financial and industrial holdings passed the Law of 1986 which paved the way for privatization of a total of 65 companies over a five-year period to which was added TF-1, the television company. Although the list was wide-ranging, it did not include two major categories of public enterprises, public services utilities and monopolies and companies with a poor financial performance. French citizens and residents were initially promised 10 shares a piece and allocated a total roughly of one-half of the available shares, a further minimum of 10 per cent was offered at a preferential rate to employees, 15 per cent was offered to foreigners and between 15 and 30 per cent was offered to core buyers to provide a stable nucleus. The minimum selling price of each public enterprise was to be publicly fixed by an independent Commission after audit and valuation. The government was to sell shares at a price recommended by the commission or higher than that. Under these provisions, 30 financial and industrial groups were privatized in 14 months, representing an aggregate market capitalization of over FF 120 billion of total work force of more than 4,50,000 people. The number of these enterprises ranked among the world leaders in their sectors such as the financial institutions Société Générale, Paribas, Suez, Credit Agricole and the industrial groups Saint Gobain, Compagnie Generale. All the privatizations succeeded, excepting one. The public flotations were over-subscribed up to 40 times.[11] About 17 million applications for subscription were received including the majority of employees of the enterprises concerned. Of the FF 85 billion raised, 56 billion was used to pay off the public debt and 28 billion to increase the capital of public enterprises including 5 billion for companies to be privatized. The privatization programme was interrupted by the return of a government in 1988. The second wave of privatization took place between 1993 and 1995. It intended to raise FF 40 billion during 1993 and proposed to put on block 21 large groups of public enterprises including Air France, Bank of France, Bull, Pechiney, Renault, Rhône-Poulenc, Elf-Aquitaine and Thomson. 9 of the 21 groups did not appear in the list of the enterprises taken up during the first wave of privatization. The chief features of the second wave were increased allocation of shares for the domestic investor, retention of a golden share of unlimited duration by the government for the protection of national interests, increase in allocation of bonus shares to a maximum of 1 for 1 up to a maximum of FF 30,000 of shares and reduction of political

TABLE 2: VALUATION OF PUBLIC ENTERPRISE GROUPS COMPARED DURING NATIONALIZATION AND POST-PRIVATIZATION PERIOD

(FF in millions)

Name of the Public Enterprise Group	*Valuation during Nationalization Period*	*Valuation during Post-Privatization Period*
Alcatel-Alsthom	4.00	22.00
BIMP	0.20	0.40
BNP	*	46.00
BTP (Compagnie)	0.30	0.40
CCF	1.70	4.50
CLF	**	1.40
ELF-Aquitaine	**	100.00
HAVAS	–	6.50
Matra-Hachette	1.70	2.50
Paribas	5.10	20.00
Renault	–	40.00
Rhône-Poulenc	3.00	33.00
Saint Gobain	6.10	14.00
Seita	**	7.00
Société Générale	–	23.00
Sogenal	0.40	1.60
Suez	4.00	24.00
TFI	–	3.40
UAP	**	45.00
Usinor-Sacilor	–	20.00

SOURCE: Privatisees Guide 1996, Inventaire & Patrimoine, Paris, 1995, p. 12.
NOTES: * BNP was constituted in 1966.
** UAP was constituted in 1968.

patronage to the independent commission of privatization. The performance of the privatized enterprises in the bourses showed a widespread gain in the first quarter which subsequently marginally pitted out in the second quarter. As shown in Table 2, the price of the privatized firms as compared to their price during the nationalization period, had a large upward swing indicating the success of privatization.

The French experience in privatization reveals the factors critical for success. They include among others, transparency, independent machinery, involvement of foreign buyers, regulation and adherence to a strict time frame. The experience also brings out the role of political economy in the success/failure of privatization exercise.

THE INDIAN EXPERIENCE

India launched its economic reforms programme in 1991 to meet the challenges of chronic fiscal deficits, adverse balance of payments position, and stagflation.[12] Public enterprise reforms were initiated in 1992 as a part of the package of overall economic reforms. The public enterprise reforms initiative[13] included withdrawal from non-core areas, reduction of government stake to a bare minimum in such enterprises, and mobilization of funds from disinvestments to fund the fiscal deficits. For the enterprises to be retained the package contained measures to provide greater autonomy by improving the public enterprise-government interface through memorandum of understanding (MOU), strengthening the institution of the Board of Directors, recognition of flagship enterprises as 'navaratnas' and 'miniratnas' and their restructuring. This section concerns itself with the measures taken relating to the enterprises which were to be offloaded from the public enterprise portfolio. As the first generation of economic reforms dealt with the central government, the focus of public sector reforms was limited to the central public enterprises. It was for the first time that the central government announced its intention to go all out for privatization as indicated in the national budget presented in 1999. Between 1991 and January 2001, only one central public enterprise, Modern Foods Ltd., was privatized in 1999 to the Hindustan Lever Ltd. Nevertheless, disinvestment has dominated the entire public enterprises reforms programme during this decade. However, several state governments have privatized their enterprises on outright basis. During 1991-2, shares of 31 central public enterprises were disinvested in two tranche to short listed financial institutions an mutual funds in the form of bundles. The pricing formula adopted for referral price was stated to be the average of the net asset value and the profit earning capacity value at 10 per cent industry capitalization rate. The level of disinvestments for individual undertakings varied between 5 and 20 per cent. In 1992-3, disinvestments were done in three phases. The reserve price fixed for sale was the average of price recommended by three bankers, the Industrial Credit and Investment Corporation of India, Industrial Development Bank of India and SBI Capital Market Ltd. The next round of disinvestment took place in 1993-4. The reserve price was fixed internally by the Inter-Ministerial Committee on the basis of the recommendations. During 1994-5, two rounds of disinvestment took place, in 1995-6, only one round, in 1996-7 one round and in 1997-8 one round. From 1998-9, the disinvestment process took a new turn. Hereafter, the disinvestments were carried out through buy back and cross holdings of shares. Another mechanism, the Special Purpose Vehicle (SPV), was suggested for effeting disinvestment, which did not cut ice with the government. According to this technique, the SPV was to warehouse the shares and advance the money for the receipt of the shares to the companies that divested. The SPV was to offload the shares at an opportune time. The buy back/cross holdings of shares, made a dent in the cash reserves of the companies that divested, and hence attracted criticism. The public enterprise-wise disinvestment and the present government holdings as on 31 March 1999 are given in Table 3.

In 1996 the Disinvestment Commission was set up through an executive order and was accorded an advisory status. The Commission was assigned the responsibility of drawing a comprehensive long-term disinvestment programme within five or ten years. The Commission submitted 12 reports and suggested disinvestment modalities for 53 enterprises. The government did not see eye to eye with the Commission, which was wound up in 1999. The government set up a separate Department for Disinvestment, headed by a Minister. The Ministry's approach to the implementation of the disinvestment programme is on a case to case basis. The Ministry receives inputs from the concerned enterprise, Department of Public Enterprise and the core group of Secretaries. The Ministry finally processes the recommendations and forwards such recommendations to the empowered group of ministers and/or Cabinet Committee on Disinvestments. The Ministry is advised by the merchant bankers, most of whom happen to be international financial entities. The proceeds arising out of disinvestment programme are given in Table 4.

Although privatization/disinvestment is a self-sustained exercise, India has not been able to register significant breakthroughs in it. It is very urgent to tap resources from this self-sustained exercise as the fiscal deficits of the country are still hovering around 8 per cent of the GDP, only a notch lower than what it was at the time of initiation of the economic reforms programme in 1991. The Indian disinvestment programme suffers a great deal from a wide *divergence* as related to some well established international practices. Unless this is narrowed down, the Indian disinvestment programme is not likely to taste success as was the case with the countries discussed above.

In majority of the countries where the disinvestment programmes were successfully implemented, a separate enactment was passed. The French Law on Privatization listed the enterprises to be privatized and the mechanism for privatization. This introduced transparency in the disinvestment exercise and paved the way for its smooth implementation. In the Indian

TABLE 3: PUBLIC SECTOR ENTERPRISE-WISE DISINVESTMENT AND THE PRESENT GOVT.HOLDING AS ON 31 MARCH 1999

Sl. No	*Name of the PSE*	*Total Disinvested percentage*	*Present Govt. Holding*
1.	Andrew Yule	9.60	62.84**
2.	Bharat Earthmovers Ltd.	39.19*	60.81
3.	Bharat Electronics Ltd.	24.14	75.86
4.	Bharat Heavy Electricals Ltd.	32.28	67.72
5.	Bharat Petroleum Corp. Ltd.	33.80	66.20
6.	Bongaigaon Refineries Ltd.	25.54	66.20
7.	CMC Ltd.	16.69	74.46
8.	Cochin Refineries Ltd.	6.12	83.31
9.	Container Corp. of India Ltd.	37.00**	55.04**
10.	Dredging Corp. of India Ltd.	1.44	63.00
11.	Engineers India Ltd.	5.98	98.56
12.	Fert. & Chem. (Travancore) Ltd.	1.70	94.02
13.	Gas Authority of India Ltd.	17.03*	97.38**
14.	HMT Ltd.	8.44	82.97
15.	Hindustan Cables Ltd.	1.04	91.56
16.	Hindustan Copper Ltd.	1.24	98.96
17.	Hindustan Organic Chemical Ltd.	41.39*	98.76
18.	Hindustan Petroleum Corpn. Ltd.	48.9*	51.06
19.	Hindustan Photofilms Mfg. Co. Ltd.	9.87	90.13
20.	Hindustan Zinc Ltd.	24.08	75.92
21.	Indian Oil Corp. Ltd.	18.74	81.14**
22.	Indian Petrochemicals Corp. Ltd.	40.05*	59.95
23.	Indian Telephone Industries Ltd.	0.27	99.73
24.	IRCON International Ltd.	22.98	76.67**
25.	Indian Tourism & Dev. Corp.	10.03	89.97
26.	Kundremukh Iron Ore Co. Ltd.	1.00	99.00
27.	Madras Refineries Ltd.	16.92	53.80**
28.	Mahanagar Telephone Nigam Ltd.	43.80*	56.20*
29.	Minerals & Metals Trading Corp. Ltd.	0.67	99.33
30.	National Aluminium Co. Ltd.	12.85	87.15
31.	National Fertilizers Ltd.	2.35	97.65
32.	National Mineral Dev. Corp. Ltd.	1.62	96.36**
33.	Neyveli Lignite Corp. Ltd.	6.01	93.99
34.	Oil & Natural Gas Corp.	16.38	83.62
35.	Rashtriya Chemicals & Ferti. Ltd.	7.50	92.50
36.	Shipping Corp. of India Ltd.	19.88	80.12
37.	State Trading Corp.	8.97	91.03
38.	Steel Authority of India Ltd.	14.18*	85.82
39.	Videsh Sanchar Nigam Ltd.	47.00	53.00

NOTES: * Including Dilution of Govt. Shareholding by Public Issues/GDR Issues.
** The Balance Equity is held by State Govts /Other Collaborators.

SOURCE: *Public Enterprise Survey*, vol. 1, 1998-9, Department of Public Enterprise, Govt. of India, New Delhi, February 2000.

TABLE 4: ESTIMATES AND RECEIPTS FROM DISINVESTMENT PROGRAMME

*(Rs. crore)**

Year	*Budget Estimates*	*Actual*	*Divergence*
1991-2	2,500	3,038	+538
1992-3	2,500	1,961	-539
1993-4	3,500	-48	-3,548
1994-5	4,000	5,607	+1,607
1995-6	7,000	1,397	-5,603
1996-7	5,000	455	-4,545
1997-8	4,800	912	-3,888
1998-9	9,000	5,376	-3,624
1999-00	10,000	2,000 †	-8,000
2000-1⁺	10,000	126	-9,874
Net Mobilization	58,300	20,824	-37,476

NOTES: * US $1 bn = approx. Rs. 4500 crore.
† Estimated.
⁺ Till 31 January 2001.

SOURCE: R.K. Mishra and B. Navin, 'Disinvestment Divergence', IPE Occasional Paper, Institute of Public Enterprise, Hyderbad, 2000.

case a separate law has not been enacted. This has short circuited the debate on disinvestment and resulted in the absence of mass support. There have been severe complaints about the lack of transparency in valuation of shares and the methods of their building in the disinvestment exercise carried out by the government in the first few rounds of disinvestment in the central public enterprises. The state governments have been also accused of mismanagement.

The machinery set up for carrying out disinvestment was given independent and integrated status in the case of countries having pioneered their disinvestment programmes successfully. The political and bureaucratic forces were kept out of the machinery and the final say rested with it. India has followed altogether a different practice. Initially the responsibility rested with the Department of Public Enterprise which had to report to the group of empowered secretaries whose decisions were vetted by the Cabinet Committee on Economic Affairs. Latter a Disinvestment Commission was set up in 1996 under executive order. The recommendations of the Commission had to pass through the Department of Public enterprise to the Empowered Group whose recommendations were vetted by the Cabinet Committee on Economic Affairs. In November 1999 the Disinvestment Commission ceased to exist.

A new Department was created to deal with disinvestment headed by a Minister for State supported by a Secretary to the Government of

India. Initially the Department's recommendations were referred to the Department of Public Enterprises to pass through the Empowered Group. However, this process was modified and the reference to the Department of Public Enterprise was deleted. The fragmentation of machinery has obstructed the speed and the quality of disinvestment.

Coming to *time frame*, in the case of countries successful in disinvestment, a calendar is drawn up and adhered to. The Indian time frame is uncertain. Pre-disinvestment action has held centre stage in the case of the UK, Germany, Singapore, Malaysia, Peru, Poland, Mexico, Brazil, Italy and Romania. This has taken the form of Physical, organizational, financial and manpower restructuring. In many a case mergers, acquisitions, divisionalization and formation of holding companies were effected for the success of the enterprise during the post privatization regime. India has missed the comprehensive understanding of the approach and tackled the problem in a lackadaisical manner, resorting to mostly financial restructuring, which could not produce the desired results. The success of disinvestment programme anywhere rests on the clarity of objectives. Singapore launched the disinvestment exercise to achieve the long-term objectives of enhancing competition, promoting optimum allocation of resources, debt retirement, and increasing the total factor productivity. India has fallen prey to the short-term objective of raising revenues leading to partial realization of benefits.

The policy makers abroad have used wide-ranging techniques including ownership divestment, management privatization and privatization of financing. India has preferred ownership divestment resulting in minimal benefits. Again, even in the ownership realm, the Indian model of disinvestment has placed complete reliance upon partial privatization. The country could have taken a leaf from the British experience which in a very innovative manner introduced the golden share which allowed the British Government to exercise its control on strategic matters by casting the golden share vote against any proposal mooted by the Board which was not in the public interest making such proposal null and void. The Indian Companies Act still awaits an appropriate amendment to incorporate this provision. As partial pregnancy cannot deliver a child, so is the case with partial disinvestment which has delivered a still baby. Regulation has been considered a key to successful disinvesment. In the case of the member countries of the European Common Market, the regulatory agencies were set up either ahead of privatization or concurrently with it. Barring the setting up of Central Electricity Regulatory Authority, the State Electricity Regulatory Authorities and the recently set up Insurance Regulatory and

Development Authority, the Indian scenario does not inspire any confidence in this regard. The absence of the much desired regulatory framework has adversely affected competition, quality and delivery. On the score of interlocking it may be pointed out that Italy and France could speedily privatize by directing their development financial institutions to pick up the equity stake. No such understanding exists in India and to that extent the speed of execution of the disinvestment programme stands hampered badly. The privatization exercise abroad has been punctuated by the introduction of strategic buyers to facilitate the transfer of ownership, acquisition of relevant technology and markets. The Disinvestment Commission in its recommendations had suggested the introduction of the institution of strategic buyer. Unfortunately, the policy makers have been suggesting the introduction of only one strategic buyer, without giving heed to the fact that in our situation when we have gigantic public enterprises, we may need multiple strategic buyers. Finally, any disinvestment exercise should be proactive, ushering in new methods of manufacturing, marketing, consumer care, responsiveness and accountability to society. The enterprise to be divested should be treated as the focal point. The entire disinvestment exercise has kept the enterprise to be divested and its employees at bay. Consequently, the change in management has been tardy and ineffective. There is a need to take urgent steps to remove the existing disinvestment divergence. This is necessary to create confidence in the disinvestment exercise and congenial climate for its speedier implementation.

CONCLUSION

The economic trends prevalent in India, ASEAN and the world over in case of both the developed and developing countries, converge about the need to privatize and reduce the government control. The reasons for privatization have ranged from reduction of fiscal deficits to improving the enterprise performance. The empirical evidences point out to the success of privatization in terms of efficiency and equity improvement in the ASEAN economies in particular and the world economy in general. Commercialization and Corporatization have acted as preconditions for successful privatization. The institutional set-up, selection of techniques and implementation strategy have played an important role in the success of privatization exercise. Privatization has received a popular support from the masses. Whereas ASEAN could be rated as very high on the scale of privatization completed, the global trend amount to be medium and the status of privatization in India is rated low. This divergence could be explained by the differences in the political economy framework.

NOTES

1. Commonwealth Secretariat, *Management of the Privatisation Process: A Guide to Policy Making and Implementation*, Management and Training Services Division, London, 1994, p. 23.
2. Rohdewohld Rainer, 'Management Training in Indonesian Public Enterprises: Concepts and Approaches', *Annals of Public and Cooperative Economics*, vol. 16 (2) (1996), p. 166.
3. Dhiratayakinant Kraiyudht, 'Privatisation of the Bangkok Metropolitan Transit Organisation: A Case Study', in *Privatisation and Public Enterprise: The Asia Pacific Experience*, ed. Gouri Geeta, New Delhi: Oxford University Press, 1991, p. 467.
4. R.K. Mishra, 'Disinvestment and Share Valuation in Public Enterprises: The International Experience', *Chartered Secretary*, August 1994, pp. 186-9.
5. Ariff Mohammed, Mukul Asher and Ian Thynne, 'Singapore', in *Corporatisation, Disinvestment and the Public-Private Mix: Selected Country Studies*, ed. Jen Thynne, Hong Kong: AJPA, 1995, p. 180.
6. K.S. Jomo, 'Malaysia's Privatisation Experience', in *Privatisation, Policy and Performance: International Perspectives*, ed. P. Cook and C. Kirpatrik, London: Prentice Hall, 1995, p. 237.
7. Ravi Rammurthi, 'A Multilevel Model of Privatisation in Emerging Economies', *The Academy of Management Review*, vol. 25 (3) (2000), p. 525.
8. Dunsire dwells on several distinguishable elements of privatization. Andrew Dunsire, 'The Public/Private Debate: Some United Kingdom Evidence', *International Review of Administrative Sciences*, vol. 56 (1990), pp. 30-1.
9. Helen Nankani, 'Techniques of Privatisation of State-Owned Enterprises', vol. II, Selected Country Case Studies, World Bank Technical Paper, no. 89, Washington: World Bank, 1988, p. 26.
10. Curven Peter, 'Privatisation in France: La Grande Illusion?', *Teaching Public Administration*, vol. XV (2), 1995, p. 31.
11. Andre Delion, 'Public Enterprises: Privatisation or Reform?,' *International Review of Administrative Sciences*, vol. 56 (1) (1990), p. 68.
12. The reasons leading to deregulation of public sector have been discussed at length by Rakesh Mohan in several of his works. See Rakesh Mohan, 'Public Sector Reforms and Issues in Privatisation', in Rakesh Mohan, Ahluwalia Isher Judge, Goswami Omkar and Oman Charles (eds), *Policy Reform in India*, Development Centre, OECD, Paris, 1996, pp. 55-97.
13. R.K. Mishra, 'Public Enterprise Policy in India', *Kalaeido Scope*, August-September 1999.

Index